Guide to RISC Processors

Sivarama P. Dandamudi

Guide to RISC Processors

for Programmers and Engineers

 Springer

Sivarama P. Dandamudi
School of Computer Science
Carleton University
Ottawa, ON K1S 5B6
Canada
sivarama@scs.carleton.ca

Library of Congress Cataloging-in-Publication Data
Dandamudi, Sivarama P., 1955–
    Guide to RISC processors / Sivarama P. Dandamudi.
        p.   cm.
    Includes bibliographical references and index.
    ISBN 0-387-21017-2 (alk. paper)
        1. Reduced instruction set computers.   2. Computer architecture.   3. Assembler language
    (Computer program language)   4. Microprocessors—Programming.   I. Title.
    QA76.5.D2515   2004
    004.3—dc22   2004051373

ISBN 0-387-21017-2   Printed on acid-free paper.

Printed in the United States of America.   (HAM)

9 8 7 6 5 4 3 2 1   SPIN 10984949

springeronline.com

To
my parents, **Subba Rao** and **Prameela Rani**,
my wife, **Sobha**,
and
my daughter, **Veda**

Preface

Popular processor designs can be broadly divided into two categories: Complex Instruction Set Computers (CISC) and Reduced Instruction Set Computers (RISC). The dominant processor in the PC market, Pentium, belongs to the CISC category. However, the recent trend is to use the RISC designs. Even Intel has moved from CISC to RISC design for their 64-bit processor. The main objective of this book is to provide a guide to the architecture and assembly language of the popular RISC processors. In all, we cover five RISC designs in a comprehensive manner.

To explore RISC assembly language, we selected the MIPS processor, which is pedagogically appealing as it closely adheres to the RISC principles. Furthermore, the availability of the SPIM simulator allows us to use a PC to learn the MIPS assembly language.

Intended Use

This book is intended for computer professionals and university students. Anyone who is interested in learning about RISC processors will benefit from this book, which has been structured so that it can be used for self-study. The reader is assumed to have had some experience in a structured, high-level language such as C. However, the book does not assume extensive knowledge of any high-level language—only the basics are needed.

Assembly language programming is part of several undergraduate curricula in computer science, computer engineering, and electrical engineering departments. This book can be used as a companion text in those courses that teach assembly language.

Features

Here is a summary of the special features that set this book apart.

- This probably is the only book on the market to cover five popular RISC architectures: MIPS, SPARC, PowerPC, Itanium, and ARM.
- There is a methodical organization of chapters for a step-by-step introduction to the MIPS assembly language.
- This book does not use fragments of code in examples. All examples are complete in the sense that they can be assembled and run giving a better feeling as to how these programs work.
- Source code for the MIPS assembly language program examples is available from the book's Web site (`www.scs.carleton.ca/~sivarama/risc_book`).
- The book is self-contained and does not assume a background in computer organization. All necessary background material is presented in the book.
- Interchapter dependencies are kept to a minimum to offer maximum flexibility to instructors in organizing the material. Each chapter provides an overview at the beginning and a summary at the end.
- An extensive set of programming exercises is provided to reinforce the MIPS assembly language concepts discussed in Part III of the book.

Overview and Organization

We divide the book into four parts. Part I presents introductory topics and consists of the first three chapters. Chapter 1 provides an introduction to CISC and RISC architectures. In addition, it introduces assembly language and gives reasons for programming in assembly language. The next chapter discusses processor design issues including the number of addresses used in processor instructions, how flow control is altered by branches and procedure calls, and other instruction set design issues. Chapter 3 presents the RISC design principles.

The second part describes several RISC architectures. In all, we cover five architectures: MIPS, PowerPC, SPARC, Itanium, and ARM. For each architecture, we provide many details on its instruction set. Our discussion of MIPS in this part is rather brief because we devote the entire Part III to its assembly language.

The third part, which consists of nine chapters, covers the MIPS assembly language. This part allows you to get hands-on experience in writing the MIPS assembly language programs. You don't need a MIPS-based system to do this! You can run these programs on your PC using the SPIM simulator. Our thanks go to Professor James Larus for writing the simulator, for which we provide details on installation and use.

The last part consists of several appendices. These appendices give reference information on various number systems, character representation, and the MIPS instruction set. In addition, we also give several programming exercises so that you can practice writing MIPS assembly language programs.

Acknowledgments

Several people have contributed, either directly or indirectly, to the writing of this book. First and foremost, I would like to thank Sobha and Veda for their understanding and patience!

I want to thank Ann Kostant, Executive Editor and Wayne Wheeler, Associate Editor, both at Springer, for their enthusiastic support for the project. I would also like to express my appreciation to the staff at the Springer production department for converting my camera-ready copy into the book in front of you.

I also express my appreciation to the School of Computer Science, Carleton University for providing a great atmosphere to complete this book.

Feedback

Works of this nature are never error-free, despite the best efforts of the authors, editors, and others involved in the project. I welcome your comments, suggestions, and corrections by electronic mail.

Carleton University   Sivarama Dandamudi
Ottawa, Canada   sivarama@scs.carleton.ca
April 2004   http://www.scs.carleton.ca/~sivarama

Contents

PART I
Overview

1

Introduction

We start this chapter with an overview of what this book is about. As programmers we usually write our programs in a high-level language such as Java. However, such languages shield us from the system's internal details. Because we want to explore the RISC architectures, it is best done by knowing the processor's language. That's why we look at the assembly language in the later chapters of the book.

Processor Architecture

Computers are complex systems. How do we manage complexity of these systems? We can get clues by looking at how we manage complex systems in life. Think of how a large corporation is managed. We use a hierarchical structure to simplify the management: president at the top and workers at the bottom. Each level of management filters out unnecessary details on the lower levels and presents only an abstracted version to the higher-level management. This is what we refer to as *abstraction*. We study computer systems by using layers of abstraction.

Different people view computer systems differently depending on the type of their interaction. We use the concept of abstraction to look at only the details that are necessary from a particular viewpoint. For example, a computer user interacts with the system through an application program. For the user, the application is the computer! Suppose you are interested in browsing the Internet. Your obvious choice is to interact with the system through a Web browser such as the Netscape™ Communicator or Internet Explorer. On the other hand, if you are a computer architect, you are interested in the internal details that do not interest a normal user of the system. One can look at computer systems from several different perspectives. Our interest in this book is in looking at processor architectural details.

A programmer's view of a computer system depends on the type and level of language she intends to use. From the programmer's viewpoint, there exists a hierarchy from low-level languages to high-level languages (see Figure 1.1). As we move up in this hierarchy,

3

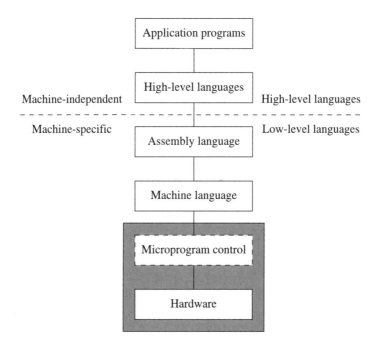

Figure 1.1 A programmer's view of a computer system.

the level of abstraction increases. At the lowest level, we have the *machine language* that is the native language of the machine. This is the language understood by the machine hardware. Because digital computers use 0 and 1 as their alphabet, machine language naturally uses 1s and 0s to encode the instructions. One level up, there is the assembly language as shown in Figure 1.1. *Assembly language* does not use 1s and 0s; instead, it uses mnemonics to express the instructions. Assembly language is closely related to the machine language.

As programmers, we use the instruction set architecture (ISA) as a useful abstraction to understand the processor's internal details. What is an ISA? It essentially describes the processor at a logical level, as opposed to giving the implementation details. This abstraction suits us very well as we are interested in the logical details of the RISC processor without getting bogged down by the myriad implementation details.

The ISA defines the personality of a processor and indirectly influences the overall system design. The ISA specifies how a processor functions: what instructions it executes and what interpretation is given to these instructions. This, in a sense, defines a logical processor. If these specifications are precise, they give freedom to various chip manufacturers to implement physical designs that look functionally the same at the ISA level. Thus, if we run the same program on these implementations, we get the same results. Different implementations, however, may differ in performance and price. For example, the Intel 32-bit ISA (IA-32) has several implementations including the Pentium processors, cheaper Celeron processors, high-performance Xeon processors, and so on.

Two popular examples of ISA specifications are the SPARC and JVM. The rationale behind having a precise ISA-level specification for the SPARC is to let multiple vendors design their own processors that look the same at the ISA level. The JVM, on the other hand, takes a different approach. Its ISA-level specification can be used to create a software layer so that the processor looks like a Java processor. Thus, in this case, we do not use a set of hardware chips to implement the specifications, but rather use a software layer to simulate the virtual processor. Note, however, that there is nothing stopping us from implementing these specifications in hardware (even though this is not usually the case).

Why create the ISA layer? The ISA-level abstraction provides details about the machine that are needed by the programmers. The idea is to have a common platform to execute programs. If a program is written in C, a compiler translates it into the equivalent machine language program that can run on the ISA-level logical processor. Similarly, if you write your program in FORTRAN, use a FORTRAN compiler to generate code that can execute on the ISA-level logical processor. At the ISA level, we can divide the designs into two categories: RISC and CISC. We discuss these two categories in the next section.

RISC Versus CISC

There are two basic types of processor design philosophies: reduced instruction set computers (RISC) and complex instruction set computers (CISC). The Intel IA-32 architecture belongs to the CISC category. The architectures we describe in the next part are all examples of the RISC category.

Before we dig into the details of these two designs, let us talk about the current trend. In the 1970s and early 1980s, processors predominantly followed the CISC designs. The current trend is to use the RISC philosophy. To understand this shift from CISC to RISC, we need to look at the motivation for going the CISC way initially. But first we have to explain what these two types of design philosophies are.

As the name suggests, CISC systems use complex instructions. What is a complex instruction? For example, adding two integers is considered a simple instruction. But, an instruction that copies an element from one array to another and automatically updates both array subscripts is considered a complex instruction. RISC systems use only simple instructions. Furthermore, RISC systems assume that the required operands are in the processor's internal registers, not in the main memory. We discuss processor registers in the next chapter. For now, think of them as scratchpads inside the processor.

A CISC design does not impose such restrictions. So what? It turns out that characteristics like simple instructions and restrictions like register-based operands not only simplify the processor design but also result in a processor that provides improved application performance. We give a detailed list of RISC design characteristics and their advantages in Chapter 3.

How come the early designers did not think about the RISC way of designing processors? Several factors contributed to the popularity of CISC in the 1970s. In those days, memory was very expensive and small in capacity. For example, even in the mid-1970s,

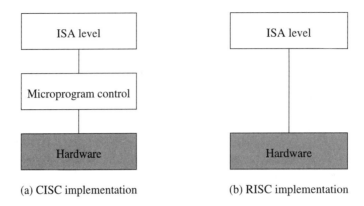

(a) CISC implementation   (b) RISC implementation

Figure 1.2 The ISA-level architecture can be implemented either directly in hardware or through a microprogrammed control.

the price of a small 16 KB memory was about $500. You can imagine the cost of memory in the 1950s and 1960s. So there was a need to minimize the amount of memory required to store a program. An implication of this requirement is that each processor instruction must do more, leading to complex instruction set designs. These designs caused another problem. How could a processor be designed that could execute such complex instructions using the technology of the day? Complex instructions meant complex hardware, which was also expensive. This was a problem processor designers grappled with until Wilkes proposed microprogrammed control in the early 1950s.

A microprogram is a small run-time interpreter that takes the complex instruction and generates a sequence of simple instructions that can be executed by the hardware. Thus the hardware need not be complex. Once it became possible to design such complex processors by using microprogrammed control, designers went crazy and tried to close the semantic gap between the instructions of the processor and high-level languages. This semantic gap refers to the fact that each instruction in a high-level language specifies a lot more work than an instruction in the machine language. Think of a `while` loop statement in a high-level language such as C, for example. If we have a processor instruction with the `while` loop semantics, we could just use one machine language instruction. This explains why most CISC designs use microprogrammed control, as shown in Figure 1.2.

RISC designs, on the other hand, eliminate the microprogram layer and use the hardware to directly execute instructions. Here is another reason why RISC processors can potentially give improved performance. One advantage of using microprogrammed control is that we can implement variations on the basic ISA architecture by simply modifying the microprogram; there is no need to change the underlying hardware, as shown in Figure 1.3. Thus it is possible to come up with cheaper versions as well as high-performance processors for the same family of processors.

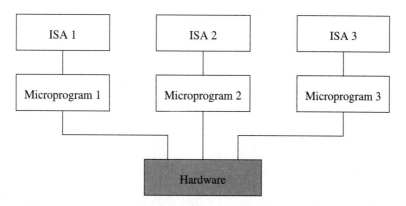

Figure 1.3 Variations on the ISA-level architecture can be implemented by changing the microprogram.

What Is Assembly Language?

Assembly language is directly influenced by the instruction set and architecture of the processor. Assembly language programming is referred to as *low-level programming* because each assembly language instruction performs a much lower-level task compared to an instruction in a high-level language. As a consequence, to perform the same task, assembly language code tends to be much larger than the equivalent high-level language code. Assembly language instructions are native to the processor used in the system. For example, a program written in the Intel assembly language cannot be executed on the PowerPC processor. Programming in the assembly language also requires knowledge about internal system details such as the processor architecture, memory organization, and so on.

Machine language is closely related to the assembly language. Typically, there is a one-to-one correspondence between the assembly language and machine language instructions. The processor understands only the machine language, whose instructions consist of strings of 1s and 0s. We say more on these two languages later.

Here are some IA-32 assembly language examples:

```
inc    result
mov    class_size,45
and    mask1,128
add    marks,10
```

The first instruction increments the variable `result`. This assembly language instruction is equivalent to

```
result++;
```

in C. The second instruction initializes `class_size` to 45. The equivalent statement in C is

```
class_size = 45;
```

The third instruction performs the bitwise and operation on mask1 and can be expressed in C as

```
mask1 = mask1 & 128;
```

The last instruction updates marks by adding 10. In C, this is equivalent to

```
marks = marks + 10;
```

As you can see from these examples, most instructions use two addresses. In these instructions, one operand doubles as a source and destination (for example, class_size and marks). In contrast, the MIPS instructions use three addresses as shown below:

```
andi    $t2,$t1,15
addu    $t3,$t1,$t2
move    $t2,$t1
```

The operands of these instructions are in processor registers. The processor registers are identified by $. The andi instruction performs bitwise and of $t1 register contents with 15 and writes the result in the $t2 register. The second instruction adds the contents of $t1 and $t2 and stores the result in $t3.

The last instruction copies the $t1 value into $t2. In contrast to our claim that MIPS uses three addresses, this instruction seems to use only two addresses. This is not really an instruction supported by the MIPS processor: it is an assembly language instruction. When translated by the MIPS assembler, this instruction is replaced by the following processor instruction.

```
addu    $t2,$0,$t1
```

The second operand in this instruction is a special register that holds constant zero. Thus, copying the $t1 value is treated as adding zero to it.

We can appreciate the readability of the assembly language instructions by looking at the equivalent machine language instructions. Here are some IA-32 and MIPS machine language examples:

IA-32 Examples

Assembly language		Operation	Machine language (in hex)
nop		No operation	90
inc	result	Increment	FF060A00
mov	class_size, 45	Copy	C7060C002D00
and	mask, 128	Logical and	80260E0080
add	marks, 10	Integer addition	83060F000A

MIPS Examples

Assembly language		Operation	Machine language (in hex)
nop		No operation	00000000
move	$t2,$t15	Copy	000A2021
andi	$t2,$t1,15	Logical and	312A000F
addu	$t3,$t1,$t2	Integer addition	012A5821

In the above tables, machine language instructions are written in the hexadecimal number system. If you are not familiar with this number system, consult Appendix A for a detailed discussion of various number systems. These examples visibly demonstrate one of the key differences between CISC and RISC designs: RISC processors use fixed-length machine language instructions whereas the machine language instructions of CISC processors vary in length.

It is obvious from this discussion that understanding the code of a program, written in an assembly language, is difficult. Before looking at why we program in assembly language, let's see the main advantages of high-level languages.

Advantages of High-Level Languages

High-level languages are preferred to program applications inasmuch as they provide a convenient abstraction of the underlying system suitable for problem solving. Here are some advantages of programming in a high-level language.

1. *Program development is faster.*
   Many high-level languages provide structures (sequential, selection, iterative) that facilitate program development. Programs written in a high-level language are relatively small compared to the equivalent programs written in an assembly language. These programs are also easier to code and debug.

2. *Programs are easier to maintain.*
   Programming a new application can take from several weeks to several months and the lifecycle of such an application software can be several years. Therefore, it is critical that software development be done with a view towards software maintainability, which involves activities ranging from fixing bugs to generating the next version of the software. Programs written in a high-level language are easier to understand and, when good programming practices are followed, easier to maintain. Assembly language programs tend to be lengthy and take more time to code and debug. As a result, they are also difficult to maintain.

3. *Programs are portable.*
   High-level language programs contain very few processor-dependent details. As a result, they can be used with little or no modification on different computer systems. In contrast, assembly language programs are processor-specific.

Why Program in Assembly Language?

The previous section gives enough reasons to discourage you from programming in assembly language. However, there are two main reasons why programming is still done in assembly language: efficiency and accessibility to system hardware.

Efficiency refers to how "good" a program is in achieving a given objective. Here we consider two objectives based on space (space-efficiency) and time (time-efficiency).

Space-efficiency refers to the memory requirements of a program (i.e., the size of the executable code). Program A is said to be more space-efficient if it takes less memory space than program B to perform the same task. Very often, programs written in an assembly language tend to be more compact than those written in a high-level language.

Time-efficiency refers to the time taken to execute a program. Obviously a program that runs faster is said to be better from the time-efficiency point of view. In general, assembly language programs tend to run faster than their high-level language versions.

The superiority of assembly language in generating compact code is becoming increasingly less important for several reasons. First, the savings in space pertain only to the program code and not to its data space. Thus, depending on the application, the savings in space obtained by converting an application program from some high-level language to an assembly language may not be substantial. Second, the cost of memory has been decreasing and memory capacity has been increasing. Thus, the size of a program is not a major hurdle anymore. Finally, compilers are becoming "smarter" in generating code that is both space- and time-efficient. However, there are systems such as embedded controllers and handheld devices in which space-efficiency is very important.

One of the main reasons for writing programs in assembly language is to generate code that is time-efficient. The superiority of assembly language programs in producing efficient code is a direct manifestation of *specificity*. That is, assembly language programs contain only the code that is necessary to perform the given task. Even here, a "smart" compiler can optimize the code that can compete well with its equivalent written in an assembly language. Although this gap is narrowing with improvements in compiler technology, assembly language still retains its advantage for now.

The other main reason for writing assembly language programs is to have direct control over system hardware. High-level languages, on purpose, provide a restricted (abstract) view of the underlying hardware. Because of this, it is almost impossible to perform certain tasks that require access to the system hardware. For example, writing a device driver to a new scanner on the market almost certainly requires programming in an assembly language. Because assembly language does not impose any restrictions, you can have direct control over the system hardware. If you are developing system software, you cannot avoid writing assembly language programs.

There is another reason for our interest in the assembly language. It allows us to look at the internal details of the processors. For the RISC processors discussed in the next part of the book, we present their assembly language instructions. In addition, Part III gives you hands-on experience in MIPS assembly language programming.

Summary

We identified two major processor designs: CISC and RISC. We discussed the differences between these two design philosophies. The Intel IA-32 architecture follows the CISC design whereas several recent processor families follow the RISC designs. Some examples belonging to the RISC category are the MIPS, SPARC, and ARM processor families.

We also introduced assembly language to prepare the ground for Part III of the book. Specifically, we looked at the advantages and problems associated with assembly language vis-à-vis high-level languages.

2

Processor Design Issues

In this chapter we look at some of the basic choices in the processor design space. We start our discussion with the number of addresses used in processor instructions. This is an important characteristic that influences instruction set design. We also look at the load/store architecture used by RISC processors.

Another important aspect that affects performance of the overall system is the flow control. Flow control deals with issues such as branching and procedure calls. We discuss the general principles used to efficiently implement branching and procedure invocation mechanisms. We wrap up the chapter with a discussion of some of the instruction set design issues.

Introduction

One of the characteristics of the instruction set architecture (ISA) that shapes the architecture is the number of addresses used in an instruction. Most operations can be divided into binary or unary operations. Binary operations such as addition and multiplication require two input operands whereas the unary operations such as the logical not need only a single operand. Most operations produce a single result. There are exceptions, however. For example, the division operation produces two outputs: a quotient and a remainder. Because most operations are binary, we need a total of three addresses: two addresses to specify the two input operands and one to specify where the result should go. Typical operations require two operands, therefore we need three addresses: two addresses to specify the two input operands and the third one to indicate where the result should be stored.

Most processors specify three addresses. We can reduce the number of addresses to two by using one address to specify a source address as well as the destination address. The Intel IA-32 processors use the two-address format. It is also possible to have instructions that use only one or even zero address. The one-address machines are called

Table 2.1 Sample three-address machine instructions

Instruction	Semantics
add dest,src1,src2	Adds the two values at src1 and src2 and stores the result in dest
sub dest,src1,src2	Subtracts the second source operand at src2 from the first at src1 (src1 − src2) and stores the result in dest
mult dest,src1,src2	Multiplies the two values at src1 and src2 and stores the result in dest

accumulator machines and the zero-address machines are called stack machines. We discuss the pros and cons of these schemes later.

RISC processors tend to use a special architecture known as the load/store architecture. In this architecture, special load and store instructions are used to move data between the processor's internal registers and memory. All other instructions expect the necessary operands to be present in the processor internal registers. Vector processors originally used the load/store architecture. We present more details on the load/store architecture later.

Instruction set design involves several other issues. The addressing mode is another important aspect that specifies where the operands are located. CISC designs typically allow a variety of addressing modes, whereas only a couple of addressing modes are supported by RISC. The addressing modes and number of addresses directly influence the instruction format. These and other issues such as instruction and operand types are discussed in the remainder of the chapter.

Number of Addresses

Most recent processors use three addresses. However, it is possible to design systems with two, one, or even zero addresses. In the rest of this section, we give a brief description of these four types of machines. After presenting these details, we discuss their advantages and disadvantages.

Three-Address Machines

In three-address machines, instructions carry all three addresses explicitly. The RISC processors we discuss in later chapters use three addresses. Table 2.1 gives some sample instructions of a three-address machine.

Table 2.2 Sample two-address machine instructions

Instruction	Semantics
load dest,src	Copies the value at src to dest
add dest,src	Adds the two values at src and dest and stores the result in dest
sub dest,src	Subtracts the second source operand at src from the first at dest (dest − src) and stores the result in dest
mult dest,src	Multiplies the two values at src and dest and stores the result in dest

In these machines, the C statement

```
A = B + C * D - E + F + A
```

is converted to the following code.

```
mult   T,C,D   ; T = C*D
add    T,T,B   ; T = B + C*D
sub    T,T,E   ; T = B + C*D - E
add    T,T,F   ; T = B + C*D - E + F
add    A,T,A   ; A = B + C*D - E + F + A
```

As you can see from this code, there is one instruction for each arithmetic operation. Also notice that all instructions, barring the first one, use an address twice. In the middle three instructions, it is the temporary T and in the last one, it is A. This is the motivation for using two addresses, as we show next.

Two-Address Machines

In two-address machines, one address doubles as a source and destination. Table 2.2 gives some sample instructions of a two-address machine. Usually, we use dest to indicate that the address is used for destination. But you should note that this address also supplies one of the source operands when required. The IA-32 architecture uses two addresses.

On these machines, the C statement

```
A = B + C * D - E + F + A
```

is converted to the following code.

Table 2.3 Sample accumulator machine instructions

Instruction	Semantics
`load addr`	Copies the value at address `addr` into the accumulator
`store addr`	Stores the value in the accumulator at the memory address `addr`
`add addr`	Adds the contents of the accumulator and value at address `addr` and stores the result in the accumulator
`sub addr`	Subtracts the value at memory address `addr` from the contents of the accumulator and stores the result in the accumulator
`mult addr`	Multiplies the contents of the accumulator and value at address `addr` and stores the result in the accumulator

```
load   T,C    ; T = C
mult   T,D    ; T = C*D
add    T,B    ; T = B + C*D
sub    T,E    ; T = B + C*D - E
add    T,F    ; T = B + C*D - E + F
add    A,T    ; A = B + C*D - E + F + A
```

Because we use only two addresses, we use a load instruction to first copy the C value into a temporary represented by T. If you look at these six instructions, you will notice that the operand T is common. If we make this our default, we don't even need two addresses: we can get away with just one.

One-Address Machines

In the early machines, when memory was expensive and slow, a special set of registers was used to provide an input operand as well as to receive the result. Because of this, these registers are called the *accumulators*. In most machines, there is just a single accumulator register. This kind of design, called the *accumulator machines*, makes sense if memory is expensive.

In accumulator machines, most operations are performed on the contents of the accumulator and the operand supplied by the instruction. Thus, instructions for these machines need to specify only the address of a single operand. There is no need to store the result in memory: this reduces the need for larger memory as well as speeds up the computation by reducing the number of memory accesses. A few sample accumulator machine instructions are shown in Table 2.3.

Table 2.4 Sample stack machine instructions

Instruction	Semantics
push addr	Places the value at address `addr` on top of the stack
pop addr	Stores the top value on the stack at memory address `addr`
add	Adds the top two values on the stack and pushes the result onto the stack
sub	Subtracts the second top value from the top value of the stack and pushes the result onto the stack
mult	Multiplies the top two values on the stack and pushes the result onto the stack

In these machines, the C statement

```
A = B + C * D - E + F + A
```

is converted to the following code.

```
load    C    ; load C into the accumulator
mult    D    ; accumulator = C*D
add     B    ; accumulator = C*D+B
sub     E    ; accumulator = C*D+B-E
add     F    ; accumulator = C*D+B-E+F
add     A    ; accumulator = C*D+B-E+F+A
store   A    ; store the accumulator contents in A
```

Zero-Address Machines

In zero-address machines, locations of both operands are assumed to be at a default location. These machines use the stack as the source of the input operands and the result goes back into the stack. A stack is a LIFO (last-in-first-out) data structure that all processors support, whether or not they are zero-address machines. As the name implies, the last item placed on the stack is the first item to be taken off the stack. A good analogy is the stack of trays you find in a cafeteria.

All operations on this type of machine assume that the required input operands are the top two values on the stack. The result of the operation is placed on top of the stack. Table 2.4 gives some sample instructions for the stack machines.

Notice that the first two instructions are not zero-address instructions. These two are special instructions that use a single address and are used to move data between memory and stack. All other instructions use the zero-address format. Let's see how the stack machine translates the arithmetic expression we have seen before.

In these machines, the C statement

```
A = B + C * D - E + F + A
```

is converted to the following code.

```
push  E      ; <E>
push  C      ; <C, E>
push  D      ; <D, C, E>
mult         ; <C*D, E>
push  B      ; <B, C*D, E>
add          ; <B+C*D, E>
sub          ; <B+C*D-E>
push  F      ; <F, B+D*C-E>
add          ; <F+B+D*C-E>
push  A      ; <A, F+B+D*C-E>
add          ; <A+F+B+D*C-E>
pop   A      ; < >
```

On the right, we show the state of the stack after executing each instruction. The top element of the stack is shown on the left. Notice that we pushed E early because we need to subtract it from (B+C*D).

Stack machines are implemented by making the top portion of the stack internal to the processor. This is referred to as the *stack depth*. The rest of the stack is placed in memory. Thus, to access the top values that are within the stack depth, we do not have to access the memory. Obviously, we get better performance by increasing the stack depth. Examples of stack-oriented machines include the earlier Burroughs B5500 system and the HP3000 from Hewlett–Packard. Most scientific calculators also use stack-based operands.

A Comparison

Each of the four address schemes has certain advantages. If you count the number of instructions needed to execute our example C statement, you will notice that this count increases as we reduce the number of addresses. Let us assume that the number of memory accesses represents our performance metric: the lower the number of memory accesses, the better.

In the three-address machine, each instruction takes four memory accesses: one access to read the instruction itself, two for getting the two input operands, and a final one to write the result back in memory. Because there are five instructions, this machine generates a total of 20 memory accesses.

In the two-address machine, each arithmetic instruction still takes four accesses as in the three-address machine. Remember that we are using one address to double as a source and destination address. Thus, the five arithmetic instructions require 20 memory accesses. In addition, we have the load instruction that requires three accesses. Thus, it takes a total of 23 memory accesses.

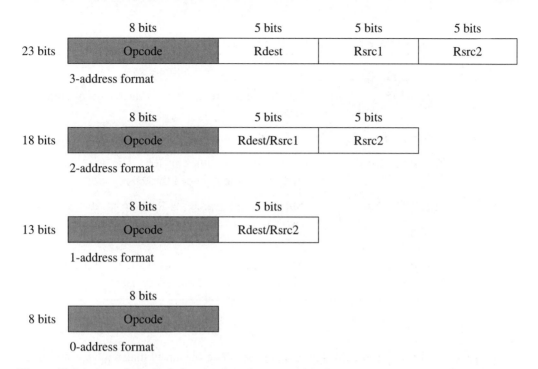

Figure 2.1 Instruction sizes for the four formats: this format assumes that the operands are located in registers.

The count for the accumulator machine is better as the accumulator is a register and reading or writing to it, therefore, does not generate a memory access. In this machine, each instruction requires just 2 accesses. Because there are seven instructions, this machine generates 14 memory accesses.

Finally, if we assume that the stack depth is sufficiently large so that all our push and pop operations do not exceed this value, the stack machine takes 19 accesses. This count is obtained by noting that each push or pop instruction takes 2 memory accesses, whereas the five arithmetic instructions take 1 memory access each.

This comparison leads us to believe that the accumulator machine is the fastest. The comparison between the accumulator and stack machines is fair because both machines assume the presence of registers. However, we cannot say the same for the other two machines. In particular, in our calculation, we assumed that there are no registers on the three- and two-address machines. If we assume that these two machines have a single register to hold the temporary T, the count for the three-address machine comes down to 12 memory accesses. The corresponding number for the two-address machine is 13 memory accesses. As you can see from this simple example, we tend to increase the number of memory accesses as we reduce the number of addresses.

Table 2.5 Sample load/store machine instructions

Instruction	Semantics
load Rd,addr	Loads the Rd register with the value at address addr
store addr,Rs	Stores the value in Rs register at address addr
add Rd,Rs1,Rs2	Adds the two values in Rs1 and Rs2 registers and places the result in the Rd register
sub Rd,Rs1,Rs2	Subtracts the value in Rs2 from that in Rs1 (Rs1 − Rs2) and places the result in the Rd register
mult Rd,Rs1,Rs2	Multiplies the two values in Rs1 and Rs2 and places the result in the Rd register

There are still problems with this comparison. The reason is that we have not taken the size of the instructions into account. The stack machine instructions do not need to specify the operand addresses, therefore each instruction takes fewer bits to encode than an instruction in the three-address machine. Of course, the difference between the two depends on several factors including how the addresses are specified and whether we allow registers to hold the operands.

Figure 2.1 shows the size of the instructions when the operands are available in the registers. This example assumes that the processor has 32 registers like the MIPS processor and the opcode takes 8 bits. The instruction size varies from 23 bits to 8 bits.

In practice, most systems use a combination of these address schemes. This is obvious from our stack machine. Even though the stack machine is a zero-address machine, it uses load and store instructions that specify a single address. Some architectures impose restrictions on where the operands can be located. For example, the IA-32 architecture allows only one of the two operands to be located in memory. RISC architectures take this restriction further by allowing most instructions to work only on the operands located in the processor registers. This architecture is called the load/store architecture, which is discussed next.

The Load/Store Architecture

In the load/store architecture, only load and store instructions move data between the registers and memory. Table 2.5 gives some sample instructions for the load/store machines.

RISC machines as well as vector processors use this architecture, which reduces the size of the instruction substantially. If we assume that memory addresses are 32 bits long,

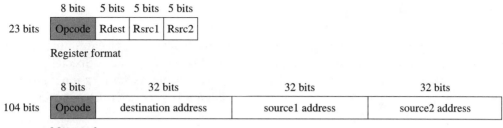

Figure 2.2 A comparison of the instruction size when the operands are in registers versus memory.

an instruction with all three operands in memory requires 104 bits whereas the register-based operands require only 23 bits, as shown in Figure 2.2.

In these machines, the C statement

```
A = B + C * D - E + F + A
```

is converted to the following code.

```
load    R1,C       ; load C
load    R2,D       ; load D
mult    R1,R1,R2   ; R1 = C*D
load    R2,B       ; load B
add     R1,R1,R2   ; R1 = B + C*D
load    R2,E       ; load E
sub     R1,R1,R2   ; R1 = B + C*D - E
load    R2,F       ; load F
add     R1,R1,R2   ; R1 = B + C*D - E + F
load    R2,A       ; load A
add     R1,R1,R2   ; R2 = B + C*D - E + F + A
store   A,R1       ; store the result in A
```

Each load and store instruction takes two memory accesses: one to fetch the instruction and the other to access the data value. The arithmetic instructions need just one memory access to fetch the instruction, as the operands are in registers. Thus, this code takes 19 memory accesses.

Note that the elapsed execution time is not directly proportional to the number of memory accesses. Overlapped execution reduces the execution time for some processors. In particular, RISC processors facilitate this overlapped execution because of their load/store architecture.

Processor Registers

Processors have a number of registers to hold data, instructions, and state information. We can divide the registers into general-purpose or special-purpose registers. Special-purpose registers can be further divided into those that are accessible to the user programs and those reserved for system use. The available technology largely determines the structure and function of the register set.

The number of addresses used in instructions partly influences the number of data registers and their use. For example, stack machines do not require any data registers. However, as noted, part of the stack is kept internal to the processor. This part of the stack serves the same purpose that registers do. In three- and two-address machines, there is no need for the internal data registers. However, as we have demonstrated before, having some internal registers improves performance by cutting down the number of memory accesses. The RISC machines typically have a large number of registers.

Some processors maintain a few special-purpose registers. For example, the IA-32 uses a couple of registers to implement the processor stack. Processors also have several registers reserved for the instruction execution unit. Typically, there is an instruction register that holds the current instruction and a program counter that points to the next instruction to be executed.

Flow of Control

Program execution, by default, proceeds sequentially. The program counter (PC) register plays an important role in managing the control flow. At a simple level, the PC can be thought of as pointing to the next instruction. The processor fetches the instruction at the address pointed to by the PC. When an instruction is fetched, the PC is automatically incremented to point to the next instruction. If we assume that each instruction takes exactly four bytes as in MIPS and SPARC processors, the PC is automatically incremented by four after each instruction fetch. This leads to the default sequential execution pattern. However, sometimes we want to alter this default execution flow. In high-level languages, we use control structures such as if-then-else and while statements to alter the execution behavior based on some run-time conditions. Similarly, the procedure call is another way we alter the sequential execution. In this section, we describe how processors support flow control. We look at both branch and procedure calls next.

Branching

Branching is implemented by means of a branch instruction. There are two types of branches: *direct* and *indirect*. The direct branch instruction carries the address of the target instruction explicitly. In indirect branch, the target address is specified indirectly via either memory or a register. We look at an indirect branch example in Chapter 14 (page 259). In the rest of this section, we consider direct branches.

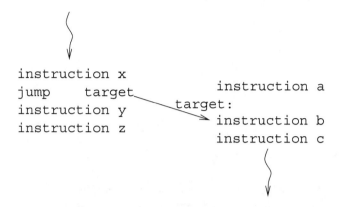

Figure 2.3 Normal branch execution.

We can divide the branches into two categories: unconditional and conditional. In both cases, the transfer control mechanism remains the same as that shown in Figure 2.3.

Unconditional Branch The simplest of the branch instructions is the *unconditional branch*, which transfers control to the specified target. Here is an example branch instruction:

```
branch     target
```

Specification of the target address can be done in one of two ways: absolute address or PC-relative address. In the former, the actual address of the target instruction is given. In the PC-relative method, the target address is specified relative to the PC contents. Most processors support absolute address for unconditional branches. Others support both formats. For example, MIPS processors support absolute address-based branch by

```
j     target
```

and PC-relative unconditional branch by

```
b     target
```

In fact, the last instruction is an assembly language instruction; the processor supports only the j instruction.

The PowerPC allows each branch instruction to use either an absolute or a PC-relative address. The instruction encoding has a bit—called the absolute address (AA) bit—to indicate the type of address. If AA = 1, absolute address is assumed; otherwise, the PC-relative address is used.

If the absolute address is used, the processor transfers control by simply loading the specified target address into the PC register. If PC-relative addressing is used, the specified target address is added to the PC contents, and the result is placed in the PC. In either case, because the PC indicates the next instruction address, the processor will fetch the instruction at the intended target address.

The main advantage of using the PC-relative address is that we can move the code from one block of memory to another without changing the target addresses. This type of code is called *relocatable code*. Relocatable code is not possible with absolute addresses.

Conditional Branch   In conditional branches, the jump is taken only if a specified condition is satisfied. For example, we may want to take a branch if the two values are equal. Such conditional branches are handled in one of two basic ways.

- *Set-Then-Jump:* In this design, testing for the condition and branching are separated. To achieve communication between these two instructions, a condition code register is used. The PowerPC follows this design, which uses a condition register to record the result of the test condition. It uses a compare (cmp) instruction to test the condition. This instruction sets the various condition bits to indicate the relationship between the two compared values. The following code fragment, which compares the values in registers r2 and r3, should clarify this sequence.

  ```
          cmpd   r2,r3      ; compare the two values in r2 and r3
          bne    target     ; if r2 ≠ r3, transfer control to target
          not    r3,r3      ; if r2 = r3, this instruction is executed
             .  .  .
  target:
          add    r4,r3,r4  ; control is transferred here if r2 ≠ r3
             .  .  .
  ```

  The bne (branch if not equal) instruction transfers control to target only if the two values in registers r2 and r3 are not equal.

- *Test-and-Jump:* In this method, testing and branching are combined into a single instruction. We use the MIPS to illustrate the principle involved in this strategy. The MIPS architecture supports several branch instructions that test and branch (for a quick peek, see Table 14.2 on page 249). For example, the branch on not equal instruction

  ```
          bne    Rsrc1,Rsrc2,target
  ```

  tests the contents of the two registers Rsrc1 and Rsrc2 for equality and transfers control to target if Rsrc1 ≠ Rsrc2. If we assume that the numbers to be compared are in registers $t0 and $t1, we can write the branch instruction as

  ```
          bne    $t1,$t0,target
  ```

This single instruction replaces the two-instruction cmp/bne sequence used by the PowerPC.

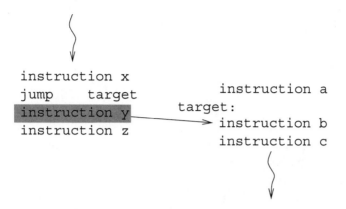

Figure 2.4 Delayed branch execution.

Some processors maintain registers to record the condition of the arithmetic and logical operations. These are called *condition code registers*. These registers keep a record of
the status of the last arithmetic/logical operation. For example, when we add two 32-bit
integers, it is possible that the sum might require more than 32 bits. This is the overflow
condition that the system should record. Normally, a bit in the condition code register is
set to indicate this overflow condition. The MIPS, for example, does not use a condition
register. Instead, it uses exceptions to flag the overflow condition. On the other hand, PowerPC and SPARC processors use condition registers. In the PowerPC, this information is
maintained by the XER register. SPARC uses a condition code register.

Some instruction sets provide branches based on comparisons to zero. Some examples
that provide this type of branch instructions include the MIPS and SPARC (see Table 14.3
on page 250 for the MIPS instructions).

Highly pipelined RISC processors support what is known as delayed branch execution. To see the difference between delayed and normal branch execution, let us look at the
normal branch execution shown in Figure 2.3. When the branch instruction is executed,
control is transferred to the target immediately.

In delayed branch execution, control is transferred to the target after executing the
instruction that follows the branch instruction. For example, in Figure 2.4, before the control is transferred, the instruction `instruction y` (shown shaded) is executed. This
instruction slot is called the *delay slot*. For example, MIPS and SPARC use delayed
branch execution. In fact, they also use delayed execution for procedure calls.

Why does the delayed execution help? The reason is that by the time the processor
decodes the branch instruction, the next instruction is already fetched. Thus, instead of
throwing it away, we improve efficiency by executing it. This strategy requires reordering
of some instructions. In Chapter 5 we give some examples of how it affects the programs.

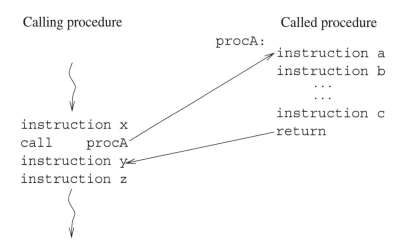

Figure 2.5 Control flow in procedure calls.

Procedure Calls

The use of procedures facilitates modular programming. Procedure calls are slightly different from the branches. Branches are one-way jumps: once the control has been transferred to the target location, computation proceeds from that location, as shown in Figure 2.3. In procedure calls, we have to return control to the calling program after executing the procedure. Control is returned to the instruction following the call instruction as shown in Figure 2.5.

From Figures 2.3 and 2.5, you will notice that the branches and procedure calls are similar in their initial control transfer. For procedure calls, we need to return to the instruction following the procedure call. This return requires two pieces of information: an end-of-procedure indication and a return address.

End of Procedure   We have to indicate the end of the procedure so that the control can be returned. This is normally done by a special return instruction. For example, the IA-32 uses `ret` and the MIPS uses the `jr` instruction to return from a procedure. We do the same in high-level languages as well. For example, in C, we use the `return` statement to indicate an end of procedure execution.

Return Address   How does the processor know where to return after completing a procedure? This piece of information is normally stored when the procedure is called. Thus, when a procedure is invoked, it not only modifies the PC as in a branch instruction, but also stores the return address. Where does it store the return address? Two main places are used: a special register or the stack. In processors that use a register to store the return address, some use a special dedicated register, whereas others allow any register to be

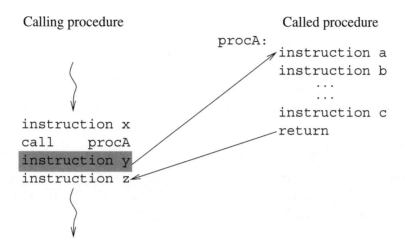

Calling procedure   Called procedure

Figure 2.6 Control flow in delayed procedure calls.

used for this purpose. The actual return address stored depends on the architecture. For example, SPARC stores the address of the `call` instruction itself. Others like MIPS store the address of the instruction *following* the `call` instruction.

The IA-32 uses the stack to store the return address. Thus, each procedure call involves pushing the return address onto the stack before control is transferred to the procedure code. The return instruction retrieves this value from the stack to send the control back to the instruction following the procedure call.

MIPS processors allow any general-purpose register to store the return address. The return statement can specify this register. The format of the return statement is

```
jr    $ra
```

where `ra` is the register that contains the return address.

The PowerPC has a dedicated register, called the link register (LR), to store the return address. Both the MIPS and the PowerPC use a modified branch to implement a procedure call. The advantage of these processors is that simple procedure calls do not have to access memory.

Most RISC processors that support delayed branching also support delayed procedure calls. As in the branch instructions, control is transferred to the target after executing the instruction that follows the call (see Figure 2.6). Thus, after the procedure is done, control should be returned to the instruction after the delay slot, that is, to `instruction z` in the figure. We show some SPARC examples of this in Chapter 5.

Parameter Passing

The general architecture dictates how parameters are passed on to the procedures. There are two basic techniques: register-based or stack-based. In the first method, parameters are placed in processor registers and the called procedure reads the parameter values from these registers. In the stack-based method, parameters are pushed onto the stack and the called procedure would have to read them off the stack.

The advantage of the register method is that it is faster than the stack method. However, because of the limited number of registers, it imposes a limit on the number of parameters. Furthermore, recursive procedures cannot use the simple register-based mechanism. Because RISC processors tend to have more registers, register-based parameter passing is used in RISC processors. The IA-32 tends to use the stack for parameter passing due to the limited number of processor registers.

Some architectures use a register window mechanism that allows a more flexible parameter passing. The SPARC and Intel Itanium processors use this parameter passing mechanism. We describe this method in detail in later chapters.

Handling Branches

Modern processors are highly pipelined. In such processors, flow-altering instructions such as branch require special handling. If the branch is not taken, the instructions in the pipeline are useful. However, for a taken branch, we have to discard all the instructions that are in the pipeline at various stages. This causes the processor to do wasteful work, resulting in a *branch penalty*.

How can we reduce this branch penalty? We have already mentioned one technique: the delayed branch execution, which reduces the branch penalty. When we use this strategy, we need to modify our program to put a useful instruction in the delay slot. Some processors such as the SPARC and MIPS use delayed execution for both branching and procedure calls.

We can improve performance further if we can find whether a branch is taken without waiting for the execution of the branch instruction. In the case where the branch is taken, we also need to know the target address so that the pipeline can be filled from the target address. For direct branch instructions, the target address is given as part of the instruction. Because most instructions are direct branches, computation of the target address is relatively straightforward. But it may not be that easy to predict whether the branch will be taken. For example, we may have to fetch the operands and compare their values to determine whether the branch is taken. This means we have to wait until the instruction reaches the execution stage. We can use branch prediction strategies to make an educated guess. For indirect branches, we have to also guess the target address. Next we discuss several branch prediction strategies.

Branch Prediction

Branch prediction is traditionally used to handle the branch problem. We discuss three branch prediction strategies: fixed, static, and dynamic.

Table 2.6 Static branch prediction accuracy

Instruction type	Instruction distribution (%)	Prediction: Branch taken?	Correct prediction (%)
Unconditional branch	$70 \times 0.4 = 28$	Yes	28
Conditional branch	$70 \times 0.6 = 42$	No	$42 \times 0.6 = 25.2$
Loop	10	Yes	$10 \times 0.9 = 9$
Call/return	20	Yes	20
Overall prediction accuracy = 82.2%			

Fixed Branch Prediction   In this strategy, prediction is fixed. These strategies are simple to implement and assume that the branch is either never taken or always taken. The Motorola 68020 and VAX 11/780 use the branch-never-taken approach. The advantage of the never-taken strategy is that the processor can continue to fetch instructions sequentially to fill the pipeline. This involves minimum penalty in case the prediction is wrong. If, on the other hand, we use the always-taken approach, the processor would prefetch the instruction at the branch target address. In a paged environment, this may lead to a page fault, and a special mechanism is needed to take care of this situation. Furthermore, if the prediction were wrong, we would have done a lot of unnecessary work.

The branch-never-taken approach, however, is not proper for a loop structure. If a loop iterates 200 times, the branch is taken 199 out of 200 times. For loops, the always-taken approach is better. Similarly, the always-taken approach is preferred for procedure calls and returns.

Static Branch Prediction   From our discussion, it is obvious that, rather than following a fixed strategy, we can improve performance by using a strategy that is dependent on the branch type. This is what the static strategy does. It uses instruction opcode to predict whether the branch is taken. To show why this strategy gives high prediction accuracy, we present sample data for commercial environments. In such environments, of all the branch-type operations, the branches are about 70%, loops are 10%, and the rest are procedure calls/returns. Of the total branches, 40% are unconditional. If we use a never-taken guess for the conditional branch and always-taken for the rest of the branch-type operations, we get a prediction accuracy of about 82% as shown in Table 2.6.

The data in this table assume that conditional branches are not taken about 60% of the time. Thus, our prediction that a conditional branch is never taken is correct only 60% of the time. This gives us $42 \times 0.6 = 25.2\%$ as the prediction accuracy for conditional branches. Similarly, loops jump back with 90% probability. Loops appear about 10% of the time, therefore the prediction is right 9% of the time. Surprisingly, even this simple static prediction strategy gives us about 82% accuracy!

Table 2.7 Impact of using the knowledge of past n branches on prediction accuracy

n	Type of mix		
	Compiler	Business	Scientific
0	64.1	64.4	70.4
1	91.9	95.2	86.6
2	93.3	96.5	90.8
3	93.7	96.6	91.0
4	94.5	96.8	91.8
5	94.7	97.0	92.0

Dynamic Branch Prediction   Dynamic strategy looks at the run-time history to make more accurate predictions. The basic idea is to take the past n branch executions of the branch type in question and use this information to predict the next one. Will this work in practice? How much additional benefit can we derive over the static approach? The empirical study by Lee and Smith [15] suggests that we can get significant improvement in prediction accuracy. A summary of their study is presented in Table 2.7. The algorithm they implemented is simple: the prediction for the next branch is the majority of the previous n branch executions. For example, for $n = 3$, if two or more times branches were taken in the past three branch executions, the prediction is that the branch will be taken.

The data in Table 2.7 suggest that looking at the past two branch executions will give us over 90% prediction accuracy for most mixes. Beyond that, we get only marginal improvement. This is good from the implementation point of view: we need just two bits to take the history of the past two branch executions. The basic idea is simple: keep the current prediction unless the past two predictions were wrong. Specifically, we do not want to change our prediction just because our last prediction was wrong. This policy can be expressed using the four-state finite state machine shown in Figure 2.7.

In this state diagram, the left bit represents the prediction and the right bit indicates the branch status (branch taken or not). If the left bit is zero, our prediction would be branch "not taken"; otherwise we predict that the branch will be taken. The right bit gives the actual result of the branch instruction. Thus, a 0 represents that the branch instruction did not jump ("not taken"); 1 indicates that the branch is taken. For example, state 00 represents that we predicted that the branch would not be taken (left zero bit) and the branch is indeed not taken (right zero bit). Therefore, as long as the branch is not taken, we remain in state 00. If our prediction is wrong, we move to state 01. However, we still predict "branch not taken" as we were wrong only once. If our prediction is right, we go back to state 00. If our prediction is wrong again (i.e., two times in a row), we change our

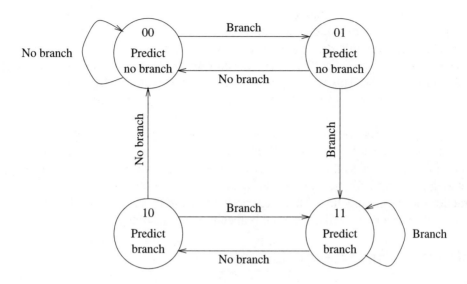

Figure 2.7 State diagram for branch prediction.

Valid bit	Branch instruction address	Prediction bits
.		
.		
.		
.		

(a)

Valid bit	Branch instruction address	Target address	Prediction bits
.	.		
.	.		
.	.		
.	.		

(b)

Figure 2.8 Implementation of dynamic branch prediction: (a) using a 2-bit branch history; (b) including the target address facilitates prefetching.

prediction to "branch taken" and move to state 11. You can verify that it always takes two wrong predictions in a row to change our prediction.

Implementation of this strategy requires maintaining two bits for each branch instruction, as shown in Figure 2.8a. These two bits correspond to the two bits of the finite state machine in Figure 2.7. This works well for direct branch instructions, where the address of the target is specified as part of the instruction. However, in indirect branch instructions, the target is not known until instruction execution. Therefore, predicting whether the branch is taken is not particularly useful to fill the pipeline if we do not know the target address in advance. It is reasonable to assume that the branch instruction, if the branch is taken, jumps to the same target address as the last time. Thus, if we store the target address along with the branch instruction, we can use this target address to prefetch instructions to fill the pipeline. This scenario is shown in Figure 2.8b. In Part III we look at some processors that use the dynamic branch prediction strategy.

Instruction Set Design Issues

There are several design issues that influence the instruction set of a processor. We have already discussed one issue, the number of addresses used in an instruction. In this section, we present some other design issues.

Operand Types

Processor instructions typically support only the basic data types. These include characters, integers, and floating-point numbers. Because most memories are byte addressable, representing characters does not require special treatment. In a byte-addressable memory, the smallest memory unit we can address, and therefore access, is one byte. We can, however, use multiple bytes to represent larger operands. Processors provide instructions to load various operand sizes. Often, the same instruction is used to load operands of different sizes. For example, the IA-32 instruction

```
mov    AL,address      ; Loads an 8-bit value
```

loads the AL register with an 8-bit value from memory at `address`. The same instruction can also be used to load 16- and 32-bit values as shown in the following two instructions.

```
mov    AX,address      ; Loads a 16-bit value
mov    EAX,address     ; Loads a 32-bit value
```

In these instructions, the size of the operand is indirectly given by the size of the register used. The AL, AX, and EAX are 8-, 16-, and 32-bit registers, respectively. In those instructions that do not use a register, we can use size specifiers. This type of specification is typical for the CISC processors.

RISC processors specify the operand size in their load and store operations. Note that only the load and store instructions move data between memory and registers. All other instructions operate on registerwide data. Below we give some examples of the MIPS load instructions:

```
lb      Rdest,address    ; Loads a byte
lh      Rdest,address    ; Loads a halfword (16 bits)
lw      Rdest,address    ; Loads a word (32 bits)
ld      Rdest,address    ; Loads a doubleword (64 bits)
```

The last instruction is available only on 64-bit processors. In general, when the size of the data moved is smaller than the destination register, it is sign-extended to the size of Rdest. There are separate instructions to handle unsigned values. For unsigned numbers, we use lbu and lhu instead of lb and lh, respectively.

Similar instructions are available for store operations. In store operations, the size is reduced to fit the target memory size. For example, storing a byte from a 32-bit register causes only the lower byte to be stored at the specified address. SPARC also uses a similar set of instructions.

So far we have seen operations on operands located either in registers or in memory. In most instructions, we can also use constants. These constants are called immediate values because the constants are encoded as part of the instruction. In RISC processors, instructions excluding the load and store use registers only; any nonregister value is treated as a constant. In most assembly languages, a special notation is used to indicate registers. For example, in MIPS assembly language, the instruction

```
add    $t0,$t0,-32    ; $t0 = $t0 - 32
```

subtracts 32 from the $t0 register and places the result back in the $t0 register. Notice the special notation to represent registers. But there is no special notation for constants. Some assemblers, however, use the "#" sign to indicate a constant.

Addressing Modes

Addressing mode refers to how the operands are specified. As we have seen in the last section, operands can be in one of three places: in a register, in memory, or part of the instruction as a constant. Specifying a constant as an operand is called the *immediate addressing mode*. Similarly, specifying an operand that is in a register is called the *register addressing mode*. All processors support these two addressing modes.

The difference between the RISC and CISC processors is in how they specify the operands in memory. CISC designs support a large variety of memory addressing modes. RISC designs, on the other hand, support just one or two addressing modes in their load and store instructions. Most RISC architectures support the following two memory addressing modes.

- The address of the memory operand is computed by adding the contents of a register and a constant. If this constant is zero, the contents of the register are treated as the operand address. In this mode, the memory address is computed as

Address = contents of a register + constant.

- The address of the memory operand is computed by adding the contents of two registers. If one of the register contents is zero, this addressing mode becomes the same as the one above with zero constant. In this mode, the memory address is computed as

Address = contents of register 1 + contents of register 2.

Among the RISC processors we discuss, ARM and Itanium provide slightly different addressing modes. The Itanium uses the computed address to update the register. For example, in the first addressing mode, the register is loaded with the value obtained by adding the constant to the contents of the register.

The IA-32 provides a variety of addressing modes. The main motivation for this is the desire to support high-level language data structures. For example, one of its addressing modes can be used to access elements of a two-dimensional array.

Instruction Types

Instruction sets provide different types of instructions. We describe some of these instruction types here.

Data Movement Instructions   All instruction sets support data movement instructions. The type of instructions supported depends on the architecture. We can divide these instructions into two groups: instructions that facilitate movement of data between memory and registers and between registers. Some instruction sets have special data movement instructions. For example, the IA-32 has special instructions such as `push` and `pop` to move data to and from the stack.

In RISC processors, data movement between memory and registers is restricted to load and store instructions. Some RISC processors do not provide any explicit instructions to move data between registers. This data transfer is accomplished indirectly. For example, we can use the `add` instruction

```
add     Rdest,Rsrc,0      ; Rdest = Rsrc + 0
```

to copy contents of `Rsrc` to `Rdest`. The IA-32 provides an explicit `mov` instruction to copy data. The instruction

```
mov     dest,src
```

copies the contents of `src` to `dest`. The `src` and `dest` can be either registers or memory. In addition, `src` can be a constant. The only restriction is that both `src` and `dest` cannot be located in memory. Thus, we can use the `mov` instruction to transfer data between registers as well as between memory and registers.

Arithmetic and Logical Instructions   Arithmetic instructions support floating-point as well as integer operations. Most processors provide instructions to perform the four basic arithmetic operations: addition, subtraction, multiplication, and division. Because the 2's complement number system is used, addition and subtraction operations do not need separate instructions for unsigned and signed integers. However, the other two arithmetic operations need separate instructions for signed and unsigned numbers.

Some processors do not provide division instructions, whereas others support only partially. What do we mean by partially? Remember that the division operation produces two outputs: a quotient and a remainder. We say that the division operation is fully supported if the division instruction produces both results. For example, the IA-32 and MIPS provide full division support. On the other hand, SPARC and PowerPC provide only the quotient.

Logical instructions provide the basic bitwise logical operations. Processors typically provide logical `and` and `or` operations. Other logical operations including the `not` and `xor` operations are also supported by most processors.

Most of these instructions set the condition code bits, either by default or when explicitly instructed. In the IA-32 architecture, the condition code bits are set by default. In other processors, two versions of arithmetic and logical instructions are provided. For example, in SPARC, `ADD` does not update the condition codes, whereas the `ADDcc` instruction updates the condition codes.

Instruction Formats

Processors use two types of basic instruction format: fixed-length or variable-length instructions. In the fixed-length encoding, all (or most) instructions use the same size instructions. In the latter encoding, the length of the instructions varies quite a bit. Typically, RISC processors use fixed-length instructions and the CISC designs use variable-length instructions.

All 32-bit RISC architectures discussed in this book use instructions that are 32 bits wide. Some examples are the SPARC, MIPS, ARM, and PowerPC. The Intel Itanium, which is a 64-bit processor, uses fixed-length, 41 bit wide instructions. We discuss instruction encoding schemes of these processors in Part II of the book.

The size of the instruction depends on the number of addresses and whether these addresses identify registers or memory locations. Figure 2.1 shows how the size of the instruction varies with the number of addresses when all operands are located in registers. This format assumes that eight bits are reserved for the operation code (opcode). Thus we can have 256 different instructions. Each operand address is five bits long, which means we can have 32 registers. This is the case in architectures like the MIPS. The Itanium, for example, uses seven bits as it has 128 registers.

As you can see from this figure, using fewer addresses reduces the length of the instruction. The size of the instruction also depends on whether the operands are in memory or in registers. As mentioned before, RISC designs keep their operands in registers. In

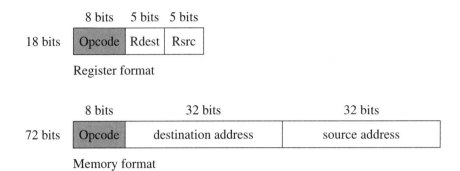

Figure 2.9 Instruction size depends on whether the operands are in registers or memory.

CISC architectures, operands can be in memory. If we use 32-bit memory addresses for each of the two addresses, we would need 72 bits for each instruction (see Figure 2.9) whereas the register-based instruction requires only 18 bits. For this and other efficiency reasons, the IA-32 does not permit both addresses to be memory addresses. It allows at most one address to be a memory address.

The instruction size in IA-32 varies from one byte to several bytes. Part of the reason for using variable length instructions is that CISC tends to provide complex addressing modes. For example, in the IA-32 architecture, if we use register-based operands, we need just 3 bits to identify a register. On the other hand, if we use a memory-based operand, we need up to 32 bits. In addition, if we use an immediate operand, we need an additional 32 bits to encode this value into the instruction. Thus, an instruction that uses a memory address and an immediate operand needs 8 bytes just for these two components. You can realize from this description that providing flexibility in specifying an operand leads to dramatic variations in instruction sizes.

The opcode is typically partitioned into two fields: one identifies the major operation type, and the other defines the exact operation within that group. For example, the major operation could be a branch operation, and the exact operation could be "branch on equal." These points become clearer as we describe the instruction formats of various processors in later chapters.

Summary

When designing a processor, several design choices will have to be made. These choices are dictated by the available technology as well as the requirements of the target user group. Processor designers will have to make compromises in order to come up with the best design. This chapter looked at some of the important design issues involved in such an endeavor.

Here we looked at how the processor design at the ISA level gets affected by various design choices. We stated that the number of addresses in an instruction is one of the choices that can have an impact on the instruction set design. It is possible to have instruction sets with zero, one, two, or three addresses; however, most recent processors use the three-address format. The IA-32, on the other hand, uses the two-address format.

The addressing mode is another characteristic that affects the instruction set. RISC designs tend to use the load/store architecture and use simple addressing modes. Often, they support just one or two addressing modes. In contrast, CISC architectures provide a wide variety of addressing modes.

Both of these choices—the number of addresses and the complexity of addressing modes—affect the instruction format. RISC architectures use fixed-length instructions and support simple addressing modes. In contrast, CISC designs use variable-length instructions to accommodate various complex addressing modes.

3

RISC Principles

In the last chapter, we presented many details on the processor design space as well as the CISC and RISC architectures. It is time we consolidated our discussion to give details of RISC principles. That's what we do in this chapter. We describe the historical reasons for designing CISC processors. Then we identify the reasons for the popularity of RISC designs. We end our discussion with a list of the principal characteristics of RISC designs.

Introduction

The dominant architecture in the PC market, the Intel IA-32, belongs to the Complex Instruction Set Computer (CISC) design. The obvious reason for this classification is the "complex" nature of its Instruction Set Architecture (ISA). The motivation for designing such complex instruction sets is to provide an instruction set that closely supports the operations and data structures used by Higher-Level Languages (HLLs). However, the side effects of this design effort are far too serious to ignore.

The decision of CISC processor designers to provide a variety of addressing modes leads to variable-length instructions. For example, instruction length increases if an operand is in memory as opposed to in a register. This is because we have to specify the memory address as part of instruction encoding, which takes many more bits. This complicates instruction decoding and scheduling. The side effect of providing a wide range of instruction types is that the number of clocks required to execute instructions varies widely. This again leads to problems in instruction scheduling and pipelining.

For these and other reasons, in the early 1980s designers started looking at simple ISAs. Because these ISAs tend to produce instruction sets with far fewer instructions, they coined the term Reduced Instruction Set Computer (RISC). Even though the main goal was not to reduce the number of instructions, but the complexity, the term has stuck.

There is no precise definition of what constitutes a RISC design. However, we can identify certain characteristics that are present in most RISC systems. We identify these RISC design principles after looking at why the designers took the route of CISC in the first place. Because CISC and RISC have their advantages and disadvantages, modern processors take features from both classes. For example, the PowerPC, which follows the RISC philosophy, has quite a few complex instructions.

Evolution of CISC Processors

The evolution of CISC designs can be attributed to the desire of early designers to efficiently use two of the most expensive resources, memory and processor, in a computer system. In the early days of computing, memory was very expensive and small in capacity. This forced the designers to devise high-density code: that is, each instruction should do more work so that the total program size could be reduced. Because instructions are implemented in hardware, this goal could not be achieved until the late 1950s due to implementation complexity.

The introduction of microprogramming facilitated cost-effective implementation of complex instructions by using microcode. Microprogramming has not only aided in implementing complex instructions, it has also provided some additional advantages. Microprogrammed control units use small fast memories to hold the microcode, therefore the impact of memory access latency on performance could be reduced. Microprogramming also facilitates development of low-cost members of a processor family by simply changing the microcode.

Another advantage of implementing complex instructions in microcode is that the instructions can be tailored to high-level language constructs such as `while` loops. For example, the `loop` instruction of the IA-32 can be used to implement `for` loops. Similarly, memory block copying can be done by using its string instructions. Thus, by using these complex instructions, we close the "semantic gap" between HLLs and machine languages.

So far, we have concentrated on the memory resource. In the early days, effective processor utilization was also important. High code density also helps improve execution efficiency. As an example, consider the VAX-11/780, the ultimate CISC processor. It was introduced in 1978 and supported 22 addressing modes as opposed to 11 on the Intel 486 that was introduced more than a decade later. The VAX instruction size can range from 2 to 57 bytes, as shown in Table 3.1.

To illustrate how code density affects execution efficiency, consider the autoincrement addressing mode of the VAX processor. In this addressing mode, a single instruction can read data from memory, add contents of a register to it, write back the result to memory, and increment the memory pointer. Actions of this instruction are summarized below:

```
(R2) = (R2)+ R3;  R2 = R2+1
```

In this example, the R2 register holds the memory pointer. To implement this CISC instruction, we need four RISC instructions:

Table 3.1 Characteristics of some CISC and RISC processors

Characteristic	CISC		RISC
	VAX 11/780	Intel 486	MIPS R4000
Number of instructions	303	235	94
Addressing modes	22	11	1
Instruction size (bytes)	2–57	1–12	4
Number of general-purpose registers	16	8	32

```
R4 = (R2)        ; load memory contents
R4 = R4+R3       ; add contents of R3
(R2) = R4        ; store the result
R2 = R2+1        ; increment memory address
```

The CISC instruction, in general, executes faster than the four RISC instructions. That, of course, was the reason for designing complex instructions in the first place. However, execution of a *single* instruction is not the only measure of performance. In fact, we should consider the overall system performance.

Why RISC?

Designers make choices based on the available technology. As the technology—both hardware and software—evolves, design choices also evolve. Furthermore, as we get more experience in designing processors, we can design better systems. The RISC proposal was a response to the changing technology and the accumulation of knowledge from the CISC designs. CISC processors were designed to simplify compilers and to improve performance under constraints such as small and slow memories. The rest of the section identifies some of the important observations that motivated designers to consider alternatives to CISC designs.

Simple Instructions

The designers of CISC architectures anticipated extensive use of complex instructions because they close the semantic gap. In reality, it turns out that compilers mostly ignore these instructions. Several empirical studies have shown that this is the case. One reason for this is that different high-level languages use different semantics. For example, the semantics of the C for loop is not exactly the same as that in other languages. Thus, compilers tend to synthesize the code using simpler instructions.

Few Data Types

CISC ISA tends to support a variety of data structures, from simple data types such as integers and characters to complex data structures such as records and structures. Empirical data suggest that complex data structures are used relatively infrequently. Thus, it is beneficial to design a system that supports a few simple data types efficiently and from which the missing complex data types can be synthesized.

Simple Addressing Modes

CISC designs provide a large number of addressing modes. The main motivations are (i) to support complex data structures and (ii) to provide flexibility to access operands. Although this allows flexibility, it also introduces problems. First, it causes variable instruction execution times, depending on the location of the operands. Second, it leads to variable-length instructions. For example, the IA-32 instruction length can range from 1 to 12 bytes. Variable instruction lengths lead to inefficient instruction decoding and scheduling.

Large Register Set

Several researchers have studied the characteristics of procedure calls in HLLs. We quote two studies—one by Patterson and Sequin [22] and the other by Tanenbaum [28]. Several other studies, in fact, support the findings of these two studies.

Patterson and Sequin's study of C and Pascal programs found that procedure call/return constitutes about 12 to 15% of HLL statements. As a percentage of the total machine language instructions, call/return instructions are about 31 to 33%. More interesting is the fact that call/return generates nearly half (about 45%) of all memory references. This is understandable as procedure call/return instructions use memory to store activation records. An activation record consists of parameters, local variables, and return values. In the IA-32, for example, the stack is extensively used for these activities. This explains why procedure call/return activities account for a large number of memory references. Thus, it is worth providing efficient support for procedure calls and returns.

In another study, Tanenbaum [28] found that only 1.25% of the called procedures had more than six arguments. Furthermore, more than 93% of them had less than six local scalar variables. These figures, supported by other studies, suggest that the activation record is not large. If we provide a large register set, we can avoid memory references for most procedure calls and returns. In this context, we note that the eight general-purpose registers available in IA-32 processors are a limiting factor in providing such support. The Itanium, for example, provides a large register set (128 registers), and most procedure calls on the Itanium can completely avoid accessing memory.

RISC Design Principles

The best way to understand RISC is to treat it as a concept to design processors. Although initial RISC processors had fewer instructions compared to their CISC counterparts, the new generation of RISC processors has hundreds of instructions, some of which are as complex as the CISC instructions. It could be argued that such systems are really hybrids of CISC and RISC. In any case, there are certain principles that most RISC designs follow. We identify the important ones in this section.

Simple Operations

The objective is to design simple instructions so that each can execute in one cycle. This property simplifies processor design. Note that a cycle is defined as the time required to fetch two operands from registers, perform an operation, and store the result in a register. The advantage of simple instructions is that there is no need for microcode and operations can be hardwired. If we design the cache subsystem properly to capture these instructions, the overall execution efficiency can be as good as a microcoded CISC machine.

Register-to-Register Operations

A typical CISC instruction set supports register-to-register operations as well as register-to-memory and memory-to-memory operations. The IA-32, for instance, allows register-to-register as well as register-to-memory operations; it does not allow memory-to-memory operations. The VAX 11/780, on the other hand, allows memory-to-memory operations as well.

RISC processors allow only special `load` and `store` operations to access memory. The rest of the operations work on a register-to-register basis. This feature simplifies instruction set design as it allows execution of instructions at a one-instruction-per-cycle rate. Restricting operands to registers also simplifies the control unit.

Simple Addressing Modes

Simple addressing modes allow fast address computation of operands. Because RISC processors employ register-to-register instructions, most instructions use register-based addressing. Only the load and store instructions need a memory-addressing mode. RISC designs provide very few addressing modes: often just one or two. They provide the basic register indirect addressing mode, often allowing a small displacement that is either relative or absolute.

Large Register Set

RISC processors use register-to-register operations, therefore we need to have a large number of registers. A large register set can provide ample opportunities for the com-

piler to optimize their usage. Another advantage with a large register set is that we can
minimize the overhead associated with procedure calls and returns.

To speed up procedure calls, we can use registers to store local variables as well as for
passing arguments. Local variables are accessed only by the procedure in which they are
declared. These variables come into existence at the time of procedure invocation and die
when the procedure exits.

Fixed-Length, Simple Instruction Format

RISC designs use fixed-length instructions. Variable-length instructions can cause implementation and execution inefficiencies. For example, we may not know if there is another
word that needs to be fetched until we decode the first word. Along with fixed-length
instruction size, RISC designs also use a simple instruction format. The boundaries of
various fields in an instruction such as opcode and source operands are fixed. This allows
for efficient decoding and scheduling of instructions. For example, both PowerPC and
MIPS use six bits for opcode specification.

Summary

We have introduced important characteristics that differentiate RISC designs from their
CISC counterparts. CISC designs provide complex instructions and a large number of
addressing modes. The rationale for this complexity is the desire to close the semantic
gap that exists between high-level languages and machine languages.

In the early days, effective usage of processor and memory resources was important.
Complex instructions tend to minimize the memory requirements. Empirical data, however, suggested that compilers do not use these complex instructions; instead, they use
simple instructions to synthesize complex instructions. Such observations led designers
to take a fresh look at processor design philosophy. RISC principles, based on empirical studies on CISC processors, have been proposed as an alternative to CISC. Most of
the current processor designs are based on these RISC principles. The next part looks at
several RISC architectures.

PART II

Architectures

4

MIPS Architecture

In the previous chapter, we discussed the RISC design principles. Starting with this chapter, we look at the architecture of several RISC processors. This chapter gives details about the MIPS architecture. However, we do not discuss its instruction set details here. We devote the next part of the book to this purpose.

Introduction

We have selected to present the MIPS as the first architecture. One of the reasons for this preference is the simplicity of the MIPS architecture and its faithfulness to the RISC design philosophy. Once you read details about the other architectures in the following chapters, you will see why this is so.

The MIPS architecture primarily grew out of research done at Stanford. Along with the Berkeley RISC project, these projects influenced processor design towards RISC orientation. MIPS is dominant in embedded applications including digital cameras, digital TVs, Sony PlayStation 2, network routers, and so on.

The MIPS Instruction Set Architecture (ISA) has evolved over time from MIPS I through MIPS V ISAs. In the late 1990s, MIPS formalized their designs around two basic architectures: MIPS32 for 32-bit architectures and MIPS64 for 64-bit architectures. The MIPS32 architecture is based on the MIPS II ISA with some additional instructions from MIPS III through MIPS V ISAs. The MIPS64 architecture is based on the MIPS V ISA.

MIPS first processor implementation R2000 was announced in the mid-1980s. An improved version R3000 became available three years later. Both these processors were 32-bit implementations. The first 64-bit MIPS implementation R4000 was released in the early 1990s. In the next part, which discusses the MIPS assembly language, we focus on the MIPS R2000/R3000 processor. The main reason for this selection is that the SPIM simulator is written for this processor. From a pedagogical perspective, this processor is sufficient to explain the MIPS assembly language.

Like the other RISC processors, MIPS is based on the load/store architecture. As mentioned in Chapter 3, in this architecture most instructions expect their operands to be in registers. Two instructions are used to move data between registers and memory. As we show in the next part, the MIPS architecture provides several load and store instructions to transfer data of different sizes: byte, halfword, and so on.

In the rest of the chapter, we give details on the MIPS32 architecture. The instruction set and assembly language programming aspects are covered in the next part. We start our discussion with the registers set.

Registers

The MIPS32 architecture provides 32 general-purpose registers, a Program Counter (PC), and two special-purpose registers. All registers are 32-bits wide as shown in Figure 4.1. In the assembly language, these registers are identified as $0, $1, . . . , $31. Two of the general-purpose registers—the first and the last—are reserved for a specific function:

- Register $0 is hardwired to provide zero. This register is often used as a source register when a zero value is needed. If this register is used as the destination register of an instruction, the result is discarded.
- The last register $31 is used as a link register by the jump and link (jal) instruction, which is used to invoke a procedure. Register $31 is used to store the return address of a procedure call. We discuss details about this instruction in Chapter 11.

We discussed the purpose of the PC register in Chapter 2 (see page 22). The two special-purpose registers—called HI and LO—are used to hold the results of integer multiply and divide instructions:

- In the integer multiply operation, HI and LO registers hold the 64-bit result, with the higher-order 32 bits in the HI and the lower-order 32 bits in the LO register.
- In integer divide operations, the 32-bit quotient is stored in the LO and the remainder in the HI register.

Register Usage Convention

Although there is no requirement from the processor hardware, there is an established convention on how these 30 registers should be used. Table 4.1 shows the suggested use of each register. Because these suggestions are not enforced by the hardware, we can use the general-purpose registers in an unconventional manner. However, such programs are not likely to work with other programs.

Registers $v0 and $v1 are used to return results from a procedure. Registers $a0 to $a3 are used to pass the first four arguments to procedures. The remaining arguments are passed via the stack. These registers are not preserved across procedure calls (i.e., the called procedure can freely modify the contents of these registers).

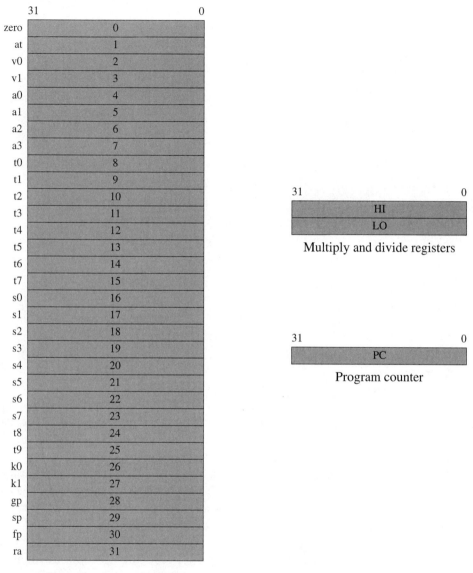

31   0

zero	0
at	1
v0	2
v1	3
a0	4
a1	5
a2	6
a3	7
t0	8
t1	9
t2	10
t3	11
t4	12
t5	13
t6	14
t7	15
s0	16
s1	17
s2	18
s3	19
s4	20
s5	21
s6	22
s7	23
t8	24
t9	25
k0	26
k1	27
gp	28
sp	29
fp	30
ra	31

General−purpose registers

31   0

| HI |
| LO |

Multiply and divide registers

31   0

| PC |

Program counter

Figure 4.1 MIPS registers. All registers are 32-bits wide.

Registers $t0 to $t9 are temporary registers that need not be preserved across a procedure call. These registers are assumed to be saved by the caller. On the other hand, registers $s0 to $s7 are callee-saved registers that should be preserved across procedure calls.

Table 4.1 MIPS registers and their conventional usage

Register name	Number	Intended usage
zero	0	Constant 0
$at	1	Reserved for assembler
$v0, $v1	2, 3	Results of a procedure
$a0, $a1, $a2, $a3	4–7	Arguments 1–4 (not preserved across call)
$t0–$t7	8–15	Temporary (not preserved across call)
$s0–$s7	16–23	Saved temporary (preserved across call)
$t8, $t9	24, 25	Temporary (not preserved across call)
$k0, $k1	26, 27	Reserved for OS kernel
$gp	28	Pointer to global area
$sp	29	Stack pointer
$fp	30	Frame pointer (if needed); otherwise, a saved register $s8
$ra	31	Return address (used to return from a procedure)

Register $sp is the stack pointer, which is useful to implement the stack. It points to the top of stack. The MIPS compiler does not use a frame pointer. As a result, the frame pointer register $fp is used as callee-saved register $s8. The $ra is used to store the return address in a procedure call. We discuss these registers in Chapter 11.

Register $gp points to the memory area that holds constants and global variables. The $at register is reserved for the assembler. The assembler often uses this register to translate pseudoinstructions. Pseudoinstructions are not the processor instructions; these instructions are supported by the assembler. Each pseudoinstruction is translated by the assembler into one or more processor instructions. In the next part, we give some examples to show how the assembler uses this register in translating pseudoinstructions (see the examples on pages 229 and 281).

Addressing Modes

As MIPS is a load/store architecture, only the load and store instructions access memory. All other instructions expect their operands in the processor registers. Thus, they use register-addressing mode. For more details on the addressing modes, see our discussion in Chapter 2 on page 33.

It is important to understand how the load and store instructions access the operands located in memory. As noted in Chapter 3, CISC processors provide a large number of addressing modes. RISC processors, on the other hand, support only one or two addressing modes. MIPS faithfully follows this RISC principle.

The bare machine provides only a single memory-addressing mode:

```
disp(Rx)
```

where displacement `disp` is a signed, 16-bit immediate value. The address is computed as

```
disp + contents of base register Rx
```

We can use any register as the base register. MIPS uses the I-type instruction encoding for the load and store instructions. As you can see from this encoding the immediate value is restricted to a 16-bit signed number.

Even though there is only one basic addressing mode, we can make one of the two components zero to get variations on this basic addressing mode. For example, if we specify `$0`, the address is the immediate value specified as this register is hardwired to zero. Similarly, if we specify zero as the immediate value, it takes the contents of the specified register as the memory address. For example, if `$a0` points to an array that contains 4-byte elements, we can specify the first element as `0($a0)`. If we want to access the next element, we can specify its address as `4($a0)`. In Chapter 12, we give some examples that use these addressing modes.

The virtual machine supported by the assembler provides additional addressing modes to help in assembly language programming. These addressing modes are described in detail in Chapter 12.

Instruction Format

MIPS, being a RISC processor, uses a fixed-length instruction format. Each instruction is 32 bits long as shown in Figure 4.2. It uses three different instruction formats.

- *Immediate (I-type)*: All load and store instructions use this instruction format. The immediate value is a signed, 16-bit integer. In addition, arithmetic and logical instructions that use an immediate value also use this format. Branch instructions use a 16-bit signed offset relative to the program counter and are encoded in this format.

- *Jump (J-type)*: Jump instructions that specify a 26-bit target address use this instruction format. These 26 bits are combined with the higher-order bits of the program counter to get the absolute address.

- *Register (R-type)*: Arithmetic and logical instructions use this instruction format. In addition, jump instructions in which the target address is specified indirectly via a register also use this instruction format.

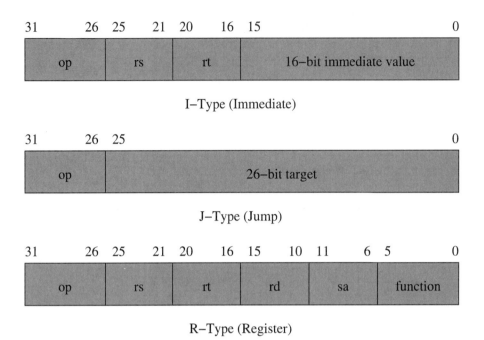

Figure 4.2 The MIPS instruction formats.

The use of a limited number of instruction formats simplifies instruction decoding. However, three instruction formats and a single addressing mode mean that complicated operations and addressing modes will have to be synthesized by the compiler. If these operations and addressing modes are less frequently used, we may not pay much penalty. This is the motivation behind the RISC processors.

Memory Usage

The MIPS uses a conventional memory layout. A program's address space consists of three parts: code, data, and stack. The memory layout of these three components is shown in Figure 4.3. The text segment, which stores instructions, is placed at the bottom of the user address space at 0x4000000.

The data segment is placed above the text segment and starts at 0x10000000. The data segment is divided into static and dynamic areas. The dynamic area grows as memory is allocated to dynamic data structures.

The stack segment is placed at the end of the user address space at 0x7FFFFFFF. It grows downward towards the lower memory address. This placement of segments allows sharing of unused memory by both data and stack segments.

Memory addresses
(in hex)

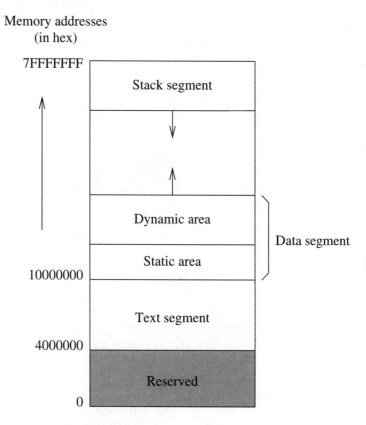

Figure 4.3 MIPS memory layout.

Summary

We have presented the basic details of the MIPS architecture. The MIPS32 architecture provides 32 general-purpose registers, a program counter register, and two special-purpose registers. Each register is 32 bits long. The two special-purpose registers are used by the multiply and divide instructions. MIPS effectively supports only a single addressing mode.

We have not discussed the MIPS instruction set and other details here. We devote the next part of the book to this purpose. In the remainder of this part, we look at a few other RISC architectures.

Web Resources

MIPS32 documentation is available from the MIPS Web site. The *MIPS32 Architecture for Programmers,* which consists of three volumes, describes the 32-bit MIPS architecture in detail [16, 17, 18]. If you are interested in the 64-bit architecture, it is also described in a three-volume manual *MIPS64 Architecture for Programmers* [19, 20, 21]. These manuals are available from www.mips.com/content/Documentation/ MIPSDocumentation.

5

SPARC Architecture

This chapter gives details about the SPARC architecture. After a brief introduction, we describe the SPARC architecture in depth. We start our discussion with a description of its register set. Following this we describe its addressing modes. It supports the two addressing modes we described in Chapter 2. The SPARC instruction set details are presented next. The following section describes how procedures are invoked in the SPARC architecture. This section also provides information on SPARC's parameter-passing mechanism and window management. We conclude the chapter with a summary.

Introduction

The SPARC architecture was initially developed by Sun and is based on the RISC II design from the University of California, Berkeley. SPARC stands for Scalable Processor ARChitecture. Unlike other companies, Sun was wise to make this an open standard and not to manufacture the processor itself. Sun licensed different chip manufacturers to fabricate the processor. Because SPARC is a specification at the ISA level, manufacturers can choose to design their version to suit the target price range and to improve efficiency. For example, implementation of the cache is completely transparent at the ISA level.

The initial SPARC specification SPARC Version 7, introduced in 1987, was a 32-bit processor. SUN and Fujitsu implemented the first SPARC processor. In the following year, SUN introduced the first VME bus-based Sun 4 SPARC workstation. In 1989, SPARC International was set up by SUN and others as the industry body to maintain SPARC as an open architecture, to facilitate distribution of SPARC information and licensing of technology.

The SPARC Version 8 was published in 1990. This is still a 32-bit architecture. The 64-bit SPARC version (Version 9) was introduced in 1993. In 1995, Fujitsu through their SPARC64 and SUN with their UltraSPARC processor introduced 64-bit workstations. A more detailed history of SPARC and its implementations is available from several sources, including [26, 13, 27].

In this chapter, we present details about the 64-bit version. Like the MIPS, it also uses the load/store architecture we discussed in Chapter 2. We start our discussion with the register set. The following sections cover the addressing mode and instruction set details.

Registers

The SPARC register set organization is different from the MIPS architecture discussed in the last chapter. At any time, a user's program sees 32 general-purpose 64-bit registers r0 through r31. These 32 registers are divided into four groups of eight registers each, as shown in Figure 5.1. As in the MIPS architecture, register zero r0 is hardwired to constant zero.

General-purpose registers r0 to r7 are used as the global registers. It also maintains another set of eight alternate global registers (see Figure 5.2). The AG (Alternate Global) field of the Processor State (PSTATE) register determines which global register set is used. By keeping global variables in the global registers, we can completely avoid accessing memory for procedure calls and returns. A similar mechanism is also used by the Itanium.

The SPARC architecture uses the register windows shown in Figure 5.2. A register window has 24 registers consisting of in, local, and out registers. The out registers of one set overlap the in registers of the adjacent set. This reduces the overhead in parameter passing. The Current Window Pointer (CWP) register gives the current window information. The value of CWP can be incremented or decremented by two instructions: the restore instruction decrements the CWP register, and the save instruction increments it. We give details of these two instructions later.

An implementation may have from 64 to 528 registers. Thus, in an implementation with the minimum number of 64 registers, we can have three register sets (8 global, 8 alternate global, three sets of 16 registers each). When the maximum number of registers is implemented, we can have 32 register sets. An implementation can define NWINDOWS to specify the number of windows, which ranges from 3 to 32. These window sets are organized as a circular buffer. Thus, the CWP arithmetic is done modulo NWINDOWS.

Condition Code Register   This register provides two 4-bit integer condition code fields: xcc and icc. Each field consists of four bits, as shown below:

7	6	5	4	3	2	1	0
n	z	v	c	n	z	v	c
	xcc				icc		

The n bit sign flag records whether the result of the last instruction that affects the condition codes is negative ($n = 1$) or positive ($n = 0$). The xcc condition codes record status information about the result of an operation when the operands are 64 bits (the "x" stands for extended). The icc records similar information for 32-bit operands. For example, if the result is 00000000F000FFFFH, the n bit of icc is set because the 32-bit result is a negative number. However, the 64-bit result is positive; therefore, the n bit is cleared.

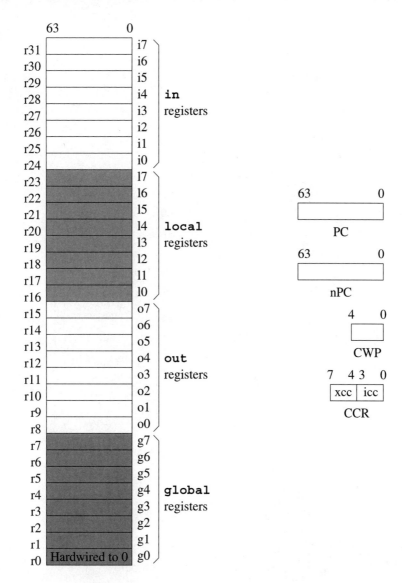

Figure 5.1 Register set in the SPARC V9 architecture (CWP: Current Window Pointer; CCR: Condition Code Register).

The zero bit indicates if the result is zero: $z = 1$ if the result is zero; otherwise, $z = 0$. The overflow bit v indicates whether the result, when treated as a signed number, is within the range of 64 bits (xcc) or 32 bits (icc). This bit is useful to detect overflow in signed arithmetic operations. The carry bit c keeps information on whether there was a carry-out from bit 63 (xcc) or bit 31 (icc). It is useful to detect overflow in unsigned arithmetic operations.

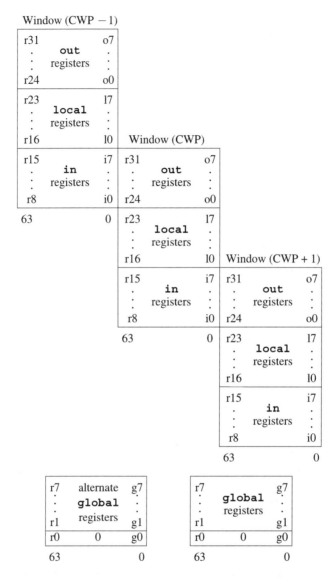

Figure 5.2 Register windows in the SPARC architecture.

Addressing Modes

The SPARC architecture supports the two addressing modes we discussed in Chapter 2: the register indirect with index and register indirect with immediate addressing modes.

- *Register Indirect with Immediate:* This addressing mode is similar to the MIPS addressing mode discussed in the last chapter. It computes the effective address as

Effective address = contents of Rx + imm13.

The base register Rx can be any general-purpose register. A 13-bit signed constant imm13 can be specified as the displacement. This constant is sign-extended to 64 bits and added to the Rx register (see our discussion on sign extension in Appendix A).

- *Register Indirect with Index:* This addressing mode computes the effective address as the sum of two register contents.

Effective address = contents of Rx + contents of Ry.

The base register Rx and the index register Ry can be any general-purpose registers.

There is no register indirect addressing mode in which the contents of a register are taken as the effective address. But we can emulate this addressing mode by making the constant zero in the first addressing mode, or using r0 as the index register in the second addressing mode. Note that r0 is hardwired to read zero.

Instruction Format

All SPARC instructions are 32 bits long. The instruction format uses two opcode fields: the most significant two bits op (bits 30 and 31) identify a major operation group and the second field, op2 or op3, specifies the actual instruction. A sample of the instruction formats is shown in Figure 5.3. The first two formats show how most instructions that use three addresses are encoded. If an immediate value is used, the second format is used. The i bit specifies whether one of the source operands is in a register (i = 0) or a constant (i = 1).

The next three formats are used for sethi and conditional branch instructions. The sethi instruction moves a 22-bit constant into a register (see page 62). The SPARC architecture supports two types of conditional branch instructions. These branch instructions are also discussed later.

The final format is used for procedure calls. We can specify a 30-bit signed displacement value as part of this instruction.

Instruction Set

This section gives details about the SPARC instruction set. Procedure invocation and parameter-passing details are discussed in the next section.

Data Transfer Instructions

Because the SPARC follows the load/store architecture, only load and store instructions can move data between a register and memory. The load instruction

General Format

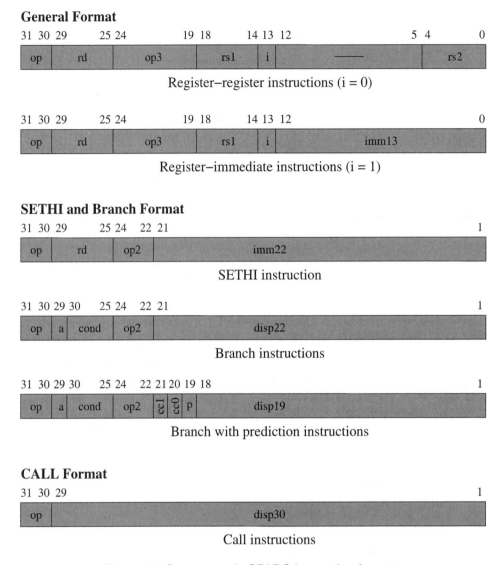

Register–register instructions (i = 0)

Register–immediate instructions (i = 1)

SETHI and Branch Format

SETHI instruction

Branch instructions

Branch with prediction instructions

CALL Format

Call instructions

Figure 5.3 Some sample SPARC instruction formats.


```
ldsb      [address],Rd
```

loads the signed byte in memory at `address` into the `Rd` register. Because it is a signed byte, it is sign-extended to 64 bits and loaded into `Rd`. To load signed halfword and word, use `ldsh` and `ldsw`, respectively. The corresponding unsigned load instructions are `ldub`, `lduh`, and `lduw`. These instructions zero-extend the data to 64 bits before loading into the `Rd` register. To load a 64-bit extended word, use `ldx`.

Table 5.1 The conditional data movement instructions

Mnemonic	Operation	Test condition
`movrz`	Move if register zero	$Rs1 = 0$
`movrnz`	Move if register not zero	$Rs1 \neq 0$
`movrlz`	Move if register less than zero	$Rs1 < 0$
`movrlez`	Move if register less than or equal to zero	$Rs1 \leq 0$
`movrgz`	Move if register greater than zero	$Rs1 > 0$
`movrgez`	Move if register greater than or equal to zero	$Rs1 \geq 0$

Unlike the load instructions, store instructions do not need to be sign- or zero-extended. Thus, we do not need separate signed and unsigned versions. The store instruction

```
stb     Rs,[address]
```

stores the lower byte of `rs` in memory at `address`. To store a halfword, word, and extended word, use `sth`, `stw`, and `stx`, respectively.

In addition to these load and store instructions, the SPARC provides two groups of conditional data movement instructions. One group moves data if the register contents satisfy a certain condition; the other group checks the condition codes. We briefly describe these two groups of instructions next.

There are five instructions in the first group. We describe one instruction as the others follow the same behavior except for the condition tested. The instruction

```
movrz    Rs1,Rs2,Rd      or      movrz    Rs1,imm10,Rd
```

copies the second operand (either `Rs2` or `imm10`) into `Rd` if the contents of `Rs1` are zero. The other instructions in this group test conditions such as "less than zero," and "greater than or equal to zero" as shown in Table 5.1.

The second group of move instructions tests the condition codes. The format is

```
movXX    i_or_x_cc,Rs1,Rd    or    movXX    i_or_x_cc,imm11,Rd
```

It copies the contents of the second operand (`Rs1` or `imm11`) into `Rd` if the condition `XX` is satisfied. The instruction can specify whether to look at `xcc` or `icc` condition codes. The conditions tested are the same ones used in the conditional branch instruction that we discuss later. For this reason, we just give one example instruction to explain the format and semantics. The `move` (move if equal) instruction

```
move     i_or_x_cc,Rs1,Rd
```

moves contents of `Rs1` to `Rd` if $z = 1$. For a full list of conditions tested by these instructions, see the conditional branch instructions in Table 5.3.

Loading Constants

To specify constants in registers, the SPARC architecture provides a special instruction `sethi` (set high). It stores a 22-bit value in the upper 22 bits of the destination register. To facilitate constant manipulation, SPARC assemblers provide several unary operators to extract parts of a word or extended word. These operators are as follows.

`%uhi`	Extracts bits 63 to 42 of a 64-bit extended word (i.e., extracts the high-order 22 bits of the upper word);
`%ulo`	Extracts bits 41 to 32 of a 64-bit extended word (i.e., extracts the low-order 10 bits of the upper word);
`%hi`	Extracts bits 31 to 10 of its operand (i.e., extracts the upper 22 bits);
`%lo`	Extracts bits 9 to 0 of its operand (i.e., extracts the lower 10 bits).

We are now ready to see how we can use the `sethi` instruction to load integer constants into registers. First, let us look at 32-bit words. The instruction sequence

```
sethi    %hi(value),Rd
or       Rd,%lo(value),Rd
```

stores the 32-bit constant `value` in the `Rd` register. In fact, SPARC assemblers provide the pseudoinstruction

```
set     value,Rd
```

to represent this two-instruction code sequence. If the upper 22 bits are zero, `set` uses

```
or      %g0,value,Rd
```

On the other hand, if the lower 10 bits are zero, `set` uses

```
sethi    %hi(value),Rd
```

The `setx` is similar to the `set` instruction except that it allows a 64-bit constant. The syntax is

```
setx     value,Rt,Rd
```

This instruction stores the 64-bit constant `value` in `Rd` using `Rt` as a temporary register. This pseudoinstruction can be translated into a sequence of SPARC processor instructions by using `%uhi`, `%ulo`, `%hi`, and `%lo` unary operators along with `or`, `sethi`, and `sllx` instructions. The `or` and `sllx` instructions are discussed in the next section.

Arithmetic Instructions

The SPARC instruction set supports the basic four arithmetic operations. Most arithmetic operations have two versions: one version updates the condition codes and the other does not. In most instructions, the second operand can be a register or a signed 13-bit immediate `imm13`.

Add Instructions The SPARC instruction set provides add instructions with and without the carry. The instruction

```
add     Rs1,Rs2,Rd
```

adds contents of `Rs1` and `Rs2` and stores the result in the `Rd` register. The immediate version of `add` is

```
add     Rs1,imm13,Rd
```

The immediate value is sign-extended to 64 bits and added to the contents of `Rs1`. This instruction does not update the condition codes. If you want the operation to update the condition codes, use `addcc` instead of `add`. It updates the four integer condition codes mentioned before.

If you want to add the carry bit, use `addc` as shown below:

```
addc    Rs1,Rs2,Rd
addccc  Rs1,Rs2,Rd
```

These instructions add the *icc* carry bit. As usual, the second operand can be a signed 13-bit immediate value. These instructions are useful in multiword addition operations.

Subtract Instructions The SPARC instruction set has four subtract instructions corresponding to the four `add` instructions: `sub`, `subcc`, `subc`, and `subccc`. The last two subtract instructions subtract the *icc* carry bit. The format of these instructions is similar to that of the `add` instructions. The instruction

```
sub     Rs1,Rs2,Rd
```

stores the result of `Rs1−Rs2` in the destination register `Rd`.

Multiplication Instructions Unlike the other processors, the SPARC provides a single multiplication instruction for both signed and unsigned multiplication. The multiplication instruction

```
mulx    Rs1,Rs2,Rd
```

multiplies two 64-bit values in `Rs1` and `Rs2` and places the 64-bit result in `Rd`. Strictly speaking, multiplying two 64-bit values can result in a 128-bit result. This instruction, however, provides only a 64-bit result. The input operands, obviously, should be restricted to get a valid result.

The 32-bit SPARC-V8 has two multiply instructions—one for the signed numbers and the other for unsigned numbers—as in the other processors we show in this book. The multiplication instructions do not modify any condition codes.

Division Instructions   Two division instructions are available: `udivx` for unsigned numbers and `sdivx` for signed numbers. These instructions divide two 64-bit numbers and produce a 64-bit quotient. The format is

```
udivx    Rs1,Rs2,Rd
sdivx    Rs1,Rs2,Rd
```

These instructions place the result of `Rs1÷Rs2` in the destination register `Rd`. As with the multiplication instructions, these instructions do not modify any of the condition codes. However, these instructions generate divide-by-zero exceptions. There is no remainder computed. As we show in the next chapter, the PowerPC also does not provide the remainder. However, we can easily compute the remainder as shown in the next chapter (page 90).

Logical Instructions

The three basic logical operations—and, or, and xor—are supported. These perform the bitwise logical operations. The instruction

```
and      Rs1,Rs2,Rd
```

performs the bitwise AND operation (`Rs1 AND Rs2`) and stores the result in `Rd`.

The SPARC provides three additional logical operations: `andn`, `orn`, and `xnor`. The `andn` and `orn` operations negate the second operand before applying the specified logical operation. The `xnor` operation is equivalent to a NOT operation followed by an XOR operation.

If you want to update the condition codes, use the `cc` versions of these instructions. As before, the second operand can be a 13-bit signed constant.

Shift Instructions

Two types of shift instructions are provided: 32- and 64-bit versions. The 64-bit versions use the suffix "x." For example, `sll` is the 32-bit left-shift instruction, whereas `sllx` is the 64-bit version. Both left- and right-shift operations are supported. The instruction

```
sll      Rs1,Rs2,Rd
```

left-shifts the lower 32 bits of `Rs1` by the shift count specified by `Rs2` and places the result in `Rd`. Note that only the least significant 5 bits of `Rs2` are taken as the shift count.

The 64-bit version

```
sllx     Rs1,Rs2,Rd
```

left-shifts the 64 bits of `Rs1`. The least significant 6 bits of `Rs2` are taken as the shift count.

For all shift instructions, the second operand can also be a constant specifying the shift count. The format is

Table 5.2 The test-and-jump branch instructions

Mnemonic	Operation	Test condition
brz	Branch on register zero	$Rs1 = 0$
brlz	Branch on register less than zero	$Rs1 < 0$
brlez	Branch on register less than or equal to zero	$Rs1 \leq 0$
brnz	Branch on register not zero	$Rs1 \neq 0$
brgz	Branch on register greater than zero	$Rs1 > 0$
brgez	Branch on register greater than or equal to zero	$Rs1 \geq 0$

```
sll    Rs1,count,Rd
```

The count is 5 bits long for 32-bit instructions and 6 bits long for the 64-bit versions.

Use srl and srlx for logical right-shift and sra and srax for arithmetic right-shift. For a discussion of the difference between the logical and arithmetic right-shift operations, see Chapter 15. The SPARC instruction set does not support rotate instructions.

Compare Instructions

The SPARC instruction set does not provide any compare instructions. However, SPARC assemblers provide a compare pseudoinstruction. The compare instruction

```
cmp      Rs1,Rs2        or        cmp        Rs1,imm13
```

is implemented using the subcc instruction as

```
subcc    Rs1,Rs2        or        subcc      Rs1,imm13
```

Branch Instructions

The SPARC instruction set provides test-and-jump as well as set-then-jump types of branch instructions. A discussion of these two types of branches is given in Chapter 2 (see page 24). The first group has six branch instructions. The simplest of these is shown below:

```
brz    Rs1,target
```

This instruction jumps to the specified target if the contents of Rs1 are equal to zero. This transfer is achieved by updating the nPC register with the target address. When comparing, the values are treated as signed integers. The branch instructions are summarized in Table 5.2.

The set-then-jump branch instructions check the icc or xcc condition codes. The syntax is

Table 5.3 The set-then-jump branch instructions

Mnemonic	Operation	Test condition
ba	Branch always	1 (always true)
bn	Branch never	0 (always false)
bne	Branch on not equal	NOT (Z)
be	Branch on equal	Z
bg	Branch on greater	NOT(Z OR (N XOR V))
ble	Branch on less or equal	Z OR (N XOR V)
bge	Branch on greater or equal	NOT (N XOR V)
bl	Branch on less	Z OR (N XOR V)
bgu	Branch on greater unsigned	NOT (C OR Z)
bleu	Branch on less or equal unsigned	C OR Z
bcc	Branch on carry clear (greater than or equal, unsigned)	NOT C
bcs	Branch on carry set (less than, unsigned)	C
bpos	Branch on positive	NOT N
bneg	Branch on negative	N
bvc	Branch on overflow clear	NOT V
bvs	Branch on overflow set	V

```
        bxxx    i_or_x_cc,target
```

The xxx identifies the branch condition. The first operand specifies whether the icc or xcc condition codes should be used. The target address is specified as in the other branch instructions. Table 5.3 shows the branch instructions in this group.

It is a good time to talk about the *branch delay slots* used by most RISC processors. We have introduced the concept of the delay slot in Chapter 2 (see page 25). Consider the following C program fragment.

```
i = 10;
x = 0;
while (i >= 0)
    x = x + 35;  /* loop body */
x = 2*x;
```

This code is translated into the following assembly language version.

```
100:    add    %g0,#11,%i0   ; i = 11 (i is in i0)
104:    xor    %i1,%i1,%i1   ; x = 0 (x is in i1)
```

Table 5.4 A branch execution example

PC	nPC	Executing		Fetching	
100	104	add	%g0,#11,%i0	xor	%i1,%i1,%i1
104	108	xor	%i1,%i1,%i1	brz	%g0,test
108	112	brz	%g0,test	add	%i1,#35,%i1
112	116	add	%i1,#35,%i1	sub	%i0,#1,%i0
116	120	sub	%i0,#1,%i0	brgez	%i0,top
120	124	brgez	%i0,top	add	%i1,%i1,%i1
124	128	add	%i1,%i1,%i1	...	

```
108:      brz    %g0,test      ; jump to test
   top:
112:      add    %i1,#35,%i1   ; x = x + 35
   test:
116:      sub    %i0,#1,%i0    ; i = i − 1
120:      brgez  %i0,top       ; jump if i ≥ 0
124:      add    %i1,%i1,%i1   ; x = 2 * x
```

We use registers i0 and i1 for variables i and x. We should have used the local registers for this purpose but l0 and l1 make for confusing reading as 1 and 1 look very similar in our font. The first column gives the memory address of each instruction, assuming that the first instruction is located at address 100. The third instruction at address 108 is essentially an unconditional branch as the g0 register is hardwired to zero. The while loop condition is tested by the other conditional branch instruction at address 120. The last instruction uses addition to multiply x by 2.

Table 5.4 shows how this assembly code is executed. We give the contents of the PC and nPC along with the instruction that is currently being executed and the one that is being fetched. You can see from this execution table that the code is not executed as intended. The two deviations are as follows.

1. The loop body instruction (at address 112, which adds constant 35 to x) is executed even before testing the loop condition.

2. The final instruction (at address 124), which should have been executed once, is executed during each iteration.

These two problems are caused by the execution of the instruction following the branch instruction. The reason is that, by the time the processor decodes the branch instruction, the next instruction has already been fetched. As we have seen in Chapter 2, we can improve efficiency by executing this instruction. The instruction slot after a branch is called the *delay slot*. Delay slots, however, require program modifications.

One simple solution to our problem is to do nothing (i.e., no operation) in the delay slot. We can correct our code to include a `nop` (no operation) instruction after each branch instruction, as shown below:

```
100:       add      %g0,#11,%i0    ; i = 11 (i is in i0)
104:       xor      %i1,%i1,%i1    ; x = 0 (x is in i1)
108:       brz      %g0,test       ; jump to test
112:       nop                     ; fill delay slot with a nop
     top:
116:       add      %i1,#35,%i1    ; x = x + 35
     test:
120:       sub      %i0,#1,%i0     ; i = i - 1
124:       brgez    %i0,top        ; jump if i ≥ 0
128:       nop                     ; another delay slot with a nop
132:       add      %i1,%i1,%i1    ; x = 2 * x
```

Even though we solved the problem, we defeated the purpose of the delay slot. The `nop` unnecessarily consumes processor cycles. This overhead can be substantial if the loop count is large. Branch instructions typically occur about 20% of the time, therefore we would be wasting a lot of processor cycles executing `nop` instructions.

We can avoid using the `nop`s if we could move the instruction before the branch to after the branch instruction. In our code we could apply this strategy to the unconditional branch instruction `brz`. However, we cannot move the `sub` instruction after the conditional branch instruction `brgez` due to the dependence on the `i0` register. The resulting code is shown below:

```
100:       add      %g0,#11,%i0    ; i = 11 (i is in i0)
104:       brz      %g0,test       ; jump to test
108:       xor      %i1,%i1,%i1    ; x = 0 (x is in i1)
     top:
112:       add      %i1,#35,%i1    ; x = x + 35
     test:
116:       sub      %i0,#1,%i0     ; i = i - 1
120:       brgez    %i0,top        ; jump if i ≥ 0
124:       nop                     ; another delay slot with a nop
128:       add      %i1,%i1,%i1    ; x = 2 * x
```

This is not a great improvement because we still have the main `nop` instruction in the loop body. We could improve this code further by noticing that the `add` and `sub` instructions at addresses 112 and 116 can be interchanged. Then we could move the `add` instruction after the `brgz` branch instruction, as shown below:

```
100:      add     %g0,#11,%i0    ; i = 11 (i is in i0)
104:      brz     %g0,test       ; jump to test
108:      xor     %i1,%i1,%i1    ; x = 0 (x is in i1)
   test:
112:      sub     %i0,#1,%i0     ; i = i − 1
116:      brgez   %i0,test       ; jump if i ≥ 0
120:      add     %i1,#35,%i1    ; x = x + 35
124:      add     %i1,%i1,%i1    ; x = 2 ∗ x
```

Although we eliminated the nop, we have a slight semantic problem. That is, the add
instruction at address 120 is executed one more time than needed. We don't want to
execute this instruction if the branch at 116 is not taken. We have no problem in executing
this instruction when the branch is taken. Because this requirement is very common, the
branch instruction can optionally specify whether the delay slot should be executed when
the branch is not taken. Note that the delay slot instruction is always executed when a
branch is taken. In the SPARC, we can append ", a" to the branch mnemonic to specify
that the delay slot instruction should *not* be executed when the branch is *not* taken. The
correct code is shown below:

```
100:      add       %g0,#11,%i0    ; i = 11 (i is in i0)
104:      brz       %g0,test       ; jump to test
108:      xor       %i1,%i1,%i1    ; x = 0 (x is in i1)
   test:
112:      sub       %i0,#1,%i0     ; i = i − 1
116:      brgez,a   %i0,test       ; jump if i ≥ 0
120:      add       %i1,#35,%i1    ; x = x + 35
124:      add       %i1,%i1,%i1    ; x = 2 ∗ x
```

Note that the specification of ", a" does not change the behavior when the branch is taken;
in this case, the delay slot instruction is always executed. But specifying ", a" annuls the
delay slot instruction only when the branch is not taken.

The SPARC allows giving a hint to the hardware as to whether the branch is likely
to be taken. To convey this information, append "pt" for branch taken hint or "pn" for
branch not taken hint. The default is branch taken. Thus brgez,a,pt is equivalent to
brgez,a. If you want to give the branch not taken hint, use brgez,a,pn instead. We
have discussed branch prediction strategies in Chapter 2 (see page 28). We visit this topic
again in the next couple of chapters.

Procedures and Parameter Passing

This section presents details about procedure invocation, parameter passing, and register
window management.

Procedure Instructions

Procedures in the SPARC can be invoked either by the `call` or `jmpl` instruction. The call instruction takes a label identifying the called procedure. The format is

```
call     procName
```

As shown in Figure 5.3, the called procedure's displacement is expressed as a 30-bit signed number. This displacement is PC-relative. The SPARC requires procedures to be word-aligned (i.e., the procedure address is a multiple of 4). It multiplies the 30-bit displacement value by 4 and adds to the contents of the PC to get the procedure address. As in the branch instructions, the call is also delayed. Thus, before the procedure is invoked, the instruction in the delay slot is executed. This delayed execution is achieved by placing the target address in the nPC.

To facilitate return from a procedure, the `call` instruction stores the PC value (i.e., address of the `call` instruction itself) in o7 (really r15). The following summarizes the actions taken by the `call` instruction.

```
nPC = PC + 4*30-bit displacement
r15 = PC
```

The `call` instruction allows only direct addressing. The `jmpl` instruction allows more flexibility. It allows indirect procedure calls as well as the specification of a 32-bit target address. The format is

```
jmpl     address,register
```

The target `address` can be specified in either of the two addressing modes allowed by the SPARC. It jumps to the 32-bit address given by `address` and leaves the current PC value, which is the address of the `jmpl` instruction itself, in `register`. To call a procedure indirectly, use

```
jmpl     register,%r15
```

This causes transfer of control to the address in `register` and leaves the return address in r15 as in the `call` instruction.

We can also use the `jmpl` instruction to return from a procedure. For example, the instruction

```
jmpl     %r15+8,%g0
```

adds 8 to the contents of r15 and delay jumps to that address. The current PC address is written to g0, which means it is ignored. We add 8 to the return address in r15 because r15 points to the `call`/`jmpl` instruction that called the procedure. Also, we have to skip the following delay-slot instruction. Assemblers typically provide a `ret` pseudoinstruction, which is translated into this particular `jmpl` instruction.

The SPARC also provides a return instruction that takes a return address as an operand. The format is

```
    return     address
```

For example, instead of the assembler-provided `ret` instruction, we can also use

```
    return     %r15+8
```

SPARC assemblers provide two pseudoinstructions (also called synthetic instructions) to facilitate return from procedures. The first return instruction

```
    ret        is implemented as      jmpl     %i7+8,%g0
```

There is a special return instruction `retl` to return from a leaf procedure. A leaf procedure is a procedure that does not call any other procedure. The

```
    retl       is implemented as      jmpl     %o7+8,%g0
```

We show an example use of these instructions later.

Parameter Passing

By convention, the first six arguments are passed in the `out` registers. The remaining arguments, if any, are passed via the stack. Recall that the caller's eight `out` registers become the callee's `in` registers. The following summarizes the usage of these registers.

Caller	Callee	Usage
%o0	%i0	First argument
%o1	%i1	Second argument
%o2	%i2	Third argument
%o3	%i3	Fourth argument
%o4	%i4	Fifth argument
%o5	%i5	Sixth argument
%o6	%i6	Stack pointer/frame pointer
%o7	%i7	Return address − 8

The `o6` is referred to as the stack pointer and can be accessed by its `sp` alias. The `i6` is referred to as the frame pointer by the callee and we can use the alias `fp` to access it.

We can return up to six values via the registers as shown below:

Caller	Callee	Usage
%o0	%i0	First return value
%o1	%i1	Second return value
%o2	%i2	Third return value
%o3	%i3	Fourth return value
%o4	%i4	Fifth return value
%o5	%i5	Sixth return value

As with the parameter passing, we have to use the stack to return the remaining return values.

Stack Implementation

We briefly describe the SPARC stack implementation. As in the MIPS architecture, the stack grows downward (i.e., from a higher memory address to a lower address). However, there are no explicit stack push and pop instructions. Instead, these instructions can be synthesized by manipulating the stack pointer sp. For example, to push or pop the contents of i0, we can use the following code.

Push operation	Pop operation
`sub    %sp,4,%sp`	`add    %sp,4,%sp`
`st     %i0,[%sp]`	`ld     [%sp],%i0`

To allocate an N-byte stack frame, we can use

```
sub    %sp,N,%sp
```

Window Management

SPARC processors can have up to 32 register windows. The number of windows available on a specific implementation is given by NWINDOWS. Note that NWINDOWS can range from 3 to 32. As noted, the Current Window Pointer (CWP) points to the current register set. These window sets are organized as a circular buffer (see Figure 5.4). Thus, the CWP arithmetic can be done modulo NWINDOWS.

With each procedure call, a new register window is assigned. This is done by the save instruction. This instruction can also allocate space on the stack for the stack frame. The save instruction

```
save    %sp,-N,%sp
```

slides the register window by incrementing CWP (mod NWINDOWS) and allocates N bytes of stack space. If no errors occur, save acts as the add instruction does. Thus, by specifying sp and a negative N value, it allocates N bytes of stack space. As in the add instruction, the second operand can also be a register.

The restore instruction restores the register window saved by the last save instruction. Its format is similar to that of the save. It also performs addition on its operands as does the save instruction. A trivial restore pseudoinstruction is defined as

```
restore    %g0,%g0,%g0
```

A typical procedure looks like

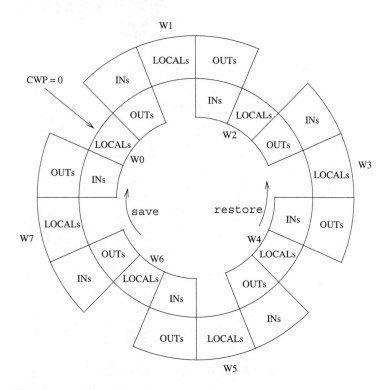

Figure 5.4 The register windows are organized as a circular buffer.

```
proc-name:
        save      %sp,-N,%sp
        . . .
        procedure body
        . . .
        ret
        restore
```

Note that the `restore` instruction is executed in the delay slot. Because the `restore` does not add N to sp, you might be wondering about how the stack allocation is released. To understand this, we should look at the way the `save` instruction performs the add operation on its operands. For this add operation, `save` uses the *old window* for the two source operands and stores the result in the *new window*. In our example, it adds $-N$ to the sp value from the previous window and stores the result in the new window's sp register. Thus, when we `restore` the previous window, we automatically see the previous sp value.

A leaf procedure does not use a new register window. It uses the registers from the caller's window. A typical leaf procedure looks like

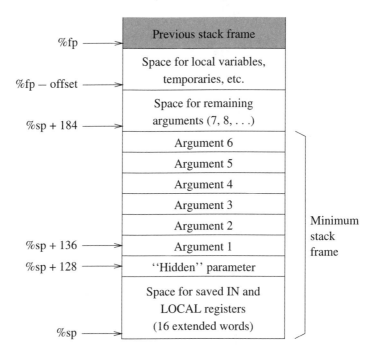

Figure 5.5 SPARC's stack frame.

```
proc-name:
        . . .
        procedure body
        . . .
        retl        /* use retl, not ret */
```

What happens if the `save` instruction cannot get a new window of registers? For this reason, the stack frame maintains space for the in, local, and six arguments. In addition, there is a "hidden parameter" to return a structure pointer. Thus, a minimum of (16 + 1 + 6) * 8 = 184 bytes of stack frame is needed. Additional space may be needed for storing temporaries, more arguments, and so on, as shown in Figure 5.5.

We give an example procedure to illustrate how these instructions are used. We use the following C code consisting of three procedures.

```
        . . .
    i = condSum (1, 2, 3, 4)
        . . .

int condSum(int a, int b, int c, int d)
{
```

```
      int   t1;

      t1 = a;
      if (a < b)
          t1 = b;
      return(sum(t1,c,d));
}

int sum(int x, int y, int z)
{
      return(x+y+z);
}
```

The corresponding SPARC assembly code is shown in three procedures. In the `main` procedure, the four arguments of `condSum` are moved to the first four `out` registers: `o0` through `o3`.

```
                 . . .
      mov     1,%o0       ; first argument
      mov     2,%o1       ; second argument
      mov     3,%o2       ; third argument
      call    condSum
      mov     4,%o3       ; fourth argument in delay slot
      ; condSum returns result in %o0. When condSum returns,
      ; the following instruction is executed
      mov     %o0,%l0     ; return result moved to %l0
                 . . .
```

Because the `call` is a delayed instruction, we use the delay slot to move the fourth argument to `o3`. Note that the `condSum` call should return to the instruction

```
  mov     %o0,%l0
```

This is the reason for adding 8 to the return address. This procedure returns the sum in the `o0` register. The above `mov` instruction copies this value to the `l0` local register.

The first instruction in the `condSum` procedure is the `save` instruction. As we have discussed, it allocates a new register window by incrementing the CWP. We also allocate 184 bytes of stack frame, which is the minimum size. The next four instructions select the minimum of the first two arguments. Note that the `out` registers of the previous window are referred to as `in` registers in the current window. We move the three arguments to `out` registers to pass them on to the `sum` procedure. When `sum` returns the total, this value is moved from `o0` to `i0` so that the result is available in `o0` in the main procedure.

```
;*********** condSum procedure **********
condSum:
    save    %sp,-184,%sp; allocate min. stack frame
    mov     %i0, %o0
    cmp     %i1, %i0    ; if %i1 is less/equal,
    ble     skip        ; skip the following mov
    mov     %i1, %o0
skip:
    mov     %i2, %o1    ; second argument
    call    sum
    mov     %i3, %o2    ; third argument in delay slot
    mov     %o0, %i0    ; move the result returned by sum to %o0
    ret
    restore             ; trivial restore in delay slot of ret
;******* end of condSum procedure *******
```

The sum procedure is a leaf procedure as it does not call any other procedure. We can
optimize a leaf procedure by not requesting a new window; instead it uses the registers
from the caller's window. Thus, there is no need for the save and restore instructions.
The only instruction that needs special care is the return: we have to use retl rather than
the ret instruction.

```
;*********** sum procedure ***********
sum:
    add     %o0, %o1, %o0 ; first addition
    retl                  ; leaf procedure, use retl
    add     %o0, %o2, %o0 ; final add in delay slot
    ; result returned in %o0
;******* end of sum procedure ********
```

Summary

We have briefly presented the architecture and instruction set of the SPARC. A user program is provided with 32 general-purpose registers, which are organized into four register
sets: in, out, local, and global. It supports a register window mechanism that facilitates
efficient parameter passing in procedure calls. We see a similar mechanism in Chapter 7.

The SPARC architecture supports two basic addressing modes. One is similar to the
addressing mode we have seen in the last chapter. The other computes the effective address as the sum of the contents of two registers. As does the MIPS architecture, SPARC
also uses 32 bits to encode instructions. After reading details about the other architectures,
you will notice that it supports a fairly standard set of instructions.

A notable difference from other processors is that it is a specification at the ISA level
that is available to chip manufacturers, which means several implementations are possible. For example, an implementation can choose to have a number of register windows be-

tween 3 and 32. Furthermore, there are also several instructions that have implementation-defined semantics. If you are interested in more details, several reference documents are available at the SPARC Web site.

Web Resources

Full specifications and other reference material on the SPARC architecture are available from `www.sparc.org`. Sun also maintains information on their SPARC processors at `www.sun.com/microelectronics/sparc`.

6

PowerPC Architecture

This chapter gives details on the PowerPC architecture. We start the chapter with an overview and a brief history of the PowerPC architecture. We then give its register set details and the addressing modes supported. As does the SPARC, PowerPC supports two addressing modes. However, PowerPC also supports update versions of these addressing modes. The update versions, for example, are useful in providing "regular" access to arrays. Unlike the MIPS architecture, PowerPC supports a variety of instruction formats. The instruction set details are presented next. After reading this section, you will notice that the PowerPC branch instructions are flexible and can take branch prediction hints from the compiler. We conclude the chapter with a summary.

Introduction

The PowerPC defines a 64-bit architecture that can operate in two modes: 64-bit and 32-bit mode. It supports dynamic switching between these two modes. In the 32-bit mode, a 64-bit PowerPC processor can execute 32-bit application binaries.

Here is a short history of the PowerPC architecture [9]. IBM developed many of the concepts in 1975 for a prototype system. An unsuccessful commercial version of this prototype was introduced around 1986. Four years later, IBM introduced the RS/6000 family of processors based on their POWER architecture. In early 1991, a group from Motorola, IBM, and Apple began work on the PowerPC architecture using the IBM POWER architecture as the base. The PowerPC includes many of the POWER instructions. PowerPC dropped some of the POWER instructions, but these were not frequently used. The first implementation of the PowerPC architecture, the PowerPC 601, implemented all but two POWER instructions so that POWER applications run on the PowerPC.

The PowerPC family of processors is available in both 32- and 64-bit implementations. Here we discuss the 64-bit implementation. As are the MIPS and SPARC, the PowerPC architecture is based on the load/store architecture. It satisfies many of the RISC characteristics we mentioned in Chapter 2.

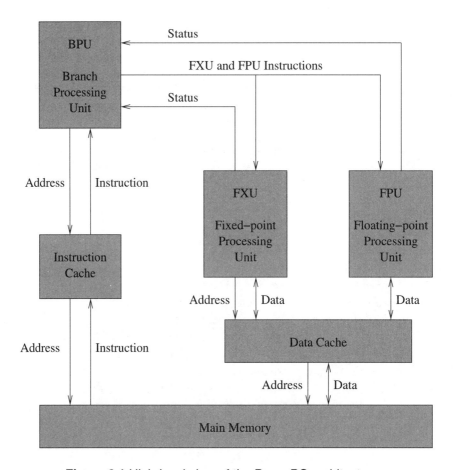

Figure 6.1 High-level view of the PowerPC architecture.

A high-level view of the PowerPC architecture is shown in Figure 6.1. It consists of three functional units to facilitate superscalar implementation in which multiple functional units concurrently work on independent instructions.

- *Branch Processing Unit:* The BPU is responsible for fetching instructions and executing branch and related instructions. In addition, the BPU also dispatches instructions for the fixed-point and floating-point units as shown in Figure 6.1.

- *Fixed-point Processing Unit:* The FXU executes the fixed-point instructions, which we discuss later in this chapter. It also computes the addresses of store and load instructions for the floating-point unit.

- *Floating-point Processing Unit:* The FPU executes the floating-point instructions, which operate on floating-point numbers that conform to the IEEE 754 standard (see our discussion of this format in Appendix A). It is also responsible for managing the floating-point loads and stores. Note that the fixed-point unit generates addresses for these operations.

The PowerPC instructions can be divided into three classes, depending on which unit executes them: branch instructions, fixed-point instructions, and floating-point instructions. Fixed-point instructions operate on byte (8 bits), halfword (16 bits), word (32 bits), and doubleword (64 bits) operands. Floating-point instructions operate on single-precision and double-precision floating-point numbers.

In the remainder of the chapter, we discuss the PowerPC register set, its addressing modes, and fixed-point and branch instructions. For the sake of brevity, we do not discuss its floating-point instructions (see [23] for details on these instructions).

Register Set

The PowerPC has 32 general-purpose registers for integer data (GPR0 to GPR31). An equal number of registers are available for floating-point data (FPR0 to FPR31), as shown in Figure 6.2. The integer registers (GPRs) as well as the floating-point registers (FPRs) are 64 bits wide. In addition, it has the following special registers: CR, LR, CTR, FPSCR, and XER. The register set can be partitioned into three groups, each group associated with a processing unit:

- Branch processing unit uses the following three special registers: Condition Register (CR), Link Register (LR), and CounT Register (CTR). The last two registers are 64 bits long and the CR is 32 bits long.

- Fixed-point processing unit uses the 32 general-purpose registers GPR0 to GPR31 and the fiXed-point Exception Register (XER).

- Floating-point processing unit uses the 32 floating-point registers FPR0 to FPR31 and the Floating-point Status and Control Register (FPSCR).

The FPSCR register consists of two types of bits: bits 0–23 are used to record the status of the floating-point operations. The remaining bits are control bits that record any exceptions generated by floating-point operations. For example, bit 23 records the invalid operation exception which occurs when an operand is invalid for the specified floating-point operation. The floating-point divide-by-zero exception is captured in bit 5. The functionality of the remaining four special registers is described next.

Condition Register (CR)

The 32-bit register is divided into eight CR fields of 4 bits each (CR0 to CR7). CR0 is used to capture the result of a fixed-point instruction. The four CR0 bits are interpreted as follows [23].

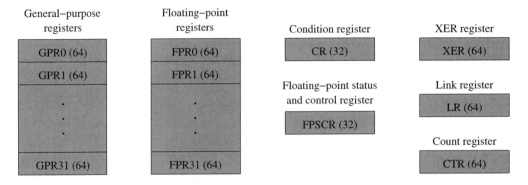

Figure 6.2 PowerPC registers: general-purpose, link, XER, and count registers are 32-bits long in 32-bit implementations and 64-bits long in 64-bit implementations. The other registers are of fixed size independent of the implementation.

Bit	Description
0	Negative (LT) The result is negative.
1	Positive (GT) The result is positive.
2	Zero (EQ) The result is zero.
3	Summary overflow (SO) This is a copy of the SO bit from XER register (discussed later).

The first bit can be interpreted as representing the "less than" (LT) relationship. Similarly, the second and third bits represent "greater than" (GT) and "equal to" (EQ) relationships, respectively.

The CR1 field is used to capture floating-point exception status. These four bits are a copy of the least significant four bits of the FPSCR register. Because we do not discuss the floating-point unit details here, we skip the interpretation of these four bits (see [23] for details).

The remaining CR fields can be used for either integer or floating-point instructions to capture integer or floating-point LT, GT, EQ, and SO conditions. Instructions are available to perform logical operations on individual CR bits. Branch instructions are available to test a specific CR field bit. These instructions can specify the CR field that should be used.

Link Register (LR)

The 64-bit link register is used to store the return address in a procedure call. Procedure calls are implemented by branch (bl/bla) or conditional branch (bc/bca) instructions. For these instructions, the LR register receives the effective address of the instruction following the branch instruction.

Count Register

The 64-bit CTR register holds the loop count value. Branch instructions can specify a variety of conditions under which branching should take place. For example, a conditional branch instruction can decrement CTR and branch only if CTR $\neq$ 0 or if CTR = 0. Even more complex branch conditions can be tested. More details on the branch instruction are presented later in this chapter (page 93).

XER Register

The XER register serves two distinct purposes. Bits 0, 1, and 2 are used to record Summary Overflow (SO), OVerflow (OV), and CArry (CA). The OV bit records the fact that an overflow has occurred during the execution of an instruction. The SO bit is different in the sense that it is set whenever the OV bit is set. However, once set, the SO bit remains set until a special instruction is executed to clear it. The CA bit is set by add and subtract arithmetic operations and right-shift instructions.

Bits 57 to 63 are used as a 7-bit byte count to specify the number of bytes to be transferred between memory and registers. This field is used by Load String Word Indexed (lswx) and Store String Word Indexed (stswx) instructions. Using just one lswx instruction we can load 128 contiguous bytes from memory into all 32 general-purpose registers. Similarly, reverse transfer can be done by stswx instruction.

Addressing Modes

The PowerPC supports two basic addressing modes as does the SPARC. We can specify three general-purpose registers rA, rB, and rD/rS in load/store instructions. Registers rA and rB are used to compute the effective address. The third register is treated either as the destination register rD in load operations or as the source register rS in store operations.

Register Indirect with Immediate

In this addressing mode, instructions contain a signed immediate value imm. The effective address is computed by adding this value to the contents of a general-purpose register rA specified in the instruction. Interestingly, we can specify a 0 in place of rA. In this case, the effective address is the immediate value given in the instruction. Thus, it is straightforward to convert indirect addressing to direct addressing.

$$\text{Effective address} = \text{Contents of } rA \text{ or } 0 + imm$$

The immediate constant is either 14 or 16 bits depending on the instruction encoding used. We discuss instruction formats in the next section. Also, note that this is the only addressing supported by the MIPS architecture.

Register Indirect with Index

Instructions using this addressing mode specify two general-purpose registers rA and rB. The effective address is computed as the sum of the contents of these two registers. As in the other addressing modes, we can specify 0 in place of rA.

Effective address = Contents of rA or 0 + Contents of rB

These addressing modes are also available in the update version. In this version, the computed effective address is loaded into the base register rA. We look at these two versions next.

Register Indirect with Immediate Update

This is the update version of the first addressing mode. The semantics are shown below:

Effective address = Contents of rA or 0 + imm
rA = Effective address

•

Register Indirect with Index Update

The indexed version has the following semantics.

Effective address = Contents of rA or 0 + Contents of rB
rA = Effective address

We later show how these update versions are useful in accessing arrays by means of an example.

In our discussion so far, we assumed 64-bit mode. In 32-bit mode, computation of the effective address is the same. However, only the lower-order 32 bits are used as the effective address to access memory.

Instruction Format

As with the MIPS and SPARC, all PowerPC instructions are encoded using four bytes. Instructions are assumed to be word-aligned, so that the processor can ignore the least significant two bits of all instruction addresses.

As shown in Figure 6.3, bits 0 to 5 specify the primary opcode. Many instructions also have an extended opcode. The remaining bits are used for various fields depending on the instruction type. Here we discuss some basic instruction formats.

Most instructions use the register format shown in Figure 6.3a. In arithmetic, logical, and other similar instruction types, registers rA and rB specify the source operands and rD specifies the destination register. The OE and rC bits are explained later.

The immediate format shown in Figure 6.3b is used by instructions that specify an

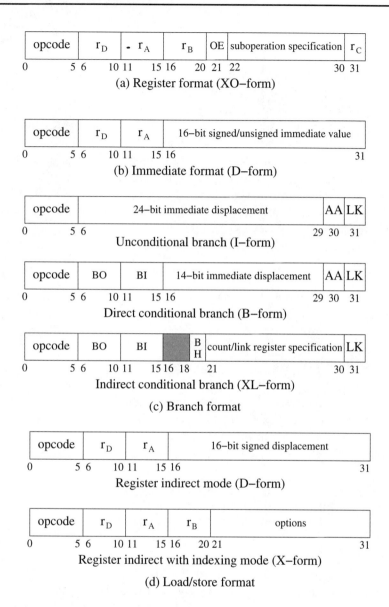

Figure 6.3 Sample PowerPC instruction formats.

immediate operand. For example, the addi instruction, described in the next section, uses this format.

The format shown in Figure 6.3c is used by branch instructions. The unconditional branch format allows specification of a 24-bit target address. This figure also shows the format used by direct and indirect conditional branch instructions. The AA bit is used to indicate whether the address is an absolute address or a relative address. The LK bit is used to link the return address so that we can use the branch instruction for procedure calls. More details on the branch instruction fields, including the BO and BI fields, are given later in this chapter (page 94).

The format of load/store instructions is shown in Figure 6.3d. The first format is used by load/store instructions that specify the address in the first addressing mode. As mentioned before, these instructions use rA and the signed 16-bit operand (imm) to compute the effective address. The second format is used by load/store instructions that use the index addressing mode (i.e., the second addressing mode).

Note that we have skipped several other formats used by the PowerPC to encode instructions. The PowerPC manual [23] contains a more detailed description of these instruction formats.

Instruction Set

This section presents a sample of the PowerPC instructions. As in the last chapter, we organize our presentation into instruction groups. Let us begin with the data transfer instructions.

Data Transfer Instructions

The PowerPC instruction set supports a variety of load and store instructions to move data between memory and registers. We discuss some of these instructions to convey the type of instructions available. The load and store instructions do not affect any of the status bits. There are no instructions to move data between registers. However, we can use a logical instruction to affect such moves. We give an example of this later.

Load Instructions Load instructions operate on byte, half-word, word, and doubleword data. Note that load instructions that operate on floating-point numbers are also available, but we do not discuss them here. The following is a list of load instructions that work on byte data.

lbz	rD,disp(rA)	Load Byte and Zero
lbzu	rD,disp(rA)	Load Byte and Zero with Update
lbzx	rD,rA,rB	Load Byte and Zero Indexed
lbzux	rD,rA,rB	Load Byte and Zero with Update Indexed

The first instruction lbz loads the byte at the Effective Address (EA) into the lower-order byte of rD. The remaining three bytes in rD are cleared (i.e., zeroed). The EA is computed as the sum of the contents of rA and the displacement disp. Note that if we specify 0 for rA, disp becomes the effective address.

The second instruction lbzu performs the same operation as the lbz instruction. In addition, it loads the computed effective address into rA (i.e., it updates rA with EA).

87

The last two instructions use the indexed addressing mode. The effective address is computed as the sum of the contents of registers rA and rB. Except for the computation of the EA, lbzx is similar to the lbz instruction, and lbzxu is similar to the lbzu instruction.

The update forms of these instructions are useful to access arrays. For example, suppose that rA initially points to an array of bytes and disp is 1. We can use lbzu to access successive bytes from this array by repeatedly executing this instruction. There is no need to update the array pointer. If we want to access every 4th element of this array, all we have to do is change disp value to 4.

To move halfwords, there are four instructions corresponding to the four-byte load instructions. Halfword instructions use the mnemonics lhz, lhzu, lhzx, and lhzux. Similarly, word instructions use the mnemonics lwz, lwzu, lwzx, and lwzux.

When loading halfwords, instead of zeroing the upper two bytes, we can also sign-extend halfword to word (see our discussion in Appendix A). Remember that sign extension copies the sign bit to the remaining higher-order bits. We can use the following load instructions to sign-extend the halfword in rD:

lha	rD,disp(rA)	Load Halfword Algebraic
lhau	rD,disp(rA)	Load Halfword Algebraic with Update
lhax	rD,rA,rB	Load Halfword Algebraic Indexed
lhaux	rD,rA,rB	Load Halfword Algebraic with Update Indexed

Similar instructions for loading words are also available. The mnemonics for these instructions are lwa, lwax, and lwaux. Finally, the instructions ld, ldu, ldx, and ldux can be used to load doublewords.

The PowerPC provides some interesting multiword load instructions. As an example, consider the instruction:

| lmw | rD,disp(rA) | Load Multiple Words |

It loads n consecutive words from memory starting at EA, which is computed as in the previous instructions. Inasmuch as the target is a register, what is n? This instruction loads words starting with rD and proceeds until r31. Note that it loads only the lower-order 32 bits in each register. For example, if we specify r20 as rD, 12 consecutive words from memory are loaded into lower-order 32 bits of registers r20, r21, ..., r31.

Store Instructions   There is a store instruction corresponding to each load instruction to move data to memory. For example, to move a byte into memory, these instructions can be used:

stb	rS,disp(rA)	Store Byte
stbu	rS,disp(rA)	Store Byte with Update
stbx	rS,rA,rB	Store Byte Indexed
stbux	rS,rA,rB	Store Byte with Update Indexed

There are corresponding instructions to store halfwords: sth, sthu, sthx, and sthux. Similar instructions are available to store words and doublewords (just substitute "w" for words and "d" for doublewords in the mnemonics for the byte instructions).

To store multiple words, we can use the following:

```
stmw        rS,disp(rA)        Store Multiple Words
```

This instruction has the same semantics as the lmw instruction except for the direction of data movement. As in the lmw instruction, it loads the lower-order 32 bits from these registers.

Arithmetic Instructions

The PowerPC supports the four basic arithmetic instructions: add, subtract, multiply, and divide. We start our discussion with the addition instructions.

Addition Instructions   The basic add instruction

```
add      rD,rA,rB
```

adds contents of registers rA and rB and stores the result in rD. Status and overflow bits of the CR0 field as well as the XER register are not altered. Three variations on the basic add are possible to affect these bits:

add.	rD,rA,rB	LT, GT, EQ bits of CR0 field are altered
addo	rD,rA,rB	SO and OV bits of XER register are altered
addo.	rD,rA,rB	LT, GT, EQ bits of CR0 field and
		SO and OV bits of XER register are altered

The OE bit in Figure 6.3a indicates whether the SO and OV bits of the XER register are altered (OE = 1) or not (OE = 0). Thus, this bit is set for the last two add instructions (addo and addo.) and cleared for the other two instructions.

The rc bit specifies if the LT, GT, and EQ bits of CR0 field should be altered. This bit is set for those instructions that alter these bits. Thus, rc = 1 for the two "dot" versions of the add instruction (add. and addo.).

These four add instructions do not affect the CA bit in the XER register. To alter the carry bit, we have to use addc, addc., addco, and addco. instructions. The other bits are updated as in the basic add instruction variations. Yet another variation is the adde instruction. The instruction

```
adde     rD,rA,rB
```

adds contents of registers rA, rB and the CA bit of the XER register. As usual, the result goes into the rD register. As with the add instruction, it does not alter any of the status bits. We can use adde., addeo, or addeo. to affect these status and condition bits. The addc and adde instructions are useful in performing multiword addition operations.

We can also have an immediate operand specified in an add instruction. The add instruction

```
addi      rD,rA,Simm16
```

is similar to the `add` instruction except that the second operand is a signed 16-bit imme-diate value. It does not affect any status/condition bits. If `rA` is specified as 0, it uses the value 0, not the contents of GPR0. Thus, we can use the `addi` instruction to implement load immediate (`li`), load address (`la`), and subtract immediate (`subi`) as shown below:

```
li      rD,value       equivalent to  addi    rD,0,value
la      rD,disp(rA)    equivalent to  addi    rD,rA,disp
subi    rD,rA,value    equivalent to  addi    rD,rA,-value
```

Because the processor does not directly support these instructions, we refer to these instructions as pseudoinstructions. The assembler translates these pseudoinstructions to equivalent processor instructions. As we show in Part III, the MIPS also uses pseudoin-structions to simplify assembly language programming.

Subtract Instructions   Subtract instructions use the mnemonic `subf` standing for "sub-tract from." The subtract instruction

```
subf     rD,rA,rB           /* rD = rB-rA */
```

subtracts the contents of `rA` from `rB` and places the result in the `rD` register. As with the `add` instruction, no status/condition bits are affected. We can also use the simplified mnemonic `sub` for this instruction. Other subtract instructions—`subf.`, `subfo`, and `subfo.`—are available to alter these bits as in the `add` instruction.

To alter the carry (CA) bit, use `subfc` instead of the `subf` mnemonic. Similarly, to include carry, use the `subfe` mnemonic. There is no "subtract immediate" instruction as it can be implemented using the `addi` instruction, as discussed before.

The PowerPC also provides a negate instruction. The negate instruction

```
neg     rD,rA                /* rD = 0-rA */
```

essentially negates the sign of the integer in the `rA` register. The processor actually per-forms a 2's complement operation (i.e., complements the bits of `rA` and adds 1).

Multiply Instructions   The PowerPC multiply instruction is slightly different from the other processors in that it does not produce the full 64-bit result. Remember that we get a 64-bit result when multiplying two 32-bit integers. The PowerPC provides two instructions to get the lower- and higher-order 32 bits of the 64-bit result. First, we look at the signed integers. The instruction

```
mullw     rD,rA,rB
```

multiplies the contents of registers `rA` and `rB` and stores the lower-order 32 bits of the result in the `rD` register. We have to use

```
mulhw      rD,rA,rB
```

to get the higher-order 32 bits of the result.

For unsigned numbers, we have to use `mulhwu` instead of `mulhw` to get the higher-order 32 bits of the result. The lower-order 32 bits are given by `mullw` for both signed and unsigned integers.

There is also a multiply immediate instruction that takes an immediate value. The format is

```
mulli      rD,rA,Simm16
```

The immediate value `Simm16` is a 16-bit signed integer. Note that this operation produces a 48-bit result. But the `mulli` instruction stores only the lower 32 bits of the result.

Divide Instructions   Like the multiply operation, two divide instructions—one for signed integers and the other for unsigned integers—are provided. The instruction

```
divw       rD,rA,rB          /* rD  = rA/rB */
```

stores the quotient of `rA/rB` in `rD`. The operands are treated as signed integers. The remainder is not available. To get both quotient and remainder, we have to use the following three-instruction sequence.

```
divw       rD,rA,rB          /* quotient in rD */
mullw      rX,rD,rB
subf       rC,rX,rA          /* remainder in rC */
```

For unsigned integers, use the `divwu` (divide word unsigned) instruction instead.

Logical Instructions

The PowerPC instruction set has several logical instructions including `and`, `or`, `nor`, `nand`, `equ`, and `xor` instructions. It does not have the `not` instruction; however, the `not` operation can be implemented using the `nor` instruction. These instructions have a similar format, therefore we discuss the complete set of `and` instructions available in the PowerPC instruction set.

```
and     rA,rS,rB            and.    rA,rS,rB
andi.   rA,rS,Uimm16        andis.  rA,rS,Uimm16
andc    rA,rS,rB            andc.   rA,rS,rB
```

The `and` instruction performs bitwise AND of `rS` and `rB` and places the result in the `rA` register. The condition register field `CR0` is not affected. The `and.` instruction is similar to `and` but updates the LT, GT, and EQ bits of the `CR0` field. This is true with all the instructions ending in a period. The `andi` takes a 16-bit unsigned integer as one of the source operands. The `andis.` instruction is similar to `andi.` except that the immediate value is left-shifted by 16 bit positions before ANDing. Note that the shifted-out bits on the right receive zeros. In the andc instruction, the contents of rB are complemented before performing the and operation.

The logical or instruction also has six versions as does the and instruction. The only difference is that the immediate versions do not update the CR0 field. That is, the immediate or instructions are ori and oris with no period. We can use the or instruction to move register contents as shown below:

    mr   rA,rS   is equivalent to   or   rA,rS,rS

A no-operation (nop) is implemented as

    ori   0,0,0

The NAND instructions (nand and nand.) perform a NOT operation followed by an AND operation. Similarly, NOR instructions (nor and nor.) perform a NOT operation after an OR operation.

The PowerPC instruction set also includes four xor instructions as shown below:

    xor   rA,rS,rB   xor.   rA,rS,rB
    xori   rA,rS,Uimm16   xoris   rA,rS,Uimm16

The semantics of these four instructions are similar to the and instructions, except for the actual operation performed.

In addition, the PowerPC provides the eqv (equivalence) logical function. The *equivalence* function is defined as the exclusive-NOR operation (i.e., the output of XOR is complemented). Two instructions—eqv and eqv.— are available.

Shift Instructions

The PowerPC provides four types of shift instructions to shift left or right. Each type of instruction is available in two forms: one that does not affect the status bits in CR0 and the other that updates these status bits (i.e., the "dot" version). We first discuss the left-shift instruction. The sld (shift left doubleword) instruction

    sld   rA,rS,rB

left-shifts the contents of rS by the shift count value specified in rB, and the result is placed in rA. Shifted-out bits on the right receive zeros. For the shift count, only the least significant seven bits are taken from the rB register. If the shift count is between 64 and 127, the result is zero. We can use sld. to update the status bits in CR0.

There are two shift right instructions—srd and srd.—that are similar to the two left-shift instructions except for the direction of shift. Zeros replace the vacated bits on the left. These two right-shift instructions perform logical shift operations. In logical shifts, vacated bits receive zeros. On the other hand, in an arithmetic right-shift operation, vacated bits receive the sign bit. For details on the differences and the need for logical and arithmetic shift operations and why we need them only for the right-shifts, see our discussion in Chapter 15.

These shift instructions are also available for word operands. For example, the instruction

        slw   rA,rS,rB

left-shifts the lower-order 32 bits of rS by the shift count value specified in rB, and the result is placed in the lower-order 32 bits of rA. The upper 32 bits are cleared to zero. The shift count is taken from the lower-order six bits of rB. A shift count value between 32 and 63 gives a zero result. The dot version of this instruction (slw.) is also available. The instructions are srw and srw. can used to right-shift word operands.

The PowerPC provides two types of arithmetic right-shift operations: one type assumes that the shift count is in a register as in the previous shift instructions, and the other type can accept the shift count as an immediate value. The register versions use the following format.

        srad   rA,rS,rB
        sard.   rA,rS,rB

The instructions sraw and sraw. work on word operands. All these shift instructions are encoded using the X-form instruction format shown on page 85.

Let us next look at the immediate versions of the arithmetic shift instructions. The instructions

        sradi   rA,rS,count
        sardi.   rA,rS,count

use the 6-bit immediate value count as the shift count. The instructions srawi and srawi. work on word operands and take a 5-bit immediate value as the shift count. One difference between the arithmetic shift instructions and the other shift instructions is that the shift arithmetic instructions affect the CA bit in the XER register.

Rotate Instructions

The PowerPC provides several rotate-left instructions. We describe only one of them to see an interesting feature of these instructions. The rlwnm (rotate-left word then AND with mask) instruction takes five operands as shown below:

        rlwnm   rA,rS,rB,MB,ME

The contents of rS are rotated left by the count value specified in the lower-order five bits of rB. A mask value that contains 1s from the MB+32 bit to the ME+32 bit and 0s in all the other bit positions is generated. The rotated value is ANDed with the mask value and the result is placed in rA. This instruction is useful to extract and rotate bit fields. It is straightforward to implement a simple rotate-left instruction as shown below:

        rotlw   rA,rS,rB   is equivalent to   rlwnm   rA,rS,rB,0,31

Comparison Instructions

We describe two compare instructions: one for comparing signed numbers and the other for unsigned numbers. Each of these instructions is available in two formats: register version and immediate version. We first look at the signed compare instructions. This instruction compares two numbers and updates the specified CRx field of the CR register. The format is

```
cmp      crfD,L,rA,rB
```

The L field controls the operand size: 32 bits (L = 0) or 64 bits (L = 1). If the contents of rA are less than the contents of rB, the LT bit in the crfD is set; if greater, the GT bit is set; otherwise, the EQ bit is set. It also updates the SO field by copying it from the XER register. The CR0 field is used if no CR field is specified as shown below:

```
cmpw     rA,rB        is equivalent to     cmp      0,0,rA,rB
cmpd     cr3,rA,rB    is equivalent to     cmp      3,1,rA,rB
```

These instructions use the X-form format shown on page 85. The immediate version of this statement

```
cmpi     crfD,L,rA,Simm16
```

takes an immediate 16-bit signed integer in place of rB. These instructions are encoded using the D-form instruction format.

To treat the operands as unsigned integers, we can use cmpl (compare logical) and cmpli (compare logical immediate) instructions.

Branch Instructions

The PowerPC implements branch and procedure invocation operations using more flexible branch instructions. As we see in Part III, MIPS also uses a similar mechanism to invoke procedures. Some of the branch instruction encodings are shown in Figure 6.3 on page 85.

As in the other instructions, the most significant 6 bits are used for op-code. The remaining 26 bits are used for specifying the target. All instructions take four bytes and are aligned, thus the least significant 2 bits are always zero. These 2 bits are used to make the branch instruction more flexible. The AA bit is used to indicate whether the address is the absolute address (AA = 1) or PC-relative address (AA = 0). In the absolute address mode, the 26-bit value is treated as the branch target address. In the PC-relative mode, this value is used as an offset relative to the contents of the program counter (PC). Thus, the PC-relative mode works as do the Pentium's jump instructions.

The second bit LK is used to convert the branch instruction into a procedure call instruction. When the LK bit is set, the return address (i.e., the address of the instruction following the branch) is placed in the Link Register (LR). In this case, LR is loaded with a value equal to the branch instruction address + 4 as each instruction takes four bytes.

There are four unconditional branch variations, depending on the values specified for the AA and LK bits:

b	target	(AA = 0, LK = 0)	Branch
ba	target	(AA = 1, LK = 0)	Branch Absolute
bl	target	(AA = 0, LK = 1)	Branch then Link
bla	target	(AA = 1, LK = 1)	Branch Absolute then Link

All instructions transfer control to the `target` address. These instructions use the I-form instruction format. The last two instructions, `bl` and `bla`, also load the LR register with the return address. Thus these instructions are useful to invoke procedures.

There are also three types of conditional branch instructions. The first type uses direct address as do the previous branch instructions. The remaining two types use register indirect branching. One uses the count register to supply the target address, and the other uses the link register for this purpose. This last type of branch where the target is given by the link register is essentially used to return from a procedure.

Just as with the unconditional branch instructions, four versions are available:

bc	BO,BI,target	(AA = 0, LK = 0)	Branch Conditional
bca	BO,BI,target	(AA = 1, LK = 0)	Branch Conditional Absolute
bcl	BO,BI,target	(AA = 0, LK = 1)	Branch Conditional then Link
bcla	BO,BI,target	(AA = 1, LK = 1)	Branch Conditional Absolute then Link

The BO (Branch Options) operand, which is five bits long, specifies the condition under which the branch is taken. The BI (Branch Input) operand specifies the bit in the CR field that should be used as the branch condition. These instructions use the B-form instruction format.

We can specify the following nine different branch conditions.

- Decrement CTR; branch if CTR $\neq$ 0 and the condition is false.

- Decrement CTR; branch if CTR = 0 and the condition is false.

- Decrement CTR; branch if CTR $\neq$ 0 and the condition is true.

- Decrement CTR; branch if CTR = 0 and the condition is true.

- Branch always.

- Branch if the condition is false (*).

- Branch if the condition is true (*).

- Decrement CTR; branch if CTR $\neq$ 0 (*).

- Decrement CTR; branch if CTR = 0 (*).

In the last four conditions, marked with (*), two bits of the BI field are used to provide hints on whether the branch is likely to be taken. These two bits, called `at` bits, have the following meaning.

at   Hint

00   No hint.

01   Reserved.

10   The branch is likely not taken.

11   The branch is likely taken.

The link register-based branch instructions are shown below:

```
bclr    BO,BI,BH    (LK = 0)    Branch Conditional to Link Register
bclrl   BO,BI,BH    (LK = 1)    Branch Conditional to Link Register then
                                   Link
```

For these instructions, the target address is taken from the LR register. These instructions can be used to return from a procedure call. The BO and BI operands play the same role as in the previous direct conditional branch instructions. The final two branch instructions

```
bcctr   BO,BI,BH    (LK = 0)    Branch Conditional to Count Register
bcctrl  BO,BI,BH    (LK = 1)    Branch Conditional to Count Register then
                                   Link
```

use the CTR register instead of the LR register. These four instructions use the XL-form instruction format shown in Figure 6.3 on page 85.

The indirect conditional branch instructions have a Branch Hint (BH) operand. This operand gives branch hints and has the following interpretation.

BH   Hint

00   The instruction is a return from a procedure.

01   The instruction is not a procedure return. The target address is likely to be the same as the target address used the last time branch was taken.

10   Reserved.

11   The target address is not predictable.

As noted in our discussion in Chapter 2 (page 32), for indirect branch instructions, branch prediction is not particularly useful to prefetch instructions as we do not know the target address in advance. The BH operand gives hints on the target address. Note that the BH hint is different from the at hint given in the conditional direct branch instructions. The at field gives a hint on whether the branch is likely to be taken, whereas the BH operand gives hints about the target address.

Summary

We have presented details on the PowerPC architecture. The PowerPC architecture consists of three main functional units: branch processor, fixed-point processor, and floating-point processor. This partitioning facilitates superscalar implementation in which multiple functional units can concurrently work on independent instructions.

PowerPC provides two basic addressing modes for the load and store instructions. These modes are similar to the addressing modes in the SPARC. Unlike MIPS, PowerPC has several instruction formats. We have presented only a few instruction formats here. Although most instructions are similar to the SPARC instructions discussed in the last chapter, there are some instructions that are not simple. In addition, the division operation is supported only partially—it produces only the quotient.

You can see from this description that the PowerPC does not closely adhere to all the principles of the RISC philosophy. Although it uses simple addressing modes and fixed-size instructions, some of its instructions are not simple. For example, the `lswx` and `stlwx` instructions mentioned earlier are not simple by any stretch of the imagination. This observation also holds for the Itanium that we discuss in the next chapter.

Web Resources

PowerPC documentation is available from the IBM Web site. The *PowerPC Architecture Book,* which consists of three volumes, describes the PowerPC architecture in detail [23, 24, 25]. These three volumes are available from `www.ibm.com/developerworks/ eserver/articles/archguide.html`.

7

Itanium Architecture

This chapter describes the Itanium architecture, which is the Intel 64-bit architecture. Unlike their 32-bit architecture, this is a RISC architecture. In addition to the standard RISC features, the Itanium incorporates several advanced architectural features such as instruction-level parallelism, register stacks, speculative execution, and predication to improve instruction reordering. These features are discussed in detail. We conclude the chapter with a summary.

Introduction

Intel has moved from the CISC architecture used in their 32-bit processors to a RISC orientation for their 64-bit processors. The Itanium architecture defines their 64-bit processor architecture. Implementations of this architecture include the Itanium and Itanium 2 processors. As do the other processors discussed before, the Itanium architecture also uses the load/store architecture. Furthermore, the RISC features discussed in Chapter 3 are also present. In addition, it incorporates several advanced architectural features to improve performance. We discuss these features in detail in this chapter. More specifically, we discuss instruction-level parallelism, register stacks, speculative execution, and predication to improve instruction reordering.

The Itanium's ISA is based on the EPIC (Explicit Parallel Instruction Computing) design philosophy. Of course, it also maintains backward compatibility to the IA-32 ISA. EPIC design features include the following.

- *Explicit Parallelism:* The ISA provides necessary support for the compiler to convey information on the instructions that can be executed in parallel. In traditional architectures, hardware extracts this Instruction-Level Parallelism (ILP) within a fairly small window of instructions (or reorder buffer). In contrast, the Itanium allows the compiler to do the job. Because ILP extraction is done in software, a more detailed analysis can be done on a much larger window at compile time.

It also provides hardware support to execute instructions in parallel by reading three instructions as a bundle. The compiler packs only instructions that have no dependencies into a bundle. Thus, the processor does not have to spend time in analyzing the instruction stream to extract ILP. We present details on this and other features of the Itanium later in this chapter.

- *Features to Enhance ILP:* The Itanium allows the compiler to detect and extract ILP, therefore we can use more elaborate methods to improve ILP. Two such schemes are speculative execution and predication. Speculative execution allows high-latency load instructions to be advanced so that the latency can be masked. Branch handling is improved by using predication. In some instances, branch instructions can be completely eliminated. We present details on these two techniques later.

- *Resources for Parallel Execution:* It is imperative that to successfully exploit the ILP detected by the compiler, the processor should provide ample resources to execute instructions in parallel. The Itanium provides a large number of registers and functional units. It has 128 integer registers and an equal number of floating-point registers. The large number of registers, for example, can be effectively used to make procedure calls and returns very efficient. Most procedure calls/returns need not access memory for parameter values and local and global variables.

To summarize, the Itanium architecture improves performance by

- Increasing instruction-level parallelism by providing large register sets and a three-instruction wide word;
- Hiding memory latency by speculative loads;
- Improving branch handling by using predication; and
- Providing hardware support for efficient procedure calls and returns.

The Itanium supports both integer and floating-point data types. Integer data types can be 1, 2, 4, or 8 bytes wide. With a few exceptions, integer operations are done on 64-bit data. Furthermore, registers are always written as 64 bits. Thus, 1-, 2-, and 4-byte operands loaded from memory are zero-extended to 64 bits. Floating-point data types include IEEE single, double, and double-extended formats. In the remainder of this chapter, we look at the various features of the Itanium architecture.

Registers

The Itanium has 128 general registers, which are labeled gr0 through gr127 as shown in Figure 7.1. Each register is 64 bits wide. In addition, a bit is associated with each register to indicate whether the register is free or contains something valid. This bit is called NaT, which stands for *Not-a-Thing.* We explain later how this bit is used in speculative loading.

The general registers are divided into *static* and *stacked* registers. Static registers are comprised of the first 32 registers: gr0 through gr31. Of these, gr0 is essentially a

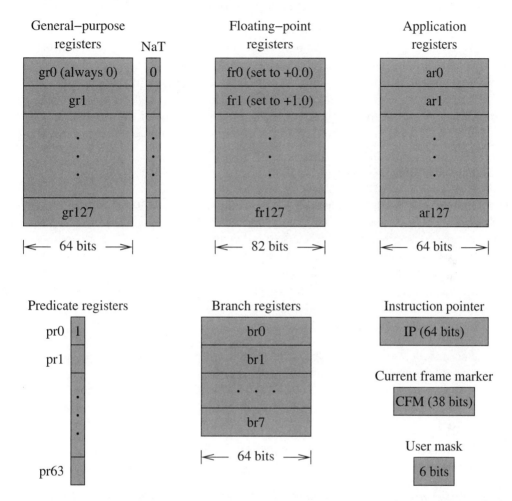

Figure 7.1 Itanium registers: the general-purpose register gr0 and its NaT bit are hard-wired to zero. Similarly, the first two floating registers are set to 0 and 1. The predicate register pr0 is set to 1.

read-only register. As in the MIPS and SPARC architectures, this register always provides a zero value when used as a source operand. Writing to this register generates an "illegal operation" fault.

General registers gr32 through gr127 are classified as stacked registers. These registers are available for use by a program as a register stack frame. This is similar to the register window mechanism used in the SPARC architecture.

The eight 64-bit branch registers, br0 through br7, hold the target address for indirect branches. These registers are used to specify the target address for conditional branch, procedure call, and return instructions.

The user mask (UM) register is used to control memory access alignment, byte ordering (little-endian or big-endian), and user-configurable performance monitors. If the byte order bit is 0, little-endian order is used; otherwise, big-endian order is assumed. In IA-32 memory accesses, data access always uses little-endian order and ignores this bit.

The uses of the remaining registers—predicate registers, applications registers, and current frame marker—are discussed later. The instruction pointer register plays the same role as the PC register in the other architectures discussed before.

Addressing Modes

The Itanium provides three addressing modes, somewhat similar to the addressing modes in the PowerPC architecture. As mentioned in Chapter 3, RISC architectures provide only a few, simple addressing modes. Because the Itanium follows the load/store architecture, only the load and store instructions can access memory. These instructions use three general registers: r1, r2, and r3. Two of these registers, r2 and r3, are used to compute the effective address. The third register r1 either receives (in load) or supplies (in store) the data. These three addressing modes are very similar to the PowerPC addressing modes, therefore we briefly describe them here:

- *Register Indirect Addressing:* In this mode, load and store instructions use the contents of r3 as the effective address.

$$\text{Effective address} = \text{Contents of } r3.$$

    The PowerPC does not directly support this addressing mode. However, it provides the following two addressing modes.

- *Register Indirect with Immediate Addressing:* In this addressing mode, the effective address is computed by adding the contents of r3 and a signed 9-bit immediate value imm9 specified in the instruction. The computed effective address is placed in r3.

$$\text{Effective address} = \text{Contents of } r3 + imm9,$$
$$r3 = \text{Effective address.}$$

- *Register Indirect with Index Addressing:* In this addressing mode, two general registers r2 and r3 are used to compute the effective address as in the PowerPC. As in the previous addressing mode, r3 is updated with the computed effective address.

$$\text{Effective address} = \text{Contents of } r3 + \text{Contents of } r2,$$
$$r3 = \text{Effective address.}$$

The last two addressing modes are similar to the update addressing modes supported by the PowerPC. As discussed in Chapter 6, the update feature of the last two addressing modes gives more flexibility. For example, we can use the second addressing mode to access successive elements of an array by making imm9 equal to the element size.

Procedure Calls

The Itanium provides hardware support for efficient procedure invocation and return. An Itanium procedure call typically does not involve the stack. Instead, it uses a register stack for passing parameters, local variables, and the like. For this purpose, the 128 general register set is divided into two subsets.

- *Static Registers:* The first 32 registers, gr0 though gr31, are called static registers. These registers are used to store the global variables and are accessible to all procedures.
- *Stacked Registers:* The upper 96 registers, gr32 through gr127, are called stack registers. These registers, instead of the stack, are used for passing parameters, returning results, and storing local variables.

A *register stack frame* is the set of stacked registers visible to a given procedure. This stack frame is partitioned into local area and output area. The size of each area can be specified by each procedure by using the alloc instruction. The local area consists of input area and space for local variables of the procedure. The input area is used to receive parameters from the caller and the output area is used to pass parameters to the callee. When a procedure is called, the alloc instruction can be used to allocate the required number of registers for the local and output areas. As mentioned, the local area includes the storage to receive arguments in addition to local variable storage.

The Itanium aligns the caller's output area with the callee's local area so that passing of parameters does not involve actual copying of register values (for a similar discussion on SPARC, see Figure 5.2 on page 58). Furthermore, the Itanium uses register renaming. That is, independent of the actual set of registers allocated to a procedure, the allocated register set is renamed such that the first register is always labeled as gr32.

The Current Frame Marker (CFM) register maintains information on the current stack frame. It keeps two values: Size of Frame (SOF) and Size of Locals (SOL). As the names indicate, SOF gives the total stack frame size, and SOL specifies the local area size. The difference (SOF − SOL) is the output area size. The alloc statement takes three immediate values that specify the size of inputs, locals, and outputs. The SOF value is determined by adding these three values; SOL is given by the sum of the first two values (i.e., size of inputs and locals).

Another interesting feature is that a procedure's stack frame can be up to 90 registers. What happens if some of the registers are allocated to other procedures? Itanium uses a hardware mechanism called a Register Stack Engine (RSE) to transparently manage registers. When allocation exceeds the available registers on the stack, it moves data from the registers to memory. The stored registers are restored when returning from the procedure. This mechanism is transparent, but the cost is not. If we use RSE to move data between registers and memory, the overhead is similar to what we see in processors such as the Pentium that use the stack for activation records.

Instruction Format

A typical Itanium instruction uses a three-operand format. The general syntax is

```
[(qp)] mnemonic[.comp] dests = srcs
```

The syntax is quite different from what we have seen before for other architectures. The optional qualifying predicate (qp) specifies a predicate register that indicates whether the instruction should be executed. Recall that the Itanium has 64 1-bit predicate registers (see Figure 7.1). An instruction is executed only if the specified predicate register has a true (1) value; otherwise, the instruction is treated as a nop (No OPeration). If a predicate register is not specified in an instruction, predicate register p0 is used, which is always true. Note that some instructions cannot be predicated.

The mnemonic field identifies an instruction and is similar to the mnemonic field in other architectures. However, for some instructions, mnemonic identifies only a generic instruction such as comparison. Such instructions require more information to completely specify the operation. For example, in comparison instructions, we have to specify the type of comparison: equality, greater than, and so on. One or more completers comp can be used for this purpose. Completers indicate optional variations on the basic operation. dests is typically a register to receive the result. Most instructions require two source operands and srcs specifies these input operands. Some examples of Itanium instructions are given below:

Simple instruction	`add r1 = r2,r3`
Predicated instruction	`(p4)add r1 = r2,r3`
Instruction with an immediate value	`add r1 = r2,r3,1`
Instructions with completers	`cmp.eq p3 = r2,r4`
	`cmp.gt p2,p3 = r3,r4`
	`br.cloop.sptk loop_back`

Each instruction is encoded using 41 bits as shown in Figure 7.2. This figure shows some sample Itanium instruction formats. In every instruction, the least significant 6 bits are used to specify one of the 64 predicate registers. The leftmost 4 bits specify a major opcode that identifies a major operation group such as comparison, floating-point operation, and so on. Opcode extension fields are used to specify subcases of the major operations. In the register format, source and destination register specification take a total of 21 bits. Each register specification needs 7 bits as Itanium has 128 registers (see Figure 7.2a).

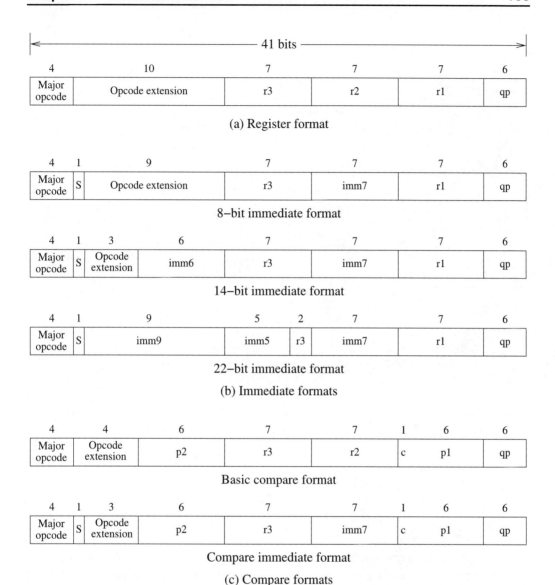

Figure 7.2 Sample Itanium instruction formats (continued on the next page).

The Itanium supports three types of immediate formats: 8-, 14-, and 22-bit immediate values can be specified. In the immediate format, the sign of the immediate value is always placed in the fifth leftmost bit (the S bit in Figure 7.2b). When a 22-bit immediate value is specified, the destination register must be one of the first four registers (r0 through r3), as we have only two bits to specify this register.

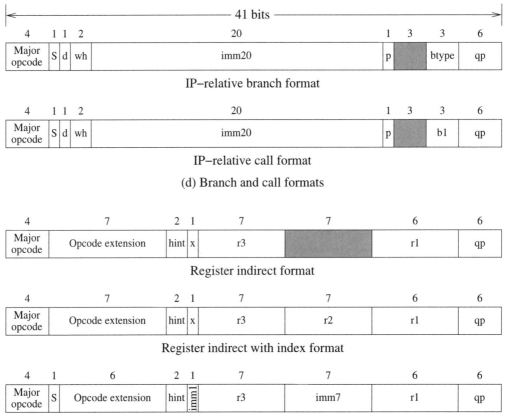

IP–relative branch format

IP–relative call format

(d) Branch and call formats

Register indirect format

Register indirect with index format

Register indirect with immediate format

(e) Integer load formats

Figure 7.2 *Continued.*

Two sample compare instruction formats are presented in Figure 7.2c. As we show later, compare instructions can specify two predicate registers p1 and p2. In a typical compare operation, the two source operands are compared, and the result is placed in p1 and its complement in p2. The c bit extends the opcode to specify the complement compare relation. For example, if the encoding with c = 0 represents a "less than" comparison, c = 1 converts this to a "greater than or equal to" type of comparison.

Figure 7.2d shows a sample format for branch and call instructions. Each instruction takes a 21-bit signed IP-relative displacement to the target. Note that the Itanium also supports indirect branch and call instructions. For both instructions, d and wh fields are opcode extensions to specify hints. The d bit specifies the branch cache deallocation hint, and the wh field gives the branch whether hint. These two hints are discussed later.

In the branch instruction, the `btype` field indicates the type of branch instruction (e.g., branch on equality, less than, etc.). In the call instruction, the `b1` field specifies the register that should receive the return address.

The integer load instruction formats are shown in Figure 7.2e. The `x` bit is used for opcode extension. In the indexed addressing mode, the 9-bit immediate value is split into three pieces: `S`, `imm1`, and `imm7`. The `hint` field, which gives the memory reference hint, is discussed later in this chapter.

Instruction-Level Parallelism

The Itanium enables instruction-level parallelism by letting the compiler/assembler explicitly indicate parallelism by providing run-time support to execute instructions in parallel, and by providing a large number of registers to avoid register contention. First we discuss the instruction groups, and then see how the hardware facilitates parallel execution of instructions by bundling nonconflicting instructions together.

Itanium instructions are bound into instruction groups. An instruction group is a set of instructions that do not have conflicting dependencies among them (read-after-write or write-after-write dependencies, as discussed later on page 115), and may execute in parallel. The compiler or assembler can indicate instruction groups by using the `;;` notation. Let us look at a simple example to get an idea. Consider evaluating a logical expression consisting of four terms. For simplicity, assume that the results of these four logical terms are in registers `r10`, `r11`, `r12`, and `r13`. Then the logical expression in

```
if (r10 || r11 || r12 || r13) {
      /* if-block code */
}
```

can be evaluated using `or`-tree reduction as

```
or      r1 = r10,r11        /* Group 1 */
or      r2 = r12,r13;;
or      r3 = r1,r2;;        /* Group 2 */
other instructions          /* Group 3 */
```

The first group performs two parallel `or` operations. Once these results are available, we can compute the final value of the logical expression. This final value in `r3` can be used by other instructions to test the condition. Inasmuch as we have not discussed Itanium instructions, it does not make sense to explain these instructions at this point. We have some examples in a later section.

In any given clock cycle, the processor executes as many instructions from one instruction group as it can, according to its resources. An instruction group must contain at least one instruction; the number of instructions in an instruction group is not limited. Instruction groups are indicated in the code by cycle breaks (`;;`). An instruction group may also end dynamically during run-time by a taken branch.

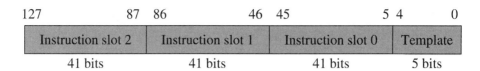

Figure 7.3 Itanium instruction bundle format.

An advantage of instruction groups is that they reduce the need to optimize the code for each new microarchitecture. Processors with additional resources can take advantage of the existing ILP in the instruction group.

By means of instruction groups, compilers package instructions that can be executed in parallel. It is the compiler's responsibility to make sure that instructions in a group do not have conflicting dependencies. Armed with this information, instructions in a group are bundled together as shown in Figure 7.3. Three instructions are collected into 128-bit, aligned containers called *bundles*. Each bundle contains three 41-bit instruction slots and a 5-bit template field.

The main purpose of the template field is to specify mapping of instruction slots to execution instruction types. Instructions are categorized into six instruction types: integer ALU, non-ALU integer, memory, floating-point, branch, and extended. A specific execution unit may execute each type of instruction. For example, floating-point instructions are executed by the F-unit, branch instructions by the B-unit, and memory instructions such as load and store by the M-unit. The remaining three types of instructions are executed by the I-unit. All instructions, except extended instructions, occupy one instruction slot. Extended instructions, which use long immediate integers, occupy two instruction slots.

Instruction Set

As in the other chapters, we discuss several sample groups of instructions from the Itanium instructions set.

Data Transfer Instructions

The Itanium's load and store instructions are more complex than those in a typical RISC processor. The Itanium supports speculative loads to mask high latency associated with reading data from memory.

The basic load instruction takes one of the three forms shown below depending on the addressing mode used:

```
(qp)  ldSZ.ldtype.ldhint   r1 = [r3]         /* No update form */
(qp)  ldSZ.ldtype.ldhint   r1 = [r3],r2      /* Update form 1 */
(qp)  ldSZ.ldtype.ldhint   r1 = [r3],imm9    /* Update form 2 */
```

The load instruction loads SZ bytes from memory, starting at the effective address. The SZ completer can be 1, 2, 4, or 8 to load 1, 2, 4, or 8 bytes. In the first load instruction, register r3 provides the address. In the second instruction, contents of r3 and r2 are added to get the effective address. The third form uses a 9-bit signed immediate value, instead of register r2. In the last two forms, as explained earlier, the computed effective address is stored in r3.

The ldtype completer can be used to specify special load operations. For normal loads, the completer is not specified. For example, the instruction

```
ld8     r5 = [r6]
```

loads eight bytes from the memory starting from the effective address in r6. As mentioned before, the Itanium supports speculative loads. Two example instructions are shown below:

```
ld8.a     r5 = [r6]        /* advanced load */
ld8.s     r5 = [r6]        /* speculative load */
```

We defer a discussion of these load instruction types to a later section that discusses the speculative execution model of Itanium.

The ldhint completer specifies the locality of the memory access. It can take one of the following three values.

ldhint	Interpretation
None	Temporal locality, level 1
ntl	No temporal locality, level 1
nta	No temporal locality, all levels

A prefetch hint is implied in the two "update" forms of load instructions. The address in r3 after the update acts as a hint to prefetch the indicated cache line. In the "no update" form of load, r3 is not updated and no prefetch hint is implied. Level 1 refers to the cache level. Because we don't cover temporal locality and cache memory in this book, we refer the reader to [6] for details on cache memory. It is sufficient to view the ldhint completer as giving a hint to the processor as to whether a prefetch is beneficial.

The store instruction is simpler than the load instruction. There are two types of store instructions, corresponding to the two addressing modes, as shown below:

```
(qp) stSZ.sttype.sthint  r1 = [r3]         /* No update form */
(qp) stSZ.sttype.sthint  r1 = [r3],imm9    /* Update form */
```

The SZ completer can have four values as in the load instruction. The sttype can be none or rel. If the rel value is specified, an ordered store is performed. The sthint gives a prefetch hint as in the load instruction. However, it can be either none or nta. When no value is specified, temporal locality at level 1 is assumed. The nta has the same interpretation as in the load instruction.

The Itanium also has several move instructions to copy data into registers. We describe three of these instructions:

```
(qp) mov  r1 = r3
(qp) mov  r1 = imm22
(qp) movl r1 = imm64
```

These instructions move the second operand into the `r1` register. The first two `mov` in-structions are actually pseudoinstructions. That is, these instructions are implemented using other processor instructions. The `movl` is the only instruction that requires two instruction slots within the same bundle.

Arithmetic Instructions

The Itanium provides only the basic integer arithmetic operations: addition, subtraction, and multiplication. There is no divide instruction, either for integers or floating-point numbers. Division is implemented in software. Let's start our discussion with the add instructions.

Add Instructions   The format of the add instructions is given below:

```
(qp) add r1 = r2,r3      /* register form */
(qp) add r1 = r2,r3,1    /* plus 1 form */
(qp) add r1 = imm,r3     /* immediate form */
```

In the *plus 1* form, the constant 1 is added as well. In the immediate form, `imm` can be a 14- or 22-bit signed value. If we use a 22-bit immediate value, `r3` can be one of the first four general registers GR0 through GR3 (i.e., only 2 bits are used to specify the second operand register as shown in Figure 7.2).

The immediate form is a pseudoinstruction that selects one of the two processor immediate `add` instructions,

```
(qp) add r1 = imm14,r3
(qp) add r1 = imm22,r3
```

depending on the size of the immediate operand size and value of `r3`.

The move instruction

```
(qp) mov r1 = r3
```

is implemented as

```
(qp) add  r1 = 0,r3
```

The move instruction

```
(qp) mov r1 = imm22
```

is implemented as

```
(qp) add  r1 = imm22,r0
```

Remember that `r0` is hardwired to value zero.

Subtract Instructions The subtract instruction sub has the same format as the add instruction. The contents of register r3 are subtracted from the contents of r2. In the *minus 1* form, the constant 1 is also subtracted. In the immediate form, imm is restricted to an 8-bit value.

The instruction shladd (shift left and add)

```
(qp) shladd r1 = r2,count,r3
```

is similar to the add instruction, except that the contents of r2 are left-shifted by count bit positions before adding. The count operand is a 2-bit value, which restricts the shift to 1-, 2-, 3-, or 4-bit positions.

Multiply Instructions Integer multiply is done using the xmpy and xma instructions. These instructions do not use the general registers; instead, they use the floating-point registers.

The xmpy instruction has the following formats.

```
(qp) xmpy.l    f1 = f3,f4
(qp) xmpy.lu   f1 = f3,f4
(qp) xmpy.h    f1 = f3,f4
(qp) xmpy.hu   f1 = f3,f4
```

The two source operands, floating-point registers f3 and f4, are treated either as signed or unsigned integers. The completer u in the second and fourth instructions specifies that the operands are unsigned integers. The other two instructions treat the two integers as signed. The l or h indicate whether the lower or higher 64 bits of the result should be stored in the f1 floating-point register.

The xmpy instruction multiplies the two integers in f3 and f4 and places the lower or upper 64-bit result in the f1 register. Note that we get a 128-bit result when we multiply two 64-bit integers.

The xma instruction has four formats as does the xmpy instruction, as shown below:

```
(qp) xma.l    f1 = f3,f4,f2
(qp) xma.lu   f1 = f3,f4,f2
(qp) xma.h    f1 = f3,f4,f2
(qp) xma.hu   f1 = f3,f4,f2
```

This instruction multiplies the two 64-bit integers in f3 and f4 and adds the zero-extended 64-bit value in f2 to the product.

Logical Instructions

Logical operations and, or, and xor are supported by three logical instructions. There is no not instruction. However, the Itanium has an and-complement (andcm) instruction that complements one of the operands before performing the bitwise-and operation.

All instructions have the same format. We illustrate the format of these instructions for the and instruction:

```
(qp) and r1 = r2,r3
(qp) and r1 = imm8,r3
```

The other three operations use the mnemonics `or`, `xor`, and `andcm`. The and-complement instruction complements the contents of `r3` and `and`s it with the first operand (contents of `r2` or immediate value `imm8`).

Shift Instructions

Both left- and right-shift instructions are available. The shift instructions

```
(qp) shl r1 = r2,r3
(qp) shl r1 = r2,count
```

left-shift the contents of `r2` by the `count` value specified by the second operand. The `count` value can be specified in `r3` or given as a 6-bit immediate value. If the `count` value in `r3` is more than 63, the result is all zeros.

Right-shift instructions use a similar format. Because right-shift can be arithmetical or logical depending on whether the number is signed or unsigned, two versions are available. The register versions of the right-shift instructions are shown below:

```
(qp) shr     r1 = r2,r3     (signed right shift)
(qp) shr.u   r1 = r2,r3     (unsigned right shift)
```

In the second instruction, the completer `u` is used to indicate the unsigned shift operation. We can also use a 6-bit immediate value for shift count as in the `shl` instruction.

Comparison Instructions

The compare instruction uses two completers as shown below:

```
(qp) cmp.crel.ctype p1,p2=r2,r3
(qp) cmp.crel.ctype p1,p2=imm8,r3
```

The two source operands are compared and the result is written to the two specified destination predicate registers. The type of comparison is specified by `crel`. We can specify one of 10 relations for signed and unsigned numbers. The relations "equal" (`eq`) and "not equal" (`neq`) are valid for both signed and unsigned numbers. For signed numbers, there are 4 relations to test for "<" (`lt`), "≤" (`le`), ">" (`gt`), and "≥" (`ge`). The corresponding relations for testing unsigned numbers are `ltu`, `leu`, `gtu`, and `geu`. The relation is tested as "r2 rel r3".

The `ctype` completer specifies how the two predicate registers are to be updated. The normal type (default) writes the comparison result in the `p1` register and its complement in the `p2` register. This would allow us to select one of the two branches (we show an example on page 113). The `ctype` completer allows specification of other types such as `and` and `or`. If `or` is specified, both `p1` and `p2` are set to 1 only if the comparison result is 1; otherwise, the two predicate registers are not altered. This is useful for implementing `or`-type simultaneous execution. Similarly, if `and` is specified, both registers are set to 0 if the comparison result is 0 (useful for `and`-type simultaneous execution).

Branch Instructions

As in the other architectures, the Itanium uses branch instruction for traditional jumps as well as procedure call and return. The generic branch is supplemented by a completer to specify the type of branch. The branch instruction supports both direct and indirect branching. All direct branches are IP relative (i.e., PC relative). Some sample branch instruction formats are shown below:

IP Relative Form:

(qp)	`br.btype.bwh.ph.dh`	`target25`	(Basic form)
(qp)	`br.btype.bwh.ph.dh`	`b1=target25`	(Call form)
	`br.btype.bwh.ph.dh`	`target25`	(Counted loop form)

Indirect Form:

(qp)	`br.btype.bwh.ph.dh`	`b2`	(Basic form)
(qp)	`br.btype.bwh.ph.dh`	`b1=b2`	(Call form)

As can be seen, branch uses up to four completers. The `btype` specifies the type of branch. The other three completers provide hints and are discussed later.

For the basic branch, `btype` can be either `cond` or none. In this case, the branch is taken if the qualifying predicate is 1; otherwise, the branch is not taken. The IP-relative target address is given as a label in the assembly language. The assembler translates this into a signed 21-bit value that gives the difference between the target bundle and the bundle containing the branch instruction. The target pointer is to a bundle of 128 bits, therefore the value (`target25−IP`) is shifted right by 4 bit positions to get a 21-bit value. Note that the format shown in Figure 7.2d uses a 21-bit displacement value.

To invoke a procedure, we use the second form and specify `call` for `btype`. This turns the branch instruction into a condition call instruction. The procedure is invoked only if the qualifying predicate is true. As part of the call, it places the current frame marker and other relevant state information in the previous function state application register. The return link value is saved in the `b1` branch register for use by the return instruction.

There is also an unconditional (no qualifying predicate) counted loop version. In this branch instruction (the third one), `btype` is set to `cloop`. If the Loop Count (LC) application register `ar65` is not zero, it is decremented and the branch is taken.

We can use `ret` as the branch type to return from a procedure. It should use the indirect form and specify the branch register in which the `call` has placed the return pointer. In the indirect form, a branch register specifies the target address. The return restores the caller's stack frame and privilege level.

The last instruction can be used for an indirect procedure call. In this branch instruction, the `b2` branch register specifies the target address and the return address is placed in the `b1` branch register.

Let us look at some examples of branch instructions. The instruction

```
      (p3) br  skip      or      (p3) br.cond  skip
```

transfers control to the instruction labeled `skip`, if the predicate register `p3` is 1.
    The code sequence

```
            mov   lc = 100
      loop_back:
            . . .
            br.cloop    loop_back
```

executes the loop body 100 times. A procedure call may look like

```
      (p0)  br.call    br2 = sum
```

whereas the return from procedure `sum` uses the indirect form

```
      (p0)  br.ret    br2
```

Because we are using predicate register 0, which is hardwired to 1, both the call and return
become unconditional.
    The `bwh` (branch whether hint) completer can be used to convey whether the branch
is taken (see page 119). The `ph` (prefetch hint) completer gives a hint about sequential
prefetch. It can take either `few` or `many`. If the value is `few` or none, few lines are
prefetched; many lines are prefetched when `many` is specified. The two levels—`few` and
`many`—are system defined. The final completer `dh` (deallocation hint) specifies whether
the branch cache should be cleared. The value `clr` indicates deallocation of branch information.

Handling Branches

Pipelining works best when we have a linear sequence of instructions. Branches cause
pipeline stalls, leading to performance problems. How do we minimize the adverse effects
of branches? There are three techniques to handle this problem.

- *Branch Elimination:* The best solution is to avoid the problem in the first place. This
  argument may seem strange as programs contain lots of branch instructions. Although we cannot eliminate all branches, we can eliminate certain types of branches.
  This elimination cannot be done without support at the instruction-set level. We
  look at how the Itanium uses predication to eliminate some types of branches.

- *Branch Speedup:* If we cannot eliminate a branch, at least we can reduce the amount
  of delay associated with it. This technique involves reordering instructions so that
  instructions that are not dependent on the branch/condition can be executed while
  the branch instruction is processed. Speculative execution can be used to reduce
  branch delays. We describe the Itanium's speculative execution strategies later.

- *Branch Prediction:* If we can predict whether the branch will be taken, we can load the pipeline with the right sequence of instructions. Even if we predict correctly all the time, it would only convert a conditional branch into an unconditional branch. We still have the problems associated with unconditional branches. We described three types of branch prediction strategies in Chapter 2 (see page 28).

Inasmuch as we covered branch prediction in Chapter 2, we discuss the first two techniques next.

Predication to Eliminate Branches   In the Itanium, branch elimination is achieved by a technique known as *predication*. The trick is to make execution of each instruction conditional. Thus, unlike the instructions we have seen so far, an instruction is not automatically executed when the control is transferred to it. Instead, it will be executed only if a condition is true. This requires us to associate a predicate with each instruction. If the associated predicate is true, the instruction is executed; otherwise, it is treated as a nop instruction. The Itanium architecture supports full predication to minimize branches. Most of the Itanium's instructions can be predicated.

To see how predication eliminates branches, let us look at the following example.

```
if (R1 == R2)                              cmp      r1,r2
    R3 = R3 + R1;                          je       then_part
else                                       sub      r3,r1
    R3 = R3 - R1;                          jmp      end_if
                            then_part:
                                           add      r3,r1
                      end_if:
```

The code on the left-hand side, expressed in C, is a simple if-then-else statement. The IA-32 assembly language equivalent is shown on the right. The cmp instruction compares the contents of the r1 and r2 registers and sets the condition code bits (in the IA-32, these are called the flag bits). If r1 = r2, the jump equal (je) instruction transfers control to the then_part. Otherwise, the sub instruction is executed (i.e., the else_part). Then the unconditional jump (jmp) instruction transfers control to end_if. As you can see from this code, it introduces two branches: unconditional (jmp) and conditional (je).

Using the Itanium's predication, we can express the same as

```
      cmp.eq p1,p2 = r1,r2
(p1)  add r3 = r3,r1
(p2)  sub r3 = r3,r1
```

The compare instruction sets two predicates after comparing the contents of r1 and r2 for equality. The result of this comparison is placed in p1 and its complement in p2. Thus, if the contents of r1 and r2 are equal, p1 is set to 1 (true) and p2 to 0 (false). Because the add instruction is predicated on p1, it is executed only if p1 is true. It should be clear that either the add or the sub instruction is executed, depending on the comparison result.

To illustrate the efficacy of predicated execution, we look at the following switch statement in C.

```
switch (r6)
{
    case 1:
            r2 = r3 + r4;
            break;
    case 2:
            r2 = r3 - r4;
            break;
    case 3:
            r2 = r3 + r5;
            break;
    case 4:
            r2 = r3 - r5;
            break;
}
```

For simplicity, we are using the register names in the switch statement. Translating this statement would normally involve a series of compare and branch instructions. Predication avoids this sequence as shown below:

```
cmp.eq  p1,p0 = r6,1
cmp.eq  p2,p0 = r6,2
cmp.eq  p3,p0 = r6,3
cmp.eq  p4,p0 = r6,4 ;;

(p1) add  r2 = r3,r4
(p2) sub  r2 = r3,r4
(p3) add  r2 = r3,r5
(p4) sub  r2 = r3,r5
```

In the first group of instructions, the four compare instructions set p1/p2/p3/p4 if the corresponding comparison succeeds. If the processor has resources, all four instructions can be executed concurrently. Because p0 is hardwired to 1, failure conditions are ignored in the above code. Depending on the compare instruction that succeeds, only one of the four arithmetic instructions in the second group is executed.

Speculative Execution

Speculative execution refers to the scenario where instructions are executed in the expectation that they will be needed in actual program execution. The main motivation, of course, is to improve performance. There are two main reasons to speculatively execute instructions: to keep the pipeline full and to mask memory access latency. We discuss two types of speculative execution supported by the Itanium: one type handles data dependencies, and the other deals with control dependencies. Both techniques are compiler optimizations that allow the compiler to reorder instructions. For example, we can speculatively move high-latency load instructions earlier so that the data are available when they are actually needed.

Data Speculation

Data speculation allows the compiler to schedule instructions across some types of ambiguous data dependencies. When two instructions access common resources (either registers or memory locations) in a conflicting mode, data dependency exists. A conflicting access is one in which one or both instructions alter the data. Depending on the type of conflicting access, we can define the following dependencies.

- *Read-After-Write (RAW):* This dependency exists between two instructions if one instruction writes into a register or a memory location that is later read by the other instruction.

- *Write-After-Read (WAR):* This dependency exists between two instructions if one instruction reads from a register or a memory location that is later written by the other instruction.

- *Write-After-Write (WAW):* This dependency exists between two instructions if one instruction writes into a register or a memory location that is later written by the other instruction.

- *Ambiguous:* Ambiguous data dependency exists when pointers are used to access memory. Typically, in this case, dependencies between load and store instructions or store and store instructions cannot be resolved statically at compile time because we don't know the pointer values. Handling this type of data dependency requires run-time support.

There is no conflict in allowing read-after-read (RAR) access. The first three dependencies are not ambiguous in the sense that the dependency type can be statically determined at compile/assembly time. The compiler or programmer should insert stops (;;) so that the dependencies are properly maintained. The example

```
sub    r6=r7,r8 ;;
add    r9=r10,r6
```

exhibits a RAW data dependency on r6. The stop after the sub instruction would allow the add instruction to read the value written by the sub instruction.

If there is no data dependency, the compiler can reorder instructions to optimize the code. Let us look at the following example:

```
sub    r6=r7,r8 ;;    // cycle 1
```

```
sub      r9=r10,r6        // cycle 2
ld8      r4=[r5] ;;

add      r11=r12,r4       // cycle 4
```

Because there is a two-cycle latency to the first-level data cache, the add instruction is scheduled two cycles after scheduling the ld8 instruction. A straightforward optimization involves moving the ld8 instruction to cycle 1 as there are no data dependencies to prevent this reordering. By advancing the load instruction, we can schedule the add in cycle 3 as shown below:

```
ld8      r4=[r5]          // cycle 1
sub      r6=r7,r8 ;;

sub      r9=r10,r6 ;;     // cycle 2

add      r11=r12,r4       // cycle 3
```

However, when there is ambiguous data dependency, as in the following example, instruction reordering may not be possible:

```
sub      r6=r7,r8 ;;      // cycle 1

st8      [r9]=r6          // cycle 2
ld8      r4=[r5] ;;

add      r11=r12,r4 ;;    // cycle 4

st8      [r10]=r11        // cycle 5
```

In this code, ambiguous dependency exists between the first st8 and ld8 because r9 and r5 could be pointing to overlapped memory locations. Remember that each of these instructions accesses eight contiguous memory locations. This ambiguous dependency will not allow us to move the load instruction to cycle 1 as in the previous example.

The Itanium provides architectural support to move such load instructions. This is facilitated by advance load (ld.a) and check load (ld.c). The basic idea is that we initiate the load early and when it is time to actually execute the load, we will make a check to see if there is a dependency that invalidates our advance load data. If so, we reload; otherwise, we successfully advance the load instruction even when there is ambiguous dependency. The previous example with advance and check loads is shown below:

```
1:   ld8.a  r4=[r5]          // cycle 0 or earlier
         . . .
2:   sub    r6=r7,r8 ;;      // cycle 1
```

```
3:    st8     [r9]=r6          // cycle 2
4:    ld8.c   r4=[r5]
5:    add     r11=r12,r4 ;;

6:    st8     [r10]=r11        // cycle 3
```

We inserted an advance load (line 1) at cycle 0 or earlier so that r4 would have the value ready for the add instruction on line 5 in cycle 2. However, we have to check to see if we can use this value. This check is done by the check load instruction ld8.c on line 4. If there is no dependency between the store on line 3 and load on line 4, we can safely use the prefetched value. This is the case if the pointers in r9 and r5 are different. On the other hand, if the load instruction is reading the value written by the store instruction, we have to reload the value. The check load instruction on line 4 automatically reloads the value in the case of a conflict.

In the last example, we advanced just the load instruction. However, we can improve performance further if we can also advance all (or some of) the statements that depend on the value read by the load instruction. In our example, it would be nice if we could advance the add instruction on line 5. This causes a problem if there is a dependency between the store and load instructions (on lines 3 and 4). In this case, we not only have to reexecute the load but also the add instruction. The advance check (chk.a) instruction provides the necessary support for such reexecution as shown in the following example.

```
        ld8.a   r4=[r5]        // cycle -1 or earlier
            . . .
        add     r11=r12,r4     // cycle 1
        sub     r6=r7,r8 ;;

        st8     [r9]=r6        // cycle 2
        chk.a   r4,recover
back:
        st8     [r10]=r11

recover:
        ld8     r4=[r5]        // reload
        add     r11=r12,r4     // reexecute add
        br      back           // jump back
```

When the advanced load fails, the check instruction transfers control to recover to reload and reexecute all the instructions that used the value provided by the advanced load.

How does the Itanium maintain the dependency information for use by the check instructions? It keeps a hardware structure called the Advanced Load Address Table (ALAT), indexed by the physical register number. When an advanced load (ld.a) instruction is executed, it records the load address. When a check is executed (either ld.c or chk.a), it checks ALAT for the address. The check instruction must specify the same register that the advanced load instruction used. If the address is present in ALAT, execution continues. Otherwise, a reload (in the case of ld.c) or recovery code (in the case of chk.a) is executed. An entry in ALAT can be removed, for example, by a subsequent store that overlaps the load address. To determine this overlap, the size of the load in bytes is also maintained.

Control Speculation

When we want to reduce latencies of long latency instructions such as load, we advance them earlier into the code. When there is a branch instruction, it blocks such a move because we do not know whether the branch will be taken until we execute the branch instruction. Let us look at the following code fragment.

```
            cmp.eq  p1,p0 = r10,10    // cycle 0
    (p1) br.cond    skip ;;           // cycle 0
            ld8    r1 = [r2] ;;        // cycle 1
            add    r3 = r1,r4          // cycle 3
skip:
            // other instructions
```

In the above code, we cannot advance the load instruction due to the branch instruction. Execution of the *then branch* takes four clock cycles. Note that the code implies that the integer compare instruction that sets the predicate register p1 and the branch instruction that tests it are executed in the same cycle. This is the only exception; in general, there should be a stop inserted between an instruction that is setting a predicate register and the subsequent instruction testing the same predicate.

Now the question is: how do we advance the load instruction past the branch instruction? We speculate in a manner similar to the way we handled data dependency. There is one additional problem: because the execution may not take the branch, if the speculative execution causes exceptions, they should not be raised. Instead, exceptions should be deferred until we know that the instruction will indeed be executed. The Not-a-Thing bit is used for this purpose. If a speculative execution causes an exception, the NaT bit associated with that register is set. When a check is made at the point of actual instruction execution, if the deferred exception is not present, speculative execution was successful. Otherwise, the speculative execution should be redone. Let us rewrite the previous code with a speculative load.

```
            ld8.s   r1 = [r2] ;;       // cycle -2 or earlier

            // other instructions

            cmp.eq  p1,p0 = r10,10     // cycle 0
    (p1) br.cond    skip              // cycle 0
            chk.s   r1, recovery       // cycle 0
            add    r3 = r1,r4          // cycle 0
```

```
skip:
        // other instructions
recovery:
        ld8   r1 = [r2]
        br    skip
```

The load instruction is moved by at least two cycles so that the value is available in `r1` by the time it is needed by the `add` instruction. Because this is a speculative load, we use the `ld8.s` instruction. And, in place of the original load instruction, we insert a speculative check (`chk.s`) instruction with the same register `r1`. As in the data dependency example, if the speculative load is not successful (i.e., the `NaT` bit of `r1` is set), the instruction has to be reexecuted. In this case, the check instruction branches to the `recovery` code.

Branch Prediction Hints

Most processors use branch prediction to handle the branch problem. We have discussed three branch prediction strategies—fixed, static, and dynamic—in Chapter 2. Branch prediction strategies can accept hints from the compiler. In the Itanium, branch hints can be explicitly provided in branch instructions. The `bwh` completer can take one of the following four values.

spnt	Static branch not taken
sptk	Static branch taken
dpnt	Dynamic branch not taken
dpnt	Dynamic branch taken

The SPARC processor also allows providing hints in its branch instructions (see Chapter 5 for details).

Summary

We have given a detailed overview of the Itanium architecture. The Itanium is a more advanced processor in terms of the features provided. Compared to the other processors we have discussed so far, it supports explicit parallelism by providing ample resources such as registers and functional units. In addition, the Itanium architecture supports sophisticated speculative loads and predication. It also uses traditional branch prediction strategies. The Itanium, even though it follows the RISC principles mentioned in Chapter 3, is not a "simple" architecture. Some of its instructions truly belong to the CISC category.

Web Resources

Certainly, we have left out several elements. If you are interested in learning more about this architecture, visit the Intel Web site for recent information. The Itanium architecture details and manuals are available from www.intel.com/design/Itanium/ manuals/. The architecture is described in three volumes [10, 11, 12].

8

ARM Architecture

In this chapter, we take a detailed look at the ARM architecture. Unlike the other architectures we have seen so far, ARM provides only 16 general-purpose registers. Even though it follows the RISC principles, it provides a large number of addressing modes. Furthermore, it has several complex instructions. The format of this chapter is similar to that we used in the last few chapters. We start with a brief background on the ARM architecture. We then present details on its registers and addressing modes. Following this, we give details on some sample ARM instructions. We conclude the chapter with a summary.

Introduction

The ARM architecture was developed in 1985 by Acorn Computer Group in the United Kingdom. Acorn introduced the first RISC processor in 1987, targeting low-cost PCs. In 1990, Acorn formed Advanced RISC Machines. ARM, which initially stood for Acorn RISC Machine but later changed to Advanced RISC Machine, defines a 32-bit RISC architecture.

ARM's instruction set architecture has evolved over time. The first two versions had only 26-bit address space. Version 3 extended it to 32 bits. This version also introduced separate program status registers that we discuss in the next section. Version 4, ARMv4, is the oldest version supported today. Some implementations of this version include the ARM7™ core family and Intel StrongARM™ processors.

ARM architecture has been extended to support cost-sensitive embedded applications such as cell phones, modems, and pagers by introducing the Thumb instruction set. The Thumb instruction set is a subset of the most commonly used 32-bit ARM instructions. To reduce the memory requirements, the instructions are compressed into 16-bit wide encodings. To execute these 16-bit instructions, they are decompressed transparently to full 32-bit ARM instructions in real-time. The ARMv4T architecture has added these 16-bit Thumb instructions to produce compact code for handheld devices.

General–Purpose Registers

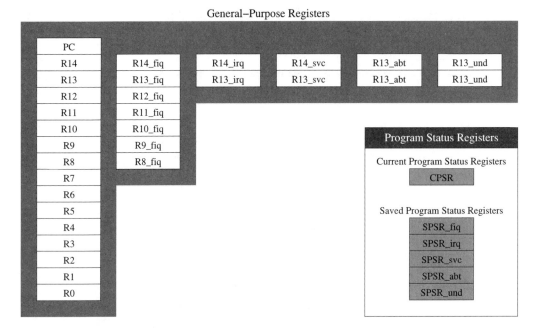

Figure 8.1 ARM register set consists of 31 general-purpose register and six status registers. All registers are 32 bits wide.

In 1999, the ARMv5TE architecture introduced several improvements to the Thumb architecture. In addition, several DSP instructions have been added to the ARM ISA. In 2000, the ARMv5TEJ architecture added the Jazelle extension to support Java acceleration technology for small memory footprint designs. In 2001, the ARMv6 architecture was introduced. This version provides support for multimedia instructions to execute in Single Instruction Multiple Data (SIMD) mode.

Like the MIPS, the ARM is dominant in the 32-bit embedded RISC microprocessor market. ARM is used in several portable and handheld devices including Dell's AXIM X5, Palm Tungsten T, RIM's Blackberry, HP iPaq, Nintendo's Gameboy Advance, and so on [4]. The ARM Web site claims that, by 2002, they shipped over 1 billion of its microprocessor cores [3].

In the remainder of this chapter we look at the ARM architecture in detail. After reading this chapter, you will notice that this architecture is somewhat different from the other processors we have seen so far. It shares some features with the Itanium architecture discussed in the last chapter. However, you should note that the ARM architecture development started in 1985.

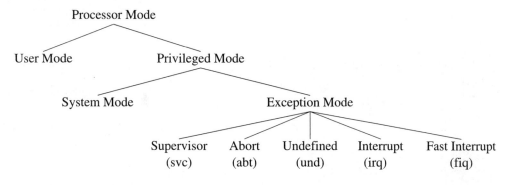

Figure 8.2 ARM processor modes.

Registers

ARM architecture has a total of 37 registers as shown in Figure 8.1. These registers are divided into two groups: general-purpose registers and program status registers.

- *General-purpose registers:* There are 31 general-purpose registers. All these registers are 32 bits wide. At any time, the user can access only 16 of these registers. The actual set of registers visible depends on the processor mode. For example, in the User and System modes, the leftmost 16 registers (R0–R14 and PC) shown in Figure 8.1 are visible.
- *Program status registers:* ARM has six status registers that keep the program status. These registers are also 32 bits wide. The Current Program Status Register (CPSR) is available in all processor modes. The visibility of the other registers depends on the processor mode.

The 16 general-purpose registers are divided into three groups: unbanked, banked, and program counter. The first eight registers (R0–R7) are unbanked registers. These registers are available in all processor modes. (We discuss the processor modes shortly.) The next seven registers (R8–R14) are banked registers. With a few exceptions, most instructions allow the banked registers to be used wherever a general-purpose register is allowed. The actual physical register used in these banks depends on the current processor mode, as shown in Figure 8.1. The last register (R15) is used as the Program Counter (PC) register.

The ARM has seven processor modes, which are divided into User and Privileged modes. The Privileged modes are further divided into System and Exception modes as shown in Figure 8.2.

Application programs typically run in the User mode. This is a nonprivileged mode, which restricts application programs from accessing protected resources. Furthermore, an exception is generated if a mode switch is attempted.

The remaining six modes are privileged modes. These modes allow access to all system resources; furthermore, we can freely switch modes. This group consists of the

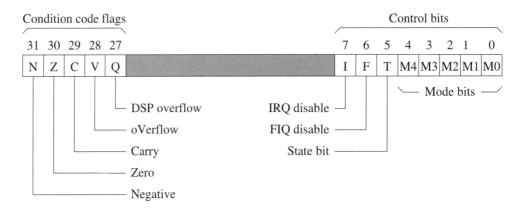

Figure 8.3 CPSR register keeps the control code flags and control bits.

System and Exception modes. The System mode has access to the same set of registers as the User mode; however, because this is a privileged mode, the User mode restrictions are not applicable. This mode is used by the operating system.

The Exception modes are entered when a specific exception occurs. The reset and software interrupts are executed under the Supervisor mode. When a Fast Interrupt request is externally asserted on the FIQ pin of the processor, an FIQ exception is generated. In response to the exception, the processor enters the Fast Interrupt mode. This mode responds to the exception with minimum context switch overhead. This mode is typically used for DMA-type data transfers. When a lesser priority interrupt request is asserted on the IRQ pin, the processor enters the IRQ mode. This mode is used for general interrupt processing.

The Undefined mode is entered when an Undefined exception is generated. This exception occurs if an attempt is made to execute an undefined instruction. The Abort mode is entered when a prefetch abort or a data abort exception occurs. The ARM manual has more details on these exceptions [1].

The general-purpose registers shown on the left in Figure 8.1 are available in the User and System modes. As mentioned before, the first eight registers (R0–R7) and the PC register are available in all modes.

- In the Fast Interrupt mode, the registers R8–R14 are replaced by the FIQ registers. By providing these banked registers, FIQ exceptions can be processed faster by minimizing the context switch overhead.

- In the remaining modes, only the two registers (R13 and R14) are replaced by the corresponding banked registers, as shown in Figure 8.1.

Each exception mode has access to a Saved Program Status Register (SPSR). This register is used to preserve the CPSR contents when the associated exception occurs. The CPSR keeps condition code information, the current processor mode, interrupt disable bits, and so on (see Figure 8.3). The CPSR is available in all modes. One of the SPSR is also available in each of the five exception modes; the actual register depends on the mode. For example, SPSR_fiq is available in FIQ mode, SPSR_irq in IRQ mode, and so on.

The condition code flags N, Z, C, and V are used to record information about the result of an operation. For example, if an instruction produces a zero result, the zero (Z) flag is set (Z = 1). The Q flag is used in DSP instructions and we do not discuss it here. The four condition code flags are modified by arithmetic, logic, and compare instructions. If you have read the previous chapters, you know what they stand for. Here is a brief description of these flags.

The N (Negative) flag indicates that the result of the operation is negative. Note that, as in the other architectures, 2's complement representation is used to represent signed numbers. This flag is essentially a copy of the sign bit of the result. The zero (Z) flag is set if the result is zero.

The remaining two flags record overflow conditions. The carry (C) flag indicates an overflow/underflow on unsigned numbers. For example, when we add two unsigned numbers, if the result does not fit the destination register, this flag is set to indicate an overflow. Similarly, in a subtract operation, a result that is less than zero indicates an underflow. The C flag records this underflow condition. The overflow (V) flag records similar information for signed numbers.

The five mode bits (M0–M4) determine the processor mode. As mentioned before, the processor operates in one of the seven modes. Thus, we do not use all combinations of these five mode bits: only the specified combinations are useful. For example, for the System mode, the mode bits are 11111.

Addressing Modes

In the last four chapters we looked at the addressing modes of four different RISC architectures. Most of these architectures provide very few memory addressing modes. At one extreme, the MIPS architecture supports only a single addressing mode. At the other end, the Itanium supports three addressing modes, some of them with an update facility. PowerPC also supports similar addressing modes. All these architectures support a single register addressing mode for instructions other than load and store.

The ARM architecture goes a few steps further. It supports effectively nine addressing modes for the load and store instructions. In addition, several other addressing modes are provided for the other instructions. In fact, the *ARM Reference Manual* devotes an entire chapter of about 65 pages to describe its addressing modes [1]. In this section, we limit our discussion to the memory addressing modes supported by the ARM architecture. Of course, full details on the addressing modes are available in [1].

In the load and store instructions, the memory address is formed by adding two components as in the other processors:

$$\text{Effective address} = \text{Contents of the base register} + \text{offset}.$$

The base register can be any general-purpose register, including the PC. When the PC is used, it allows us to use PC-relative access. Such an access facilitates position-independent code. So far, it looks as if ARM also supports addressing modes similar to those supported by the processors discussed in the previous chapters. However, the flexibility of the ARM addressing modes is due to (i) how the offset can be specified, and (ii) how the base register and offset are used to form the effective address.

Offset Specification

The offset component can be specified in one of three ways: an immediate value, a register value, or a scaled register value.

Immediate Value   The offset can be an unsigned constant that is either 8 or 12 bits long. Recall that the other architectures allow this to be a signed number. However, to compensate for this, ARM allows this number to be either added or subtracted from the contents of the base register to form the effective address. For the unsigned byte and word instructions, the immediate value is a 12-bit number. For the signed byte and halfword instructions, it is an 8-bit value. This is similar to the "Register Indirect with Immediate Addressing" mode of the Itanium and other architectures.

Register Value   In this mode, the offset can be in a general-purpose register. The effective address is formed by combining (either adding or subtracting) the contents of the base register and the offset register. This register is referred to as the index register in the previous chapters. For the index register, we can specify any general-purpose register other than the PC register. This is similar to the "Register Indirect with Index Addressing" mode discussed in the last chapter.

Scaled Register Value   This addressing mode is similar to the last one except that the index register contents are shifted before combining the contents of the base and index registers. That is, the offset is formed by taking the value from a general-purpose register and shifting it by a number of positions specified as an immediate value. As in the last mode, the PC cannot be specified as the index register. We can use any of the shift operations that we use on other operands (left-shift, right-shift, and so on). However, the left-shift operation is commonly used to scale the index register.

This addressing mode is useful to access arrays. For example, assume that the array elements are 8-byte doubles and the array index value is in the index register. In this case, we left-shift the array index in the index register by three bit positions (i.e., multiplying it by 8) so that the index value is converted to the corresponding byte displacement. If you are familiar with the Intel IA-32 architecture, you will recognize that this ARM addressing mode is similar to one of the IA-32 addressing modes.

Address Computation Mode

The effective address computation is done in one of three ways: offset, pre-indexed, and post-indexed modes.

Offset Mode   This is the basic mode of address computation and is similar to the addressing modes we have seen in previous chapters. In this mode, the address is computed as the sum of the base register value and the offset. Because we can specify the offset in three ways, the following addressing modes are available.

> Effective address = Contents of base register Rb ± imm.
>
> Effective address = Contents of base register Rb ± Contents of index register Rx.
>
> Effective address = Contents of base register Rb ± Shifted contents of index register Rx.

In all the addressing modes, we can use any general-purpose register as the base register. In the first addressing mode, the immediate value imm is either 8 or 12 bits long. In the last two addressing modes, the index can be any general-purpose register except the PC register.

Pre-Index Mode   In this mode, the memory address is computed as in the last mode. However, the computed effective address is loaded into the base register. It is similar to the update addressing modes we have seen in the PowerPC and Itanium architectures. The ARM refers to this as *write-back* rather than update. As in the last addressing mode, the following three modes are available.

> Effective address = Contents of base register Rb ± imm,
>   Rb = Effective address.
>
> Effective address = Contents of base register Rb ± Contents of index register Rx,
>   Rb = Effective address.
>
> Effective address = Contents of base register Rb ± Shifted contents of index register Rx,
>   Rb = Effective address.

Post-Index Mode   In this mode, the contents of the base register are used as the memory address. However, the effective address, computed as in the last addressing mode, is loaded into the base register. The three post-index addressing modes are shown below:

> Effective address = Contents of base register Rb,
>   Rb = Contents of base register Rb ± imm.
>
> Effective address = Contents of base register Rb,
>   Rb = Contents of base register Rb ± Contents of index register Rx.
>
> Effective address = Contents of base register Rb,
>   Rb = Contents of base register Rb ± Shifted contents of index register Rx.

The addressing modes we discussed here are available to the load and store instructions. However, ARM architecture provides several addressing modes for other instructions. We mention some of these modes in later sections. The ARM reference manual gives a complete list of all addressing modes available [1].

Instruction Format

The ARM instruction execution model is different from the MIPS, PowerPC, and SPARC models. It is somewhat similar to that of the Itanium in that most ARM instructions are conditionally executed. In the Itanium architecture, we used predicate registers to determine if an instruction should be executed. If the specified predicate register is 1, the instruction is executed; otherwise, it is treated as a nop (no operation).

The ARM architecture uses a similar scheme. However, ARM uses a 4-bit condition code field to express the condition under which the instruction should be executed. In each instruction, the most significant four bits (bits 28–31) are reserved for this purpose (see Figure 8.4).

These four bits specify a variety of conditions, as shown in Table 8.1. This table gives the condition code field value and the mnemonic used in the instructions along with a description and the condition tested. As shown in this table, the four condition code flags are used to test for the condition specified in the condition field of the instructions.

The mnemonic given in the second column is appended to the instruction mnemonic to indicate the condition. For example, to branch on equal, we use beq, whereas to branch on the less than condition, we use blt.

Out of the 16 values, two are unconditional. In particular, if the condition field is 1110, the instruction is always executed. This is the default in the sense that if no condition is specified in the instruction, it is assumed to be AL and the instruction is unconditionally executed. Thus, to branch unconditionally, we can specify either b or bal. We give more examples later on.

The last condition is used as "Never" and the instruction is never executed, essentially making it a nop. However, recent versions use it for other purposes (e.g., in DSP instructions) and, therefore, this condition should not be used.

The ARM instruction format is not as simple as that of the MIPS architecture. ARM supports a wide variety of instruction formats. What we have shown in Figure 8.4 is a small sample of the formats used by ARM. The A encoding shown in this figure is used by most arithmetic and logical instructions. The opcode field specifies the operation such as add and cmp. The Rd field identifies the destination register that receives the result. One of the source operands is in the source register Rn. Because we have 16 general-purpose registers available, each of these fields is 4 bits long. The second source operand is provided by the shifter-operand field. This field takes the least significant 12 bits and is used to specify the second source operand. How the second source operand is specified depends on the addressing mode and whether the operand is to be manipulated prior to using it. The I bit distinguishes between the immediate and register forms used

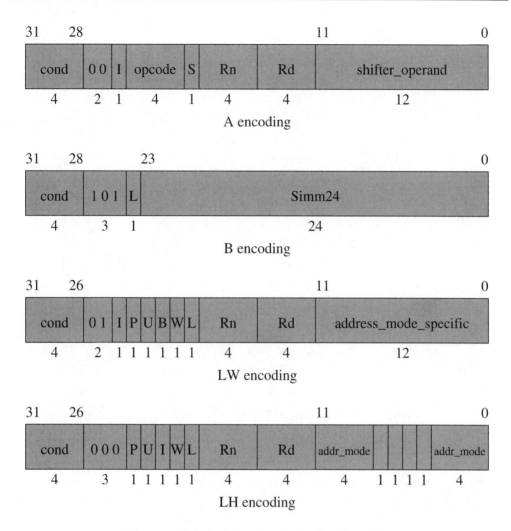

Figure 8.4 Selected ARM instruction formats.

to specify the second source operand. We defer a discussion of this topic until the next section.

Most ARM instructions can optionally update the condition code flags (N, Z, C, and V). The S bit indicates whether the condition code flags should be updated (S = 1) or not (S = 0) by the instruction.

The branch instructions use the B encoding, which can take a 24-bit signed number to specify the branch target. The L bit is used to indicate whether to store the return address in the link register. More information is given later when we discuss the branch instructions.

Table 8.1 ARM condition codes

cond	Mnemonic	Description	Condition tested
0000	EQ	Equal	$Z = 1$
0001	NE	Not equal	$Z = 0$
0010	CS/HS	Carry set/unsigned higher or same	$C = 1$
0011	CC/LO	Carry clear/unsigned lower	$C = 0$
0100	MI	Minus/negative	$N = 1$
0101	PL	Plus/positive or zero	$N = 0$
0110	VS	Overflow	$V = 1$
0111	VC	No overflow	$V = 0$
1000	HI	Unsigned higher	$C = 1$ AND $Z = 0$
1001	LS	Unsigned lower or same	$C = 0$ OR $Z = 1$
1010	GE	Signed greater than or equal	$N = V$
1011	LT	Signed less than	$N \neq V$
1100	GT	Signed greater than	$Z = 0$ AND $N = V$
1101	LE	Signed less than or equal	$Z = 1$ OR $N \neq V$
1110	AL	Always (unconditional)	—
1111	(NV)	Never (unconditional)	—

The load and store instructions use the last two formats (LW and LH encodings). As in the A encoding, the destination for load (source for store) is given by the Rd field. The Rn and the least significant 12 bits are used to give address mode specific information. The L bit indicates whether the instruction is a load ($L = 1$) or a store ($L = 0$). The B bit specifies whether the load operation is on an unsigned byte or word. The I, P, U, and W bits specify the addressing mode and other information as described here:

P bit $P = 0$ indicates post-indexed addressing.
            $P = 1$ indicates either the offset addressing or pre-indexed addressing. If $W = 0$, offset addressing is used; $W = 1$ indicates the pre-indexed addressing.

U bit   This bit indicates whether the offset value is added ($U = 1$) or subtracted ($U = 0$).

I bit $I = I$ indicates the offset is immediate value.
           $I = 0$ indicates index register-based offset.

Instruction Set

This section presents some sample instructions of the ARM instruction set. If you have read the previous chapters, you will notice that the ARM instruction semantics are somewhat different from the other architectures.

Data Transfer Instructions

We discuss three types of data transfer instructions: instructions that move data between registers, load instructions, and store instructions.

Move Instructions   Two instructions are available to copy data between registers: `mov` and `mvn`. The `mov` instruction syntax is

```
mov{cond}{s}    Rd,shifter_operand
```

It copies the value of `shifter_operand` into the destination register Rd. It uses the A encoding format shown in Figure 8.4. The fields shown in curly brackets are optional. If `s` is specified, it makes the S bit a 1. Note that this bit determines whether the condition code flags are updated (S = 1) or not (S = 0). The `cond` field takes any of the two-letter mnemonics given in Table 8.1. Also note that omitting `cond` implies unconditional execution as AL (ALways) is the default. Thus the instruction

```
mov    R1,R2
```

copies the R2 value to R1 unconditionally. We can also use this instruction to load constants, as in the following example.

```
mov    R3,#0
```

This instruction loads zero into R3. Because the PC register is also a general-purpose register, we can specify PC as the destination register to cause a branch. The instruction

```
mov    PC,LR
```

can be used to return from a procedure. Remember that the link register LR (R14) generally keeps the return address.

Now is a good time to unravel the mystery associated with the `shifter_operand`. This operand can take one of three formats.

Immediate Value: The immediate value is not given directly as in the other architectures. Instead, it takes two numbers: an 8-bit constant and a 4-bit rotate count. The 8-bit constant is rotated by rotate count bit positions to derive the constant. The 4-bit shift count can only specify 16 bit positions, therefore a zero is appended to it to make it 5 bits long. For example, if the 4-bit rotate count is `1001`, it is converted to five bits as `10010`. Thus, the rotate count is always an even number.

A limitation of this process is that not all constants can be expressed. For example, 0xFF00 is a valid constant as we can specify this value with the 8-bit constant taking the 0xFF value and using 8 as the rotate count. If we change the rotate count to 28, we get 0xF000000F as another valid constant. However, 0x7F8 is not a valid constant as it requires an odd number of rotations (three in this example). Thus, the move instruction

```
mov    R3,#0xFF00
```

is a valid one as 0xFF00 is a valid constant.

Register Value: A register can be specified to provide the second operand. This is the format used in the following instructions.

```
mov    R1,R2
mov    PC,LR
```

Shifted Register Value: This is a novel way of expressing the second operand, special to the ARM architecture. Before the value is used, the operand is shifted/rotated. In this format, three components are used to form the final value:

```
Rm, shift_op SHFT_CNT
```

The value in Rm is shifted/rotated SHFT_CNT times. The type of shift or rotate operation is specified by shift_op. The shift_op can be any of the following.

lsl	Logical Shift Left
lsr	Logical Shift Right
asr	Arithmetic Shift Right
ror	ROtate Right
rrx	Rotate Right with eXtend

The lsl specifies a left-shift operation whereas the lsr is used for the right-shift operation. The last bit shifted out will be captured in the carry flag as shown here:

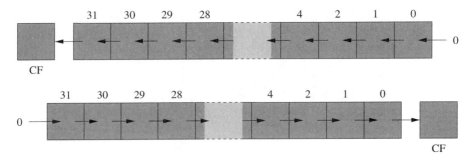

In both cases, the shifted-out bits receive zeros. These are called the logical shifts.

When we right-shift an operand, we have two choices: replace the vacated bits with zeros or with the sign bit. As we have seen, zeros replace the vacated bits in the logical right shift. On the other hand, the sign bit is copied into the vacated bits in the arithmetic right-shift `asr` as shown below:

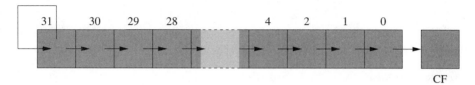

For details on the differences and the need for logical and arithmetic shift operations and why we need them only for the right-shifts, see our discussion in Chapter 15.

The rotate-right `ror` does not throw away the shifted-out bits as does the shift operation. Instead, these bits are fed at the other end as shown here.

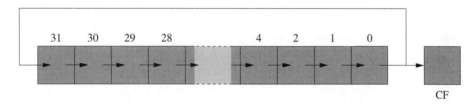

The extended version of rotate right `rrx` works on 33 bit numbers by including the carry flag as the 33rd bit as shown below:

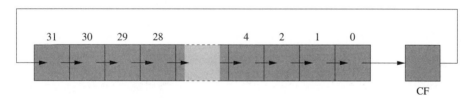

The SHFT_CNT can be an immediate value or it can be specified via a register. Here is an example that uses this format:

```
mov    R1,R2,lsl #3
```

This instruction multiplies the contents of R2 by 8 and stores the value in the R1 register. The `shift_operand` is also used in arithmetic and logical instructions that we discuss later.

The second move instruction `mvn` (MoVe Negative) has the same syntax as the `mov` except that it moves the 1's complement (i.e., bitwise `not`) of the `shifter_operand` value into Rd. For example, the instruction

```
mvn    R1,#0
```

loads 0xFFFFFFFF into R1 register.

Load Instructions   The ARM instruction set provides load instructions for words (32 bits), halfwords (16 bits), and bytes (8 bits). The `ldr` (load register) instruction has the following syntax.

```
ldr{cond}    Rd,addr_mode
```

It loads a word from the memory into the `rd` register using the addressing mode `addr_mode`. This instruction uses the LW encoding shown in Figure 8.4. The `addr_mode` can be specified in one of the following nine addressing modes.

Addressing mode	Format
Immediate offset	[Rn,#±offset12]
Register offset	[Rn,±Rm]
Scaled register offset	[Rn,±Rm, shift_op #shift_imm]
Immediate pre-indexed	[Rn,#±offset12]!
Register pre-indexed	[Rn,±Rm]!
Scaled register pre-indexed	[Rn,±Rm, shift_op #shift_imm]!
Immediate post-indexed	[Rn],#±offset12
Register post-indexed	[Rn],±Rm
Scaled register post-indexed	[Rn],±Rm, shift_op #shift_imm

The `shift_op` can take `lsl`, `lsr`, `asr`, and so on as discussed before (see page 132). Here are some example `ldr` instructions to illustrate the various formats.

Addressing mode	Example
Immediate offset	ldr R0,[R1,#-4]
Register offset	ldr R0,[R1,-R2]
Scaled register offset	ldr R0,[R1,-R2, lsl #3]
Immediate pre-indexed	ldr R0,[R1,#4]!
Register pre-indexed	ldr R0,[R1,R2]!
Scaled register pre-indexed	ldr R0,[R1,R2, lsl #3]!
Immediate post-indexed	ldr R0,[R1],#4
Register post-indexed	ldr R0,[R1],R2
Scaled register post-indexed	ldr R0,[R1],R2, lsl #3

When we load halfwords and bytes, we need to extend them to 32 bits. This can be done in one of two ways: zero-extension or sign-extension (see our discussion of these two schemes in Appendix A). Corresponding to these two extensions, two instructions are available:

```
ldrh    Load halfword (zero-extended)
ldrsh   Load halfword (sign-extended)
ldrb    Load byte (zero-extended)
ldrsb   Load byte (sign-extended)
```

The `ldrb` instruction uses the LW encoding whereas the other three instructions use the LH encoding shown in Figure 8.4.
Here is an example:

```
cmp     R0,#0
ldrneb  R1,[R0]
```

The first instruction tests if `R0` is zero (i.e., NULL pointer). If not, we load the byte at the address given by `R0`. We look at the compare (`cmp`) instructions later.

The instruction set also provides multiple loads through the `ldm` instruction. This instruction could be used to load all or a nonempty subset of the general-purpose registers. The register list can be specified as part of the instruction. The format of `ldm` is

```
ldm{cond}addr_mode  Rn{!}, register_list
```

The optional `!` is used to indicate the write-back operation. The `register_list` is a list of resisters in curly brackets. The `addressing_mode` can be one of the following four addressing modes.

- Increment After (mnemonic `ia`);
- Increment Before (mnemonic `ib`);
- Decrement After (mnemonic `da`);
- Decrement Before (mnemonic `db`).

Here are some examples:

```
ldmia   R0,{R1-R12}

ldmia   R0!,{R4-R12,LR}
```

The first instruction loads registers `R1` to `R12` from the memory address in `R0`. The register `R0` is not updated. The second instruction loads registers `R4` to `R12` and the link register (LR) as does the first one. However, because we specified `!`, the register `R0` is updated with the address after loading the registers. We can also specify a condition as in the following example.

```
cmp     R0,#0

ldmeqia R0!,{R1,R2,R4}
```

Store Instructions   The store instruction moves data from a register to the memory. They are similar to the load instructions except for the direction of data transfer, therefore our discussion of these instructions is rather brief.

To store a word, we use the `str` instruction. It uses encoding similar to that of the `ldr` instruction. The halfword and byte versions are also available. Unlike the load instructions, signed versions are not needed as we store exactly 16 or 8 bits with these instructions. We use `strh` to store the lower halfword of the specified source register. Similarly, we use the `strb` instruction to store the least significant byte of the source register. Multiple store instruction `stm` is also available.

The following example illustrates how we can use `ldm` and `stm` instructions to do memory-to-memory block copying. This example copies 50 elements from a source array to a destination array. Each element is a double, which takes 64 bits. We assume that `R0` points to the source array and `R1` to the destination array. The number of elements to be copied is maintained in `R2` as shown in the following code.

```
          mov    R2,#50          ; number of doubles to copy
copyLoop
          ldmia  R0!,{R3-R12}
          stmia  R1!,{R3-R12}
          subs   R2,R2,#5
          bne    copyLoop
```

The copy loop uses `ldmia` to copy five elements from the source array into registers R3 to R12. The `stmia` copies these elements into the destination array. Because both the load and store instructions use the write-back option (!), the pointers are automatically updated to point to successive elements. The loop iterates 10 times to copy the 50 elements.

Arithmetic Instructions

As in the Itanium, the ARM supports add, subtract, and multiply instructions. There is no divide instruction. These instructions use the A encoding shown in Figure 8.4. All instructions in the group follow the same syntax. We use the `add` instruction to illustrate their syntax.

Add Instructions   The instruction set provides two add instructions: `add` and `adc`. The `add` instruction has the following syntax.

```
add{cond}{s}   Rd,Rn,shifter_operand
```

The register Rn supplies one of the operands. The `shifter_operand` provides the second operand. As discussed in the move instructions, the `shifter_operand` pre-processes (shift/rotate) the second operand before using it in the arithmetic operation. Here are some examples of this instruction. The instruction

```
add   R0,R0,#1
```

increments R0. However, it does not update the condition code flags. The instruction

```
adds    R0,R1,R2
```

adds the contents of R1 and R2 and places the result in R0. Because we specified the s option, it updates the condition codes. Especially interesting are the carry and overflow flags. If we treat the numbers in R1 and R2 as representing unsigned numbers, we use the carry flag to see if there is an overflow (i.e., if a carry is generated out of bit 31). On the other hand, if R1 and R2 have signed numbers, we should look at the overflow flag to find if there is an overflow. If you are familiar with the Intel IA-32 architecture, you will see that these two flags are similar to the carry and overflow flags in that architecture.

Often we need to include the carry flag in the addition operation. This is particularly useful in multiword arithmetic operations. The adc is like the add except that it also adds the carry flag. If the carry flag is zero, it behaves like the add instruction.

Here is an example of how we can use add and adc to perform 64-bit additions. In this example, we assume that the first 64-bit number is in the R0 and R1 register pair with R0 holding the lower 32 bits. The second 64-bit number is in the R2 and R3 register pair (R2 has the lower 32 bits). The following two-instruction sequence

```
adds    R0,R0,R2
adcs    R1,R1,R3
```

adds these two 64-bit numbers and places the result in the R0 and R1 register pair. The conditional code flags are updated as we use the adcs instruction. It is interesting to see what these flags indicate: the N flag indicates that the 64-bit result is negative; the C flag indicates unsigned overflow as explained before; the V flag indicates signed overflow; and the Z flag indicates that the upper 32 bits of the result are zero.

Subtract Instructions   The instruction set provides a total of four subtract operations. The first two that we present are the add and adc counterparts. The sub instruction subtracts the value of shifter_operand from that in Rn. The sbc is like the sub instruction but it also subtracts the carry (the adc counterpart). These two instructions can be used to perform multiword subtract operations. Assuming that the two 64-bit numbers are in the R1:R0 and R3:R2 register pairs as in the last 64-bit addition example, the following two instructions

```
subs    R0,R0,R2
sbcs    R1,R1,R3
```

produce the difference (R1:R0 − R3:R2) in R1:R0 and set the condition code flags appropriately.

In addition to these two standard subtract instructions, which are provided by almost all architectures, ARM provides two reverse subtract operations. In the reverse subtract instructions, the value in Rn is subtracted from the shifter_operand value. The reverse instructions are not required in other architectures as the operands are in registers (we can simply switch the registers). However, in the ARM architecture, because one operand is special (given by `shifter_operand`), reverse subtract is useful. The instruction `rsb` performs the subtract operation without the carry flag and the `rsc` subtracts the carry flag as well. Here is an example that multiplies R3 by 3:

```
rsb     R3,R3,R3,lsl #2
```

The shifter operand left-shifts R3 by two bit positions, effectively multiplying it by 4. The `rsb` performs $(4 * R3 - R3)$, producing the desired result.

Multiply Instructions   The ARM instruction set supports several multiplication instructions. We can divide these instructions into short and long multiply instructions. Both versions multiply two 32-bit numbers. Note that we get a 64-bit result when we multiply two 32-bit numbers. The short multiply instructions produce only the lower 32 bits of the 64-bit result whereas the long versions generate the full 64-bit results. Let us first look at the short multiply instruction. The syntax of the `mul` instruction is

```
mul{cond}{s}      Rd,Rm,Rs
```

It multiplies the contents of Rm and Rs to produce the lower 32 bits of the 64-bit result. This value is placed in the Rd register. This instruction can be used with both signed and unsigned numbers. As usual, the s bit can be used to specify whether the condition code flags are to be updated.

The long versions have separate instructions for unsigned and signed numbers. Because both instructions use the same syntax, we illustrate the syntax using the unsigned multiply long (`umull`) instruction.

```
umull{cond}{s}      Rdlo,Rdhi,Rm,Rs
```

This instruction takes four registers: two registers specify where the 64-bit product should go (Rdlo and Rdhi with Rdlo getting the lower 32 bits) and the two numbers to be multiplied as in the `mul` instruction. The signed multiply long (`smull`) uses exactly the same format except that it treats the numbers in Rm and Rs as signed numbers.

The instruction set also supports an accumulator version of these three instructions. The `mla` (multiply accumulate) instruction has the following syntax.

```
mla{cond}{s}      Rd,Rm,Rs,Rn
```

It adds contents of Rn to the lower 32 bits of Rm * Rs and places the result in the Rd register.

The long versions have separate instructions for unsigned and signed numbers. The unsigned version has the same syntax as the `umull` instruction as shown below:

```
umlal{cond}{s}      Rdlo,Rdhi,Rm,Rs
```

It adds the 64-bit value in Rdhi:Rdlo to the 64-bit result of Rm * Rs. The result is stored back in the Rdhi:Rdlo register pair. The signed version (`smlal`) has a similar syntax.

Logical and Bit Instructions

The instruction set supports three logical operations: AND (and), OR (orr), and exclusive-or (eor). These instructions follow the same syntax as the add group of instructions discussed before. However, they do not affect the overflow (V) flag.

These instructions perform bitwise logical operations. The truth tables for these operations are given on pages 170 and 271. The usage of these logical operations is discussed in Chapter 15. Here we give some examples of these instructions. The and instruction

```
ands    R0,R0,#1
```

can be used to determine if the number in R0 is odd or even. A number is even if its least significant bit is zero; otherwise, it is odd. Essentially, this instruction isolates the least significant bit. If this bit is 1, the result of this operation is 1; else it is zero. Thus, the zero flag is set if the number is even; it is cleared if odd.

The or instruction

```
orr     R0,R0,#0x20
```

can be used to convert the uppercase letter in R0 to lowercase by forcing the 5th bit to 1. See Appendix B for details on why this conversion works.

The exclusive-or instruction

```
eor     R0,R0,#0x20
```

flips the case. That is, if it is a lowercase letter, it is converted to the uppercase and vice versa. We use the eor to flip the 5th bit while leaving the rest the bits unchanged. See Chapter 15 (page 275) for an explanation of why this is so.

There is no logical NOT instruction. However, note that the mvn instruction effectively performs the NOT operation. In addition, the instruction set has a bit clear (bic) instruction.

```
bic{cond}{s}    Rd,Rn,shifter_operand
```

It complements the value of shifter_operand and performs bitwise and of this value with the value in Rn. The result is placed in the Rd register as in the other instructions.

The last instruction we discuss in the section is the clz (count leading zeros). The syntax is

```
clz{cond}    Rd,Rm
```

It counts the number of leading zeros in Rm. It starts counting from the most significant bit and counts zeros until it encounters a 1 bit. This count is placed in the Rd register. For example, if the value in R1 is zero, the instruction

```
clz     R0,R1
```

places 32 in the R0 register.

Test Instructions

The ARM instruction set has two test instructions that perform logical and and exclusive-OR operations. Like the logical instructions, these instructions do not affect the V flag. The test instruction format is

```
tst{cond}   Rd,shifter_operand
```

It performs the logical bitwise and operation like the and instruction. However, the result of the operation is not stored. Instead, the condition code flags are updated based on this result. This instruction is useful to test the selected bits without destroying the original value. For example, we have written the following instruction to test if R0 has an even or odd value.

```
ands    R0,R0,#1
```

This instruction writes the result of the and operation back in R0. If we use the tst instruction

```
tst    R0,#1
```

we don't modify the contents of R0.

The second test instruction teq performs the exclusive-OR operation instead of and. The instruction

```
teq    R0,R1
```

can be used to compare if the contents of R0 and R1 are equal.

Shift and Rotate Operations

The ARM instruction set does not provide any shift or rotate instructions. There is really no need for this. As we have seen, every instruction has access to the shifter through the shifter_operand. If we want to perform a shift operation, we can use the mov instruction as in the following example.

```
mov    R0,R0,asr #5
```

This instruction right-shifts the contents of R0 by five bit positions. This is an arithmetic right-shift, which means the vacated bits on the left are replaced by the sign bit. Similarly, we can use any of the other shift and rotate operations allowed on shifter_operand.

Comparison Instructions

The instruction set provides two compare instructions: cmp (compare) and cmn (compare negative). These instructions can be used to compare two numbers for their relationship (less than, equal to, greater than, and so on). Because both instructions use the same syntax, we look at the compare instruction in detail. The compare instruction takes two operands:

```
cmp{cond}    Rn,shifter_operand
```

It performs $Rn - shifter\_operand$ and updates the four condition flags (N, Z, C, and V) based on the result. These flag values can be used to conditionally execute subsequent instructions. Here is an example.

Suppose we want to find the minimum of two numbers stored in registers R0 and R1. The following statements

```
cmp     R1,R0
movlt   R0,R1
```

move the minimum number to R0. The cmp instruction compares the number in R1 with that in R0. If the number in R1 is greater than or equal to the other number, we do nothing. In this case, because the "less than" condition is not true, the movlt instruction acts as a nop. Otherwise, we copy the value from R1 to R0.

This code assumes that the numbers in the two registers are treated as signed numbers as we used "lt" condition. If they are unsigned numbers, we have to use "lo" as in the following code.

```
cmp     R1,R0
movlo   R0,R1
```

As a second example, look at the following C code.

```
if (x > y)
    x = x + 4*y;
else
    y = 3*x;
```

Assuming that x and y are signed numbers, the following ARM code implements this C code.

```
;x is in R0 and y in R1
cmp     R0,R1
addgt   R0,R0,R1,lsl #2
addle   R1,R1,R1,lsl #1
```

In the last instruction, we compute 3x as $x + 2x$ with the shifter_operand supplying 2x. We can also get 3x as $4x - x$, which can be implemented by the following instruction.

```
rsble   R0,R0,R0,lsl #2
```

The cmn instruction updates the flags by adding the shifter_operand value to the value in the Rn register. In case you are wondering what is "negative" about this instruction, think of it as subtracting the negative value of the second operand.

Branch Instructions

The branch instructions are used to alter control flow. The branch instruction can also be modified for procedure invocation. These instructions use the B encoding format shown in Figure 8.4. We first discuss the branch instruction. The syntax is

```
b{l}{cond}  target_address
```

For now, ignore the `l` option. We discuss this in the next section. This instruction transfers control to `target_address` if the `cond` is true. As you can see from Figure 8.4, the target address is specified as a 24-bit value. The target instruction address is PC-relative and is computed as follows.

- The 24-bit `target_address` is sign-extended to 32 bits.
- This value is left-shifted by two bit positions. This is because ARM instructions are word aligned. The shift operation adds two zeros to the 24-bit `target_address`.
- The value computed in the last step is added to the PC register to form the branch target. Note that the PC register contains the following address:

    PC = branch instruction address + 8

    You might have thought that this is due to the delayed branching that many RISC processors implement (see our discussion in Chapter 2). Not so! ARM does not implement delayed branching. The reason for the "plus 8" is the three-stage pipeline used in the ARM cores up to ARM7. If you are not familiar with pipelining, here is a brief explanation of how this three-stage pipeline works. Each instruction that runs on this pipeline goes through three stages: fetch, decode, and execute. The pipeline consists of three units corresponding to these three stages. The pipeline works on three instructions concurrently, with each unit working on one instruction. While the first instruction is being executed by the execution unit, the next instruction is being decoded by the decode unit and a third instruction is being fetched. Thus, the PC points to this third instruction, which is 8 bytes from the first instruction. Even though the ARM9 versions use a five-stage pipeline, the "plus 8" still holds for compatibility and other reasons.

If no condition is specified, it becomes an unconditional branch as in the following example.

```
b   repeat
```

This is also equivalent to

```
bal   repeat
```

Here is an example that illustrates how the branch instruction can be used to implement a countdown loop that iterates 50 times.

```
; loop count is in R0
      mov    R0,#50        ; init loop count to 50
loop

         . . .
         . . .
      subs   R0,R0,#1      ; decrement loop count
      bne    loop          ; if R0 != 0, loop back
```

The last instruction bne can be considered as "branch on not equal to zero" as it branches to the target if the zero flag is 0.

Procedures

The branch instruction of the last section can be modified to invoke a procedure. A procedure call is like a branch with the provision that it remembers the return address. Thus, if we can make the branch instruction store the return address, it can be used as a procedure call instruction. This is what the l field does:

```
bl{cond}  target_address
```

This branch and link instruction places the return address in the link register LR, which is R14, before transferring control to the target. The return address stored is the address of the instruction following the bl instruction. For example, if we want to invoke the findMin procedure, we do so by

```
bl  findMin
```

How do we return from the procedure? It is simple: all we have to do is to copy the return address from the LR to the PC. We can do this by using the following move instruction.

```
mov  PC,LR
```

Here is an example that shows the structure of an ARM procedure:

```
; ARM code to find minimum of two signed integers
; The two input values are in R0 and R1
; The minimum is returned in R2
findMin
      cmp    R1,R0
      movge  R2,R0        ; R1 >= R0? Min = R0
      movlt  R2,R1        ; R1 < R0? Min = R1
      mov    PC,LR        ; return
```

This procedure receives two signed numbers in R0 and R1 and returns the minimum of these two values in R2.

Stack Operations

As in the MIPS, there is no special stack pointer register in the ARM architecture. By convention, register R13 is used as the stack pointer. There is another similarity with MIPS: ARM does not provide any special instructions to manipulate the stack. That is, there are no push and pop instructions. We have to implement these stack operations by using load and store instructions. This means we have complete freedom as to how the stack should behave. A stack implementation is characterized by two attributes:

- **Where the stack pointer points**

    - *Full stack:* The stack pointer points to the last full location;

    - *Empty stack:* The stack pointer points to the first empty location.

- **How the stack grows**

    - *Descending stack:* The stack grows downward (i.e., toward lower memory addresses);

    - *Ascending stack:* The stack grows upward (i.e., toward higher memory addresses).

These two attributes define the four types of stacks:

- Full Descending stack (mnemonic fd);

- Full Ascending stack (mnemonic fa);

- Empty Descending stack (mnemonic ed);

- Empty Ascending stack (mnemonic ea).

These mnemonics can be used in ldm and stm instructions to manipulate the stack. For example, we can use instructions such as ldmfd, stmfd, and so on. Most implementations, including MIPS and SPARC, prefer descending stacks for reasons discussed in Chapter 4 (page 53). Furthermore, the stack pointer points to the last item pushed on to the stack.

Using the ldmfd and stmfd instructions, we can write procedure entry and exit code as follows.

```
procName
      stmfd  R13!,{R4-R12,LR}     ; save registers and
                                  ; return address

               . . .
             <procedure body>
               . . .
      ldmfd  R13!,{R4-R12,PC}     ; restore registers and
                                  ; return address to PC
```

This code assumes that we do not have to preserve the first four registers as they are often used to pass parameters. Furthermore, we assume that the stack pointer (R13) points to a full descending stack. The `stmfd` instruction stores registers R4 to R12 and LR on the stack before executing the procedure body. Notice that we use R13! (i.e., the write-back option) so that the stack pointer is updated to point to the last full location of the stack. Before returning from the procedure, we use the `ldmfd` instruction to restore the registers and to store the return address in the PC. Because we store the return address in the PC we do not need a separate return from the procedure.

Summary

The ARM architecture is remarkably different from the other architectures we have seen in this part. It shares some features with the Itanium architecture. One feature of the ARM instruction set that sets it apart is that its instructions are executed conditionally. If the specified condition is not true, the instruction acts as a `nop`. Although Itanium also uses conditional instruction execution, the ARM uses a 4-bit condition code as opposed to the predicate bits of Itanium. Another interesting feature of ARM is that arithmetic and logical instructions can pre-process (shift/rotate) one of the input operands before operating on it.

At the beginning of this chapter, we mentioned that Thumb instructions are 16 bits long. To achieve this reduction from the 32-bit ARM instructions, several significant changes have been made. These include:

- The 4-bit `cond` field is eliminated. As a result, most Thumb instructions are executed unconditionally. In contrast, ARM instructions are executed conditionally.
- Most Thumb arithmetic and logical instructions use the 2-address format. In this format, as discussed in Chapter 2, the destination register also supplies a source operand.

Even though the ARM is a RISC architecture, it does not strictly follow the RISC principles as does the MIPS. For example, some of the ARM instructions such as `ldm` and `stm` are not simple instructions. In addition, it provides a large number of addressing modes and uses a somewhat complex instruction format. However, having looked at five different RISC designs, you will also see a lot of commonality among these architectures and the RISC principles given in Chapter 3. In the next part, we take a detailed look at the MIPS assembly language.

Web Resources

Most of the ARM documentation is available from their Web site www.arm.com. The *ARM Architecture Reference Manual* is published by Addison-Wesley [1]. The reference manual is also distributed by ARM on their documentation CD. Unfortunately, this information is not available from their Web site; you have to request this CD from ARM.

PART III

MIPS Assembly Language

9

SPIM Simulator and Debugger

SPIM is a simulator that runs MIPS 2000 programs. SPIM supports various platforms and can be downloaded from the Web. SPIM also contains a simple debugger. In this chapter, we give details on how you can download and use the SPIM simulator. We start with an introduction to the SPIM simulator. The following section gives details about SPIM settings. These settings determine how the simulator loads and runs your programs. We specify the settings you should use in order to run the example MIPS programs given in later chapters. Details about loading and running MIPS assembly language programs are discussed in the next section. This section also presents the debugging facilities provided by SPIM. We conclude the chapter with a summary.

Introduction

This chapter describes the SPIM simulator, which was developed by Professor James Larus when he was at the Computer Science Department of the University of Wisconsin, Madison. This simulator executes the programs written for the MIPS R2000/R3000 processors. This is a two-in-one product: it contains a simulator to run the MIPS programs as well as a debugger.

SPIM runs on a variety of platforms including UNIX, Linux, Windows, and DOS. In this chapter, we provide details on the Windows version of SPIM called PCSpim. The SPIM simulator can be downloaded from

```
http://www.cs.wisc.edu/~larus/spim.html
```

This page also gives information on SPIM documentation. Although SPIM is available

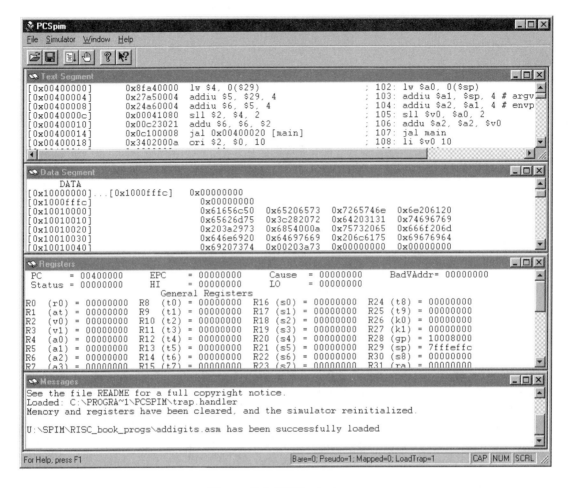

Figure 9.1 SPIM windows.

from this site at the time of this writing, use a good search engine to locate the URL if it is not available from this URL. Also, you can check this book's homepage, which provides a link to the SPIM simulator that is updated periodically.

Figure 9.1 shows the PCSpim interface. As shown in this figure, PCSpim provides a menu bar and a toolbar at the top and a status bar at the bottom of the screen. The middle area displays four windows, as discussed next.

- **Menu Bar:** The menu bar provides the following commands for the simulator operation.

    - *File:* The File menu allows you select file operations. You can open a MIPS assembly language source file using open... or save a log file of the current simulator state. In addition, you can quit PCSpim by selecting the Exit command. Of course, you can also quit PCSpim by closing the window.

- *Simulator:* This menu provides several commands to run and debug a program. We discuss these commands later in this chapter. This menu also allows you to select the simulator settings. When the `Settings...` command is selected, it opens a setting window to set the simulator settings, which are discussed in the next section.

- *Windows:* This menu allows you to control the presentation and navigation of windows. For example, in Figure 9.1, we have tiled windows to show the four windows: Text Segment, Data Segment, Register, and Messages. In addition, you can also elect to hide or display the toolbar and status bar. The console window pops up when your program needs to read/write data to the terminal. It disappears after the program has terminated. When you want to see your program's input and output, you can activate this window by selecting the Console window command.

- *Help:* This menu allows you to obtain online help on PCSpim.

• **Toolbar:** The toolbar provides mouse buttons to open and close a MIPS assembly language source file, to run and insert breakpoints, and to get help.

• **Window Display Section:** This section displays four windows: Data Segment, Text Segment, Messages, and Register.

- *Data Segment Window:* This window shows the data and stack contents of your program. Each line consists of an address (in square brackets) and the corresponding contents in hexadecimal notation. If a block of memory contains the same constant, an address range is specified as shown on the first line of the Data Segment in Figure 9.1.

- *Text Segment Window:* This window shows the instructions from your program as well as the system code loaded by PCSpim. The leftmost hex number in square brackets is the address of the instruction. The second hex number is the machine instruction encoding of the instruction. Next to it is the instruction mnemonic, which is a processor instruction. What you see after the semicolon is the source code line including any comments you have placed. This display is useful to see how the pseudoinstructions of the assembler are translated into the processor instructions. For example, the last line in the Text Segment of Figure 9.1 shows that the pseudoinstruction

```
li      $vi,10
```

is translated as

```
ori     $2,$0,10
```

- *Registers:* This window shows the contents of the general and floating-point registers. The contents are displayed in either decimal or hex notation, depending on the settings used (discussed in the next section).

- *Messages:* This window is used by PCSpim to display error messages.

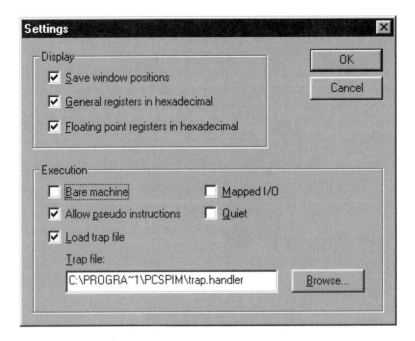

Figure 9.2 SPIM settings window.

- **Status Bar:** The status bar at the bottom of the PCSpim window presents three pieces of information:

  - The left area is used to give information about the menu items and toolbar buttons. For example, when the mouse arrow is on the open file icon (first button) on the toolbar, this area displays the "Open an assembly file" message.

  - The middle area shows the current simulator settings. Simulator settings are described in the next section.

  - The right area is used to display if the Caps Lock key (CAP), Num Lock key (NUM), and Scroll Lock key (SCRL) are latched down.

Simulator Settings

PCSpim settings can be viewed by selecting the Settings command under the Simulator menu. This opens a setting window as shown in Figure 9.2. PCSpim uses these settings to determine how to load and run your MIPS assembly language program. An incorrect setting may cause errors. The settings are divided into two groups: Display and Execution. The Display settings determine whether the window positions are saved and how the contents of the registers are displayed. When *Save window positions* is selected, PCSpim will remember the position of its windows when you exit and restore them when

you run PCSpim later. If you select the register display option, contents of the general
and floating-point registers are displayed in hexadecimal notation. Otherwise, register
contents are displayed as decimal numbers.

The Execution part of the settings shown in Figure 9.2 determines how your program
is executed.

- **Bare Machine:** If selected, SPIM simulates the bare MIPS machine. This means
  that both pseudoinstructions and additional addressing modes, which are provided
  by the assembler, are not allowed. Later chapters give details on the assembler-
  supported pseudoinstructions and addressing modes. Because the example MIPS
  programs presented in later chapters use these additional features of the assembler,
  this option should not be selected to run our example programs.

- **Allow Pseudoinstructions:** This setting determines whether the pseudoinstructions
  are allowed in the source code. You should select this option as our example programs use pseudoinstructions.

- **Mapped I/O:** If this setting is selected, SPIM enables the memory-mapped I/O
  facility. When this setting is selected, you cannot use SPIM system calls, described
  in Chapter 10 on page 161, to read from the terminal. Thus, this setting should not
  be selected to run our MIPS programs.

- **Quiet:** If this setting is selected, PCSpim will print a message when an exception
  occurs.

- **Load Trap File:** Selecting this setting causes PCSpim to load the standard exception handler and startup code. The trap handler can be selected by using the *Browse*
  button. When loaded, the startup code in the trap file invokes the `main` routine.
  In this case, we can label the first executable statement in our program as `main`.
  If the trap file is not selected, PCSpim starts execution from the statement labeled
  `__start`. Our example programs are written with the assumption that the trap file
  is loaded (we use the `main` label). If you decide not to use the trap file, you have to
  change the label to `__start` to run the programs. If the trap file is loaded, PCSpim
  transfers control to location 0x80000080 when an exception occurs. This location
  must contain an exception handler.

Running a Program

Before executing a program, you need to load the program you want to run. This can be
done either by selecting the *Open File* button from the Toolbar or from the `File` menu.
This command lets you browse for your assembly file by opening a dialog box. After
opening the file, you can issue the `Run` command either from the Toolbar or from the
`Simulator` menu to execute the program.

The Run command pops the Run window shown in Figure 9.3. It automatically fills
the start address. For our example programs, you don't have to change this value. If
desired, the command line options can be entered in this window. Command line options

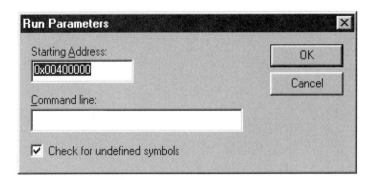

Figure 9.3 SPIM Run window.

that you can specify include the settings we discussed in the last section. For example, you enter `-bare` to simulate a bare MIPS machine, `-asm` to simulate the virtual MIPS machine provided by the assembler, and so on. The SPIM documentation contains a full list of acceptable command line options. If you have set up the settings as discussed in the last section, you don't have to enter any command line option to run our example MIPS programs.

Debugging

SPIM provides the standard facilities to debug programs. As you know, single-stepping and breakpoints are the two most popular techniques used to debug programs. As part of debugging, you often need to change the values in a register set or memory locations. As do the other debuggers you are familiar with, SPIM provides commands to alter the value of a register or memory location. All debug commands are available under the `Simulator` menu as shown in Figure 9.4. These commands are briefly explained next.

- **Clear Registers:** This command clears all registers (i.e., the values of all registers are set to zero).

- **Reinitialize:** It clears all the registers and memory and restarts the simulator.

- **Reload:** This command reinitializes the simulator and reloads the current assembler file for execution.

- **Go:** You can issue this command to run the current program. Program execution continues until a breakpoint is encountered. We have discussed the Run command before. You can also use the F5 key to execute your program.

- **Break/Continue:** This can be used to toggle between break and continue. If the program is running, execution is paused. On the other hand, if the execution is paused, it continues execution.

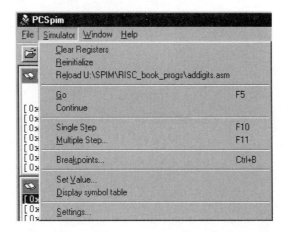

Figure 9.4 Debug commands available under the `Simulator` menu.

- **Single Step:** This is the single-step command. The simulator executes one instruction and pauses execution. You can also use the F10 key for single-stepping.
- **Multiple Step...:** This is a generalization of single-stepping. In this command, you can specify the number of instructions each step should execute. When you select this command, SPIM opens a dialog window to get the number of instructions information.
- **Breakpoints...:** This command is useful to set up breakpoints. It opens the Breakpoint dialog box shown in Figure 9.5. You can add/delete breakpoints through this dialog box. As shown in this figure, it also lists the active breakpoints. When the execution reaches a breakpoint, execution pauses and pops a query dialog box (Figure 9.6) to continue execution. Normally, you enter the address of the instruction to specify a breakpoint. However, if the instruction has a global label, you can enter this label instead of its address.
- **Set Value...:** This command can be used to set the value of a register or a memory location. It pops a window to enter the register/memory address and the value as shown in Figure 9.7. In this example, we are setting the value of the $a2 register to 7FFFF000H.
- **Display Symbol Table:** This command displays the simulator symbol table in the message window.
- **Settings...:** This opens the `Settings` dialog box shown in Figure 9.2. We have already discussed the simulator settings in detail.

When single-stepping your program, the instructions you see do not exactly correspond to your source code for two reasons: the system might have introduced some code (e.g., the startup code mentioned before), or because the pseudoinstructions are translated into

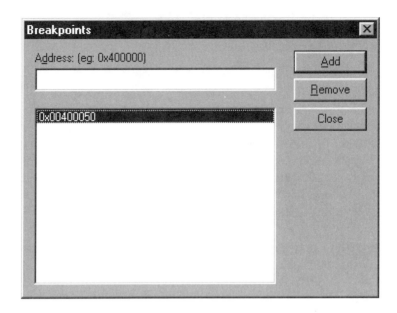

Figure 9.5 Breakpoints dialog box.

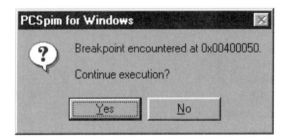

Figure 9.6 Breakpoint query window.

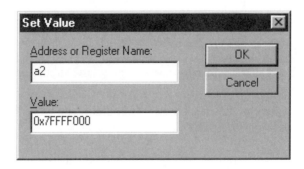

Figure 9.7 Set value dialog box.

processor instructions. For some pseudoinstructions, there is a single processor instruction. However, other pseudoinstructions may get translated into more than one processor instruction.

Summary

We have introduced the MIPS simulator SPIM. SPIM is a convenient tool to experience RISC assembly language programming. SPIM is available for a variety of platforms. It includes a simple debugger to facilitate single-stepping and setting breakpoints. In the last section, we have given an overview of its debugging facilities. However, we have not presented all the details about SPIM. Some of the missing details are given in the next chapter. Specifically, the next chapter describes the SPIM system calls and SPIM assembler directives. These details complement our discussion in this chapter.

10

Assembly Language Overview

This chapter introduces the basics of the MIPS assembly language. Assembly language statements can either instruct the processor to perform a task, or direct the assembler during the assembly process. The latter statements are called assembler directives. We start this chapter with a discussion of the format and types of assembly language statements.

Assemblers provide several directives to reserve storage space for variables. SPIM also provides several I/O system calls to facilitate input and output of basic data types including integers, strings, and floating-point numbers. These details are presented in this chapter. The instruction set can be divided into several groups of instructions (arithmetic, logical, shift, and so on). We describe the data movement, load, and store instructions in detail. To help us write useful assembly language programs, we give an overview of some of the MIPS instructions belonging to the other groups. Later chapters discuss these instruction groups more fully.

Toward the end of the chapter, we provide several assembly language program examples. In each chapter, we introduce a simple program as our first program. Then we give several examples in the "Illustrative Examples" section. Starting with this chapter, we follow this format. The chapter concludes with a summary.

Introduction

In the previous chapters we have discussed the MIPS architecture and SPIM simulator details. In the remainder of the book, we concentrate on the assembly language program structure and related details to write and execute the MIPS assembly language programs.

Assembly language programs consist of processor instructions, instructions supported only by the assembler, and assembler directives. All three statements follow the same format. We start this chapter with a description of the assembly language statement format.

The remainder of the book gives details about the MIPS instruction set as implemented by the SPIM simulator. However, to write meaningful assembly language programs, we give an overview of the instructions set. In this chapter, we present complete details on the load and store instructions. We only give a brief overview of the remaining instructions and defer a detailed discussion of these instructions to later chapters.

Assembly Language Statements

Assembly language programs are created out of three different classes of statements. Statements in the first class tell the processor what to do. These statements are called *executable instructions*, or *instructions* for short. Each executable instruction consists of an *operation code* (*opcode* for short). Executable instructions cause the assembler to generate machine language instructions.

The second class of statements consists of pseudoinstructions. These are not directly supported by the processor. The assembler supports the pseudoinstructions and generates one or more processor instructions to implement them. We clearly identify the pseudoinstructions and, where appropriate, show how they are implemented using the processor instructions.

The last class of statements provides information to the assembler on various aspects of the assembly process. These instructions are called *assembler directives*. Assembler directives are nonexecutable and do not generate any machine language instructions.

Assembly language statements are entered one per line in the source file. All three classes of the assembly language statements use the same format:

```
[label:]  mnemonic  [operands]  [#comment]
```

The fields in the square brackets are optional in some statements. As a result of this format, it is common practice to align the fields to aid readability of assembly language programs. The assembler does not care about spaces between the fields.

Label Labels are used to associate them with the address of a memory location. Labels typically appear in text and data segments. In both segments, a label is terminated by a colon. In the text segment, labels are used to identify an instruction as shown here:

```
repeat:   add      $t0,$t0,1   #increment $t0 by 1
```

In this example, the label `repeat` identifies the `add` instruction. In the data segment, labels are used for variable names as shown below:

```
number:   .word      10         #initializes number to 10
```

This example declares the variable `number` and initializes it to 10. Labels, for obvious reasons, cannot be reserved words such as instruction mnemonics like `add`.

Mnemonic This is a required field and identifies the purpose of the statement. In most statements, it represents the opcode of the instruction such as `add` and `sub`. In certain statements, this field is not required. Examples include lines consisting of a comment, or a label, or a label and a comment.

Operands Operands specify the data to be manipulated by the statement. The number of operands required depends on the specific statement. Most statements have three operands as shown here:

```
add     $t0,$t1,$t2
```

However, some instructions and pseudoinstructions have only one or two operands. Here are some examples:

```
li      $v0,5
move    $a0,$t2
la      $t3,number
mflo    $t2
```

Don't worry about the semantics of these instructions. We give details about these instructions in the remainder of the book.

Comment This is an optional field and serves the same purpose as that in a high-level language. Comments play a more important role in assembly language, as it is a low-level language. Assembler ignores all comments. Comments begin with a sharp sign (#) and extend until the end of the line. Because the readability of assembly language programs is poor, comments should be generously used to improve readability.

SPIM System Calls

SPIM provides I/O support through the system call (`syscall`) instruction. Eight of these calls facilitate input and output of the four basic data types: string, integer, float, and double. A notable service missing from this list is the character input and output. For character I/O, we have to use the string system calls.

To invoke a service, the system call service code should be placed in the `$v0` register. Any required arguments are placed in the `$a0` and `$a1` registers (use `$f12` for floating-point values). Any value returned by a system call is placed in `$v0` (`$f0` for floating-point values).

All ten system calls are summarized in Table 10.1. The first three calls are self-explanatory. The `print_string` system call takes a pointer to a NULL-terminated string and prints the string. The `read_int`, `read_float` and `read_double` system calls read input up to and including newline. Characters following the number are ignored. The `read_string` call takes the pointer to a buffer in `$a0` and the buffer size n in `$a1`. The buffer size should be expressed in bytes. It reads at most $n - 1$ characters into the buffer and terminates the string by the NULL character. The `read_string` call has the same semantics as the `fgets` function in the C library.

Table 10.1 SPIM assembler system calls

Service	System call code (in $v0)	Arguments	Result
print_int	1	$a0 = integer	
print_float	2	$f12 = float	
print_double	3	$f12 = double	
print_string	4	$a0 = string address	
read_int	5		integer in $v0
read_float	6		float in $f0
read_double	7		double in $f0
read_string	8	$a0 = buffer address $a1 = buffer size	
sbrk	9		address in $v0
exit	10		

The sbrk call returns a pointer to a block of memory containing n additional bytes. The final system call exit stops execution of a program.

SPIM Assembler Directives

SPIM supports a subset of the assembler directives provided by the MIPS assembler. This section presents some of the most common SPIM directives. The SPIM reference manual provides a complete list of directives supported by the simulator. All assembler directives begin with a period.

Segment declaration   Two segments of an assembly program—code and data—can be declared by using .TEXT and .DATA directives. The statement

```
.TEXT  <address>
```

directs the assembler to map the statements following it to the user text segment. The argument address is optional; if present, the statements are stored beginning at address. SPIM allows only instructions or words (using .WORD) in the text segment.

The data directive has a similar format as .TEXT except that the statements following it must refer to data items.

String directives   SPIM provides two directives to allocate storage for strings: `.ASCII` and `.ASCIIZ`. The `.ASCII` directive can be used to allocate space for a string that is not terminated by the NULL character. The statement

```
.ASCII   "string"
```

allocates a number of bytes equal to the number of characters in `string`. For example,

```
.ASCII   "Toy Story"
```

allocates nine bytes of contiguous storage and initializes it to "Toy Story".

Strings are normally NULL-terminated as in C. For example, to display a string using `print_string` service, the string must be NULL-terminated. Using `.ASCIIZ` instead of `ASCII` stores the specified string in the NULL-terminated format. The `.ASCII` directive is useful to break a long string into multiple string statements as shown in the following example.

```
.ASCII     "Toy Story is a good computer-animated movie. \n"
.ASCII     "This reviewer recommends it to all kids \n"
.ASCIIZ    "and their parents."
```

An associated assembler directive

```
.SPACE    n
```

can be used to allocate n bytes of uninitialized space in the current segment.

Data directives   SPIM provides four directives to store both integers and floating-point numbers. The assembler directive

```
.HALF     h1,h2, . . .,hn
```

stores the n 16-bit numbers in successive memory halfwords. For 32-bit numbers, use the `.WORD` directive. Although we refer to these 16- and 32-bit values as numbers, they can be any 16- and 32-bit quantities.

Floating-point values can be stored as single-precision or double-precision numbers. To store n single-precision floating point numbers, use

```
.FLOAT    f1,f2, . . .,fn
```

To store double precision numbers, use the `.DOUBLE` directive instead.

Miscellaneous directives   We discuss two directives that deal with data alignment and global symbol declaration. The data directives `.HALF`, `.WORD`, `.FLOAT`, and `.DOUBLE` automatically align the data. We can explicitly control data alignment using the `.ALIGN` directive. The statement

```
# Title of the program                              Filename
#
# Objective:
# Input:
# Output:
#
# Register usage
#
################ Data segment ###################
    .data
         . . .
    data go here
         . . .


################ Code segment ###################
    .text
    .globl main
main:
         . . .
    code goes here
         . . .
    li    $v0,10              # exit
    syscall
```

Figure 10.1 MIPS assembly language program template

```
.ALIGN    n
```

aligns the next datum on a 2^n byte boundary. Use

```
.ALIGN    0
```

to turn off the automatic alignment feature of the data directives until the next .DATA directive.

Before closing this section, we discuss one last directive: .GLOBL. It declares a symbol as global so that it can be referenced from other files. We normally use this directive to declare main as a global symbol so that it can be referenced by SPIM's trap file (see page 153 for details on the trap file). The program template given next shows how the global directive is used.

MIPS Program Template

Our MIPS programs follow the template shown in Figure 10.1. It consists of two main parts: a data segment and a code segment. The data segment is indicated by the .data directive. This part typically contains messages to be used in the user interface and the allocation of storage for variables, both initialized and uninitialized.

The code segment is identified by the .text directive. Program execution starts from the statement identified by the main label in the code segment. We end program execution by using the exit system call.

Here is an example code fragment that prompts the user for a name and reads the name.

```
################### Data segment #######################
        .data
prompt:
        .ASCIIZ    "Enter your name: "
in_name:
        .space    31

################## Code segment #######################
        .text
            . . .
        la    $a0,prompt      # prompt user
        li    $v0,4
        syscall

        la    $a0,in_name     # read name
        li    $a1,31
        li    $v0,8
        syscall
            . . .
```

The data segment declares a prompt message prompt and space for the input string in_name. Because we reserved 31 bytes for in_name, we can read at most 30 characters from the input into this string.

In the code segment, the first system call displays the prompt message using the print_string system call. As expected by this system call, we place the address of prompt in $a0 and load 4 into $v0. The second system call uses the read_string system call to read the name from the user into the in_name buffer. By loading 31 into $a1, we limit the input string length to 30 characters.

Data Movement Instructions

MIPS provides several data movement instructions to move data between registers. Here we discuss the move instruction that can be used to move data between the general regis-

Table 10.2 Sample MIPS load instructions

Instruction	Description
lb Rdest,address	Load Byte. Loads the byte at address in memory into the least significant byte of Rdest. The byte is treated as a signed number; sign extends to the remaining three bytes of Rdest.
lbu Rdest,address	Load Byte Unsigned. This instruction is similar to lb except that the byte is treated as an unsigned number. The upper three bytes of Rdest are filled with zeros.
lh Rdest,address	Load Halfword. Loads the half-word (two bytes) at address in memory into the least significant two bytes of Rdest. The 16-bit data are treated as a signed number; sign extends to the remaining two bytes of Rdest.
lhu Rdest,address	Load Halfword Unsigned. Same as lh except that the 16-bit halfword is treated as an unsigned number.
lw Rdest,address	Load Word. Loads the word (four bytes) at address in memory into Rdest.

Assembler pseudoinstructions

la[†] Rdest,var	Load Address. Loads the address of var into Rdest.
li[†] Rdest,imm	Load Immediate. Loads the immediate value imm into Rdest.

ters of the processor. The format is

```
move†    Rdest,Rsrc
```

It copies contents of Rsrc to Rdest. Note that we use † to indicate that the instruction is actually a pseudoinstruction supported by the assembler. Pseudoinstructions are not processor instructions; the assembler uses one or more processor instructions to implement pseudoinstructions.

Four additional data movement instructions are available for transferring data among a general register and two special registers HI and LO. These instructions are described on page 228.

Load Instructions

MIPS provides load and store instructions to move data among memory and registers. Load instructions move data from memory into registers and the store instructions move data in the opposite direction. Load and store instructions have a similar format. Therefore, we discuss the load instructions in more detail.

Several load and store instructions are available to move data of different sizes. The load byte (lb) instruction moves a byte of data from memory to a register. The format is

```
lb      Rdest,address
```

It loads the least significant byte of Rdest with the byte at the specified memory address. The byte is treated as a signed number. Consequently, a sign bit is extended to the remaining three bytes of Rdest. To load an unsigned number, use load byte unsigned (lbu) instead of lb. In this case, the remaining three bytes are filled with zeros.

Other load instructions facilitate movement of larger data items. These instructions are summarized in Table 10.2.

The assembler provides two pseudoinstructions to load the address or an immediate value into a register. For example,

```
la      $a0,marks
```

loads the address of the marks array into the $a0 register.

The li instruction shown in Table 10.2 is implemented as

```
ori     Rdest,$0,imm
```

The ori (OR immediate) instruction performs logical bitwise or of the second and third operands. Note that $0 is hardwired to zero. The logical instructions are briefly discussed later in this chapter and fully described in Chapter 15.

Store Instructions

The store byte (sb) instruction

```
sb      Rsrc,address
```

stores the least significant byte of Rsrc at the specified memory address. Because the data transfer does not involve sign extension, there is no need for separate instructions to handle signed and unsigned byte transfers. Store instructions to handle 16- and 32-bit data are also available, as shown in Table 10.3.

Addressing Modes

Both load and store instructions take a memory address. Addressing mode refers to how we specify where the operands are. We have already discussed the processor addressing modes in Chapter 4. The assembler supports several other addressing modes. Here we give some simple examples to illustrate how we can specify the address in load and store instructions.

Table 10.3 Sample MIPS store instructions

Instruction		Description
sb	Rsrc,address	Store Byte. Stores the least significant byte of Rsrc at the specified address in memory.
sh	Rsrc,address	Store Halfword. Stores the least significant two bytes (halfword) of Rsrc at the specified address in memory.
sw	Rsrc,address	Store Word. Stores the four-byte word in Rsrc at the specified address in memory.

Example 1   In a previous example, we loaded the address of the marks array into the $a0 register using the la instruction. If we want to read the first element of the marks array, we can do so by the following statement.

```
lw      $t0,($a0)
```

This instruction takes the address in $a0 and loads the word at this address into the $t0 register. Of course, we are assuming that each element of the array is four bytes long.

We can also specify a constant offset to be added to the address in a register. We illustrate this addressing mode with a couple of examples.

Example 2   Assuming that $a0 points to the marks array as in the previous example, we can access the second element of this array using the following statement.

```
lw      $t0,4($a0)
```

The address in this instruction is computed by adding 4 to the address in $a0.

Example 3   Assuming that $a0 points to the marks array, the following code interchanges the second and third elements.

```
lw      $t0,4($a0)
lw      $t1,8($a0)
sw      $t1,4($a0)
sw      $t0,8($a0)
```

In this code, we use registers $t0 and $t1 as temporary registers to hold the values to be exchanged.

Sample Instructions

The MIPS architecture provides several groups of instructions including arithmetic, logical, shift, and branch. In this section we look at some sample instructions so that we can write meaningful assembly language programs. Later chapters give a more complete and detailed discussion of these instructions.

Arithmetic Instructions

The MIPS instruction set has four arithmetic instruction types to perform addition, subtraction, multiplication, and division. Here we discuss the first two types of instructions.

Addition   The basic addition instruction

        add   Rdest,Rsrc1,Rsrc2

adds the contents of `Rsrc1` and `Rsrc2` and stores the result in `Rdest`. The numbers are treated as signed integers. In case of an overflow, an overflow exception is generated. We can use `addu` if no overflow exception is needed. Except for this, there is no difference between the `add` and `addu` instructions.

For convenience, assembler provides a pseudoinstruction that can take either a register or an immediate value as the second source operand. The format is

        add†   Rdest,Rsrc1,Src2

where `Src2` can be a 16-bit immediate value or a register. We can use `addu†` if the overflow exception is not needed.

Subtraction   The subtract instruction

        sub   Rdest,Rsrc1,Rsrc2

subtracts the contents of `Rsrc2` from `Rsrc1` (i.e., `Rsrc1 − Rsrc2`). The result is stored in `Rdest`. The contents of the two source registers are treated as signed numbers and an integer overflow exception is generated. We can use `subu` if this exception is not required.

Logical Instructions

The MIPS instruction set supports several logical instructions. In this section we discuss the two basic instructions: `and` and `or`. Chapter 15 gives a complete discussion of the logical instructions.

These instructions operate on bit-by-bit basis. The truth tables for these logical operators are given in Table 10.4. The format of these instructions is similar to that of the `add` and `sub` instructions, as shown here:

        and   Rdest,Rsrc1,Rsrc2

This instruction performs bitwise `and` on the content of the `Rsrc1` and `Rsrc2` registers and stores the result in the `Rdest` register. For example, the following sequence of instructions

Table 10.4 Truth tables for the and and or logical operations

and operation			or operation		
Input bits		Output bit	Input bits		Output bit
source1	source2	destination	source1	source2	destination
0	0	0	0	0	0
0	1	0	0	1	1
1	0	0	1	0	1
1	1	1	1	1	1

```
li    $t0,0x55
li    $t1,0xAA
and   $t2,$t1,$t0
```

leaves zero in the $t2 register.

The processor does not support the logical not operation. However, this missing logical operation is supported by a pseudoinstruction. The not pseudoinstruction takes a source operand and a destination operand, as shown below:

```
not†    Rdest,Rsrc
```

It performs bitwise logical not of the Rsrc operand and stores the result in the Rdest register.

Shift Instructions

Both left-shift and right-shift instructions are available to facilitate bit operations. The number of bit positions to be shifted (i.e., shift count) can be specified as an immediate five-bit value or via a register. If a register is used, only the least significant five bits are used as the shift count.

The basic left-shift instruction sll (shift left logical)

```
sll    Rdest,Rsrc,count
```

shifts the contents of Rsrc left by count bit positions and stores the result in Rdest. When shifting left, vacated bits on the right are filled with zeros, as shown below:

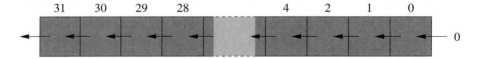

The right-shift instruction srl (shift right logical) has a similar format but shifts the bits in the opposite direction, as shown below:

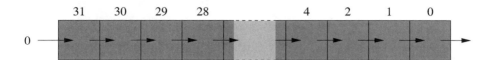

As with the sll instruction, the vacated bits are replaced by zeros. These shifts are called logical shifts. In Chapter 15 we show another category of shifts called arithmetic shifts when dealing with the right-shifts.

Branch Instructions

The MIPS instruction set provides several instructions to alter flow control. These include both unconditional and conditional branch instructions. Here we discuss a few of these instructions. The unconditional branch instruction

```
b†      target
```

transfers control to target unconditionally. As indicated here, this is a pseudoinstruction. Here is an example that illustrates the use of the unconditional branch instruction:

```
        li      $t0,50
repeat:
        add     $t1,$t1,1
        sub     $t0,$t0,1
        b       repeat
```

As written here, it is an infinite loop! We modify this code later to terminate the loop after 50 iterations. For this, we need a conditional branch instruction.

There are several conditional branch instructions. Recall from our discussion in Chapter 2 (on page 24) that conditional branch can be done in one of two ways: set-then-jump or test-and-jump. The MIPS instruction set provides several instructions to perform test-and-jump conditional branching. For example, the branch on not equal instruction

```
bne     Rsrc1,Rsrc2,target
```

tests the contents of the two registers Rsrc1 and Rsrc2 for equality and transfers control to target if Rsrc1 $\neq$ Rsrc2. If we assume that the numbers to be compared are in registers $t0 and $t1, we can write the branch instruction as

```
bne     $t1,$t0,target
```

The condition tested can be changed to "equal to", "less than", and so on. For example, the conditional branch instruction

```
blt     Rsrc1,Rsrc2,target
```

compares the contents of Rsrc1 and Rsrc2 and transfers control to target if Rsrc1 $<$ Rsrc2. In comparing the contents of these two registers, they are treated as signed numbers. For example, if $t1 = 5 and $t0 = -1, the instruction

```
bne     $t0,$t1,target
```

transfers control to `target` as $t0 < $t1. However, if we treat the contents of these registers as unsigned, the condition $t0 < $t1 is not true as $t0 contains all 1 bits (that's how −1 is stored in 2's complement notation). If you want to treat the number as unsigned, simply append the mnemonic with a u as in `bltu`. For a complete list of conditional branch instructions, see Table 14.2.

The MIPS instruction set also provides another group of conditional branch instructions that compare the value of a register to zero. For example, consider the `beqz` instruction shown below:

```
bnez    Rsrc,target
```

This instruction transfers control to `target` if the value of `Rsrc` is not equal to zero. Using this instruction, we can rewrite the previous infinite loop code fragment as

```
        li      $t0,50
repeat:
        add     $t1,$t1,1
        sub     $t0,$t0,1
        bnez    $t0,repeat
```

to terminate after 50 iterations.

We can also use other relationships such as "less then", "greater than" and so on. A complete list of these conditional branch instructions is given in Table 14.3 on page 250.

Our First Program

Let us look at our first MIPS assembly language program. The main goal is to show what MIPS programs look like. We give several other examples in the next section. The program listing shown in Program 10.1 adds three integers. The program follows the template given in Figure 10.1. The data segment consists of three messages; all three are declared as NULL-terminated ASCII strings (see lines 9–14).

Program 10.1 A simple program to add three integers

```
1:  # Find the sum of three numbers              SUM3.ASM
2:  #
3:  # Objective: Finds the sum of three integers.
4:  #      Input: Requests three numbers.
5:  #     Output: Outputs the sum.
6:  #
7:  ################## Data segment ##################
8:         .data
9:  prompt:
```

```
10:           .asciiz      "Please enter three numbers: \n"
11:  sum_msg:
12:           .asciiz      "The sum is: "
13:  newline:
14:           .asciiz      "\n"
15:
16:  ################## Code segment ##################
17:           .text
18:           .globl main
19:  main:
20:           la    $a0,prompt      # prompt user for input
21:           li    $v0,4
22:           syscall
23:
24:           li    $v0,5           # read 1st number into $t0
25:           syscall
26:           move  $t0,$v0
27:
28:           li    $v0,5           # read 2nd number into $t1
29:           syscall
30:           move  $t1,$v0
31:
32:           li    $v0,5           # read 3rd number into $t2
33:           syscall
34:           move  $t2,$v0
35:
36:           addu  $t0,$t0,$t1
37:           addu  $t0,$t0,$t2
38:
39:           la    $a0,sum_msg     # write sum message
40:           li    $v0,4
41:           syscall
42:
43:           move  $a0,$t0         # output sum
44:           li    $v0,1
45:           syscall
46:
47:           la    $a0,newline     # write newline
48:           li    $v0,4
49:           syscall
50:
51:           li    $v0,10          # exit
52:           syscall
```

The actual code begins on line 20. The program prompts the user to enter three integers by displaying the prompt string using the print_string system call (lines 20–

22). It then uses the `read_int` system call to read the three input integers. The first integer read is placed in the `$t0` register (see lines 24–26). The next two integers are placed in the `$t1` and `$t2` registers, respectively.

The three integers are added using two `add` instructions on lines 36 and 37. These instructions place the sum in the `$t0` register. It then displays the sum message on lines 39–41. The sum is output using the `print_int` system call (lines 43–45). After displaying a newline on lines 47–49, the program exits by calling the `exit` system call (lines 51 and 52).

Illustrative Examples

This section presents several examples that illustrate the use of the assembly language instructions discussed in this chapter. In order to follow these examples, you should be able to understand the difference between numeric values and their character representations. For example, when using a byte to store a number, number 5 is stored in binary as

```
00000101
```

On the other hand, character 5 is stored as

```
00110101
```

Character manipulation is easier if you understand this difference as well as the key characteristics of ASCII encoding, as discussed in Appendices A and B.

Example 10.1 *Sum of the individual digits of a number.*
The program receives a number (maximum 10 digits) and displays the sum of the individual digits of the input number. For example, if the input number is 45213, the program displays $4 + 5 + 2 + 1 + 3 = 15$.

In this example, we read the input number as a string, rather than as a number (i.e., we use the `read_string` system call, not the `read_int` system call). We revisit this example in Chapter 13 where we read the input as a number using the `read_int` system call. (The reason is that, if we read the input as a number, we need the divide instruction which we have not yet discussed.) The pseudocode for the `addigits` program is given below:

```
main()
      prompt user for input
      read input number as a string into numString
      write output sum message
      index := 0
      number := 0
      while (TRUE)
```

> char := numString[index]
> **if** ((char ≠ linefeed) AND (char ≠ NULL))
> **then**
>   number := number + (char AND 0xF)
> **else**
>   goto `exit_loop`
> **end if**
> index := index + 1
> **end while**
> `exit_loop`:
>   output sum
>   output newline
>   exit
> end `main`

The program, shown in Program 10.2, prompts the user for a number with at most 10 digits. Unlike in the last example, this number is read as a string using the `read_string` system call (lines 31–34). We use `$t0` to point to the input string (line 40). The sum is maintained in the `$t2` register, which is initialized to zero on line 41.

The sum is computed by the loop on lines 42–49. Because the input number is read as a string, the end of the string may have either a linefeed character or a NULL character depending on the number of digits entered by the user. If the user enters a 10-digit number, the string is terminated by a NULL character. On the other hand, if the user enters a number that is less than 10 digits, the string would have linefeed and NULL characters at the end of the string. Thus, we have to detect the end of the number when we encounter a linefeed (0xA) or a NULL character. These two conditions are tested on line 44 for linefeed and on line 45 for the NULL character. If either of these two conditions is met, the sum loop is terminated.

Program 10.2 Sum of individual digits of a number

```
 1:   # Add individual digits of a number            ADDIGITS.ASM
 2:   #
 3:   # Objective: To add individual digits of an integer.
 4:   #             The number is read as a string.
 5:   #      Input: Requests a number from the user.
 6:   #     Output: Outputs the sum.
 7:   #
 8:   #     $t0 - points to input string (i.e., input number)
 9:   #     $t1 - holds a digit for processing
10:   #     $t2 - maintains the running total
11:   #
12:   ################## Data segment ######################
13:           .data
14:   number_prompt:
```

```
15:         .asciiz     "Please enter a number (<11 digits): "
16:  out_msg:
17:         .asciiz     "\nThe sum of individual digits is: "
18:  newline:
19:         .asciiz     "\n"
20:  number:
21:         .space      11              # space for input string
22:
23:  ################### Code segment #######################
24:         .text
25:         .globl main
26:  main:
27:         la    $a0,number_prompt  # prompt user for input
28:         li    $v0,4
29:         syscall
30:
31:         la    $a0,number         # read the input number
32:         li    $a1,11             # as a string
33:         li    $v0,8
34:         syscall
35:
36:         la    $a0,out_msg        # write output message
37:         li    $v0,4
38:         syscall
39:
40:         la    $t0,number         # pointer to number
41:         li    $t2,0              # init sum to zero
42:  loop:
43:         lb    $t1,($t0)
44:         beq   $t1,0xA,exit_loop  # if linefeed or
45:         beqz  $t1,exit_loop      # NULL, we are done
46:         and   $t1,$t1,0x0F       # strip off upper 4 bits
47:         addu  $t2,$t2,$t1        # add to running total
48:         addu  $t0,$t0,1          # increment pointer
49:         b     loop
50:  exit_loop:
51:         move  $a0,$t2            # output sum
52:         li    $v0,1
53:         syscall
54:
55:         la    $a0,newline        # output newline
56:         li    $v0,4
57:         syscall
58:
59:         li    $v0,10             # exit
60:         syscall
```

The loop body to compute the sum follows the pseudocode given before. The input digit, which is in character form, must be converted to its numeric equivalent. Because ASCII assigns a special set of contiguous values to the digit characters, this conversion is straightforward. All we have to do is to mask off the upper half of the byte. This conversion is done by

```
and     $t1,$t1,0xF
```

on line 46. Alternatively, we could also subtract the character code for 0 as

```
sub     $t1,$t1,'0'
```

instead of masking the upper half-byte. This numeric value is added to the sum (maintained in $t2) on line 47. The string pointer in $t0 is incremented to point to the next input digit (line 48). When the loop is exited, we simply output the sum in the $t2 register.

Example 10.2 *Conversion of lowercase letters to uppercase.*

This program demonstrates how character manipulation can be used to convert lowercase letters to uppercase. The program receives a character string from the user and converts all lowercase letters to uppercase and displays the string. Characters other than the lowercase letters are not changed in any way. The pseudocode of Program 10.3 is shown below:

```
main()
      prompt user for input
      read input string
      write output sum message
      index := 0
      char := string[index]
      while (char ≠ NULL)
          if ((char ≥ 'a') AND (char ≤ 'z'))
          then
              char := char + 'A' − 'a'
          end if
          index := index + 1
          char := string[index]
      end while
          output string
          exit
   end main
```

We can see from Program 10.3 that the compound **if** condition requires two conditional branch instructions. The conditional branch instruction blt on line 41 tests if the character is less than a. If so, it is not a lowercase character and conversion is not done.

Similarly, the other condition, character $> z$, is tested by the bgt instruction on line 42. If both these tests are false, the character is a lowercase letter. In this case, we use

```
addu      $t1,$t1,-32
```

to convert it to an uppercase letter (line 43). For example, if the character is a, the character is represented by 0x61 (or 97 in decimal). By subtracting -32 (or 0x20), we get 0x41 or 65 in decimal. As you know, this value represents A in ASCII. Of course, we can do this case conversion by using the subtract instruction as shown here:

```
sub       $t1,$t1,32
```

We can also use the logical and instruction to force the 5th bit to zero. This can be easily done by

```
and       $t1,$t1,0xDF
```

The original or converted character is written back into the string using the sb instruction on line 46. After the loop is terminated, we display the converted string (lines 50–52) and exit.

Program 10.3 Conversion of lowercase letters to uppercase

```
 1:  # Uppercase conversion of characters      TOUPPER.ASM
 2:  #
 3:  # Objective: To convert lowercase letters to
 4:  #             corresponding uppercase letters.
 5:  #    Input: Requests a character string from the user.
 6:  #    Output: Prints the input string in uppercase.
 7:  #
 8:  #    $t0 - points to character string
 9:  #    $t1 - used for character conversion
10:  #
11:  ################# Data segment ####################
12:          .data
13:  name_prompt:
14:          .asciiz      "Please type your name: \n"
15:  out_msg:
16:          .asciiz      "Your name in capitals is: "
17:  in_name:
18:          .space       31          # space for input string
19:
20:  ################# Code segment ####################
21:          .text
22:          .globl main
23:  main:
24:          la    $a0,name_prompt  # prompt user for input
```

```
25:          li    $v0,4
26:          syscall
27:
28:          la    $a0,in_name       # read the input string
29:          li    $a1,31
30:          li    $v0,8
31:          syscall
32:
33:          la    $a0,out_msg       # write output message
34:          li    $v0,4
35:          syscall
36:
37:          la    $t0,in_name
38:  loop:
39:          lb    $t1,($t0)
40:          beqz  $t1,exit_loop     # if NULL, we are done
41:          blt   $t1,'a',no_change
42:          bgt   $t1,'z',no_change
43:          addu  $t1,$t1,-32        # convert to uppercase
44:                                   # 'A'-'a' = -32
45:  no_change:
46:          sb    $t1,($t0)
47:          addu  $t0,$t0,1          # increment pointer
48:          b     loop
49:  exit_loop:
50:          la    $a0,in_name        # output converted string
51:          li    $v0,4
52:          syscall
53:
54:          li    $v0,10             # exit
55:          syscall
```

Example 10.3 *Division of two integers using subtraction.*

In this example, we use subtraction to implement the division operation. Note that the MIPS instruction set supports multiplication and division instructions, even though we have not discussed them in this chapter. These instructions are described in detail in Chapter 13. For now we show how the division operation can be implemented using repeated subtraction.

```
main()
      prompt user for input
      read the two input numbers (dividend and divisor)
      quotient := 0
      remainder := number
      while (remainder < divisor)
```

```
        quotient := quotient + 1
        remainder := remainder − divisor
    end while
    output quotient
    output remainder
    exit
  end main
```

The program, shown in Program 10.4, follows the pseudocode in a straightforward manner. The user is prompted for the dividend (numerator) and divisor (denominator) on lines 23–25. The two input numbers are read on lines 27–28 and 31–32. The divisor is stored in $t1 and the dividend (also the remainder) is stored in the $t0 register. The quotient, which is maintained in $t2, is initialized to zero on line 35.

Program 10.4 Division by repeated subtraction

```
 1:  # Division using subtraction            DIVIDE.ASM
 2:  #
 3:  # Objective: Finds quotient and remainder of a division
 4:  #            using the subtract instruction.
 5:  #    Input: Requests two numbers from the user.
 6:  #   Output: Outputs the quotient and remainder.
 7:  #
 8:  ################# Data segment #################
 9:          .data
10:  prompt:
11:          .asciiz     "Please enter dividend and divisor: "
12:  quo_msg:
13:          .asciiz     "The quotient is: "
14:  rem_msg:
15:          .asciiz     "The remainder is: "
16:  newline:
17:          .asciiz     "\n"
18:
19:  ################# Code segment #################
20:          .text
21:          .globl main
22:  main:
23:          la   $a0,prompt      # prompt user for input
24:          li   $v0,4
25:          syscall
26:
27:          li   $v0,5           # read dividend into $t0
28:          syscall
29:          move $t0,$v0
```

```
30:
31:            li    $v0,5            # read divisor into $t1
32:            syscall
33:            move  $t1,$v0
34:
35:            li    $t2,0            # quotient (in $t2) = 0
36:    loop:
37:            bltu  $t0,$t1,done     # if rem < divisor, done
38:            add   $t2,$t2,1        # increment quotient
39:            sub   $t0,$t0,$t1      # compute remainder
40:            b     loop
41:
42:    done:
43:            la    $a0,quo_msg      # write quotient message
44:            li    $v0,4
45:            syscall
46:
47:            move  $a0,$t2          # output quotient
48:            li    $v0,1
49:            syscall
50:
51:            la    $a0,newline      # write newline
52:            li    $v0,4
53:            syscall
54:
55:            la    $a0,rem_msg      # write remainder message
56:            li    $v0,4
57:            syscall
58:
59:            move  $a0,$t0          # output remainder
60:            li    $v0,1
61:            syscall
62:
63:            la    $a0,newline      # write newline
64:            li    $v0,4
65:            syscall
66:
67:            li    $v0,10           # exit
68:            syscall
```

The division loop consists of the lines 36–40. The while loop termination condition (remainder < divisor) is tested on line 37. If the condition is not met, the quotient is incremented (line 38) and the remainder is updated by subtracting the divisor (line 39).

After the loop is terminated, we first display the quotient, which is in $t2, using the print_int system call. Then after displaying the remainder, the program terminates.

Summary

In this chapter, we presented the basics of the MIPS assembly language programming. We discussed three types of assembly language statements:

1. Executable statements that instruct the processor as to what to do;
2. Pseudoinstructions that are supported by the assembler;
3. Assembler directives that facilitate the assembly process.

Assembler directives to allocate storage space for data variables and to define numeric and string constants were discussed in detail. The assembler extends the processor instruction set by providing several pseudoinstructions. It translates these pseudoinstructions to one or more processor instructions. We have given an example to show how the assembler does this translation. We give more examples in later chapters.

We have given an overview of the MIPS instruction set. Although we discussed in detail the load and store instructions, there was only a brief review of the remaining instructions of the MIPS instruction set. A detailed discussion of these instructions is provided in later chapters.

11

Procedures and the Stack

We have given an overview of the MIPS assembly language in the last chapter. This chapter discusses how procedures are written in the MIPS assembly language. Procedure is an important programming construct that facilitates modular programming. Procedures can be divided into leaf and nonleaf procedures. A leaf procedure does not call other procedures. On the other hand, a nonleaf procedure calls other procedures. In the MIPS architecture, we can implement simple leaf procedures without using the stack. Nonleaf procedures always need to use the stack, at least to store the return address of the calling procedure.

In this chapter, we discuss how both leaf and nonleaf procedures are implemented in the assembly language. Our initial discussion deals with simple leaf procedures that can be implemented using the registers. Then we look at how the stack is implemented in the MIPS architecture. The details about the stack implementation are useful in understanding how we can handle nonleaf procedures in the assembly language.

Parameter passing is an important aspect of procedure invocation. As you know, we can use either the call-by-value or call-by-reference mechanism for parameter passing. Here we give details on how we can implement these two types of parameter-passing mechanisms in the assembly language programs.

Introduction

A procedure is a logically self-contained unit of code designed to perform a specific task. Procedures are sometimes called *subprograms* and play an important role in modular program development. In high-level languages, there are two types of subprograms: *procedures* and *functions*. Each function receives a list of arguments and performs a computation based on the arguments passed onto it and returns a single value.

Procedures also receive a list of arguments just as the functions do. However, procedures, after performing their computation, may return zero or more results back to the calling procedure. In C language, both these subprogram types are combined into a single function construct. For example, in the following C function

```
int sum (int x, int y, int z)
{
    return (x+y+z);
}
```

the parameters x, y, and z are called formal parameters and the function body is defined based on these parameters. When this function is called (or invoked) by a statement like

```
total = sum(number1,number2,number3);
```

the actual parameters—number1, number2, and number3—are used in the computation of the function sum.

There are two types of parameter-passing mechanisms: *call-by-value* and *call-by-reference*. In the call-by-value mechanism, the called function (sum in our example) is provided only the values of the parameters for its use. Thus, in this mechanism, the values of these actual parameters are not changed in the called function; these values can only be used as in a mathematical function. In our example, the sum function is invoked by using the call-by-value mechanism, as we simply pass the values of number1, number2, and number3 to the called function sum. Thus, if sum modifies x, y, or z, these changes are not reflected in the calling function.

To illustrate this point, let's assume that we want to exchange two values a and b passed on to the function swap. Suppose we define our swap function as follows.

```
/* Incorrect swap procedure */
int swap (int a, int b)
{
    int     temp;

    temp = a;
    a = b;
    b = temp;
    return;
}
```

If we call swap as

```
swap(value1, value2);
```

it will not exchange the two values value1 and value2 because we are using the call-by-value mechanism. We can remedy this problem by using the call-by-reference mechanism.

In the call-by-reference mechanism, the called function actually receives the addresses (i.e., pointers) of the parameters from the calling function. The function can change the contents of these parameters—and these changes are seen by the calling function—by directly manipulating the actual parameter storage space. We can rewrite the swap function as

```
/* Correct swap procedure */
void swap (int *a, int *b)
{
    int temp;

    temp = *a;
    *a = *b;
    *b = temp;
}
```

This procedure works fine as it passes the addresses of the two parameters from the calling function. Such a function can be invoked as

```
swap (&data1, &data2);
```

Often both types of parameter-passing mechanisms are used in the same function. As an example, consider finding the roots of the quadratic equation

$$ax^2 + bx + c = 0.$$

The two roots are defined as

$$\text{root1} = \frac{-b + \sqrt{b^2 - 4ac}}{2a},$$

$$\text{root2} = \frac{-b - \sqrt{b^2 - 4ac}}{2a}.$$

The roots are real if $b^2 \geq 4ac$, and imaginary otherwise.

Suppose that we want to write a function that receives a, b, and c and returns the values of the two roots (if real) and indicates whether the roots are real or imaginary.

```
int roots (double a, double b, double c,
           double *root1, double *root2)
{
    int root_type = 1;
    if (4*a*c <= b*b){   /* roots are real */
        *root1 = (-b + sqrt(b*b - 4*a*c))/(2*a);
        *root2 = (-b - sqrt(b*b - 4*a*c))/(2*a);
    }
    else    /* roots are imaginary */
        root_type = 0;
    return (root_type);
}
```

The function receives parameters a, b, and c via the call-by-value mechanism, and root1 and root2 parameters are passed using the call-by-reference mechanism. A typical invocation of roots is

```
root_type = roots (a, b, c, &root1, &root2);
```

In summary, procedures receive a list of parameters, which may be passed either by the call-by-value or by the call-by-reference mechanism. If more than one result is to be returned by a called procedure, the call-by-reference parameter-passing mechanism should be used.

Procedure Invocation

MIPS provides two instructions to support procedures: jal and jr. The jal instruction is used for calling a procedure and jr is used to return from a procedure. In this section, we discuss the jal instruction. The jr instruction is discussed in the next section.

The jal (jump and link) instruction

```
jal     proc_name
```

transfers control to proc_name just as a jump instruction does. Because we need the return address to return the called procedure, it also stores the address of the instruction following the delayed slot instruction in the $ra register. Here are the actions taken in invoking a procedure using the jal instruction:

```
$ra = PC + 8
PC = PC[31:28] || offset<<2
```

Notice that $ra (i.e., $31) is loaded with PC+8, not PC+4. This is because of the delayed slot instruction (see our discussion on page 25). Thus the control returns to the instruction following the delayed slot instruction.

This instruction uses the J-type instruction encoding shown in Figure 4.2 on page 52. As you can see from this figure, it uses 26 bits to specify the offset. The target address is computed as follows. The 26-bit offset specified in the instruction is shifted left by two bit positions because of the 32-bit alignment. This gives us 28 bits and the remaining 4 bits are taken from the PC. Before the control is transferred, the delayed branch instruction is executed.

SPIM note	Because SPIM simulates the MIPS R2000 processor, it does not simulate the delayed branch. Thus, it performs $ra = PC + 4.

An Example

To understand the procedure invocation mechanism, let's look at the program fragment, obtained from SPIM, shown in Figure 11.1. This code consists of three procedures: main, avg, and sum. The first column gives the address of each instruction (the 0x prefix

```
address          machine code
                           ; main:
                              . . .
[0x0040004c]   0x0c100022   jal 0x00400088 [sum] ; 37: jal   sum
                              . . .
                           ; end of main procedure
;*************************************************************
                           ; sum:
[0x00400088]   0x34020000   ori $2, $0, 0            ; 60: li    $v0,0
[0x0040008c]   0x0c10002c   jal 0x004000b0 [avg] ; 61: jal   avg
                              . . .
                           ; end of sum procedure
;*************************************************************
                           ; avg:
[0x004000b0]   0x00044021   addu $8, $0, $4        ; 76: move $t0,$a0
                              . . .
[0x004000c0]   0x0c100022   jal 0x00400088 [sum] ; 80: jal   sum
                              . . .
                           ; end of avg procedure
;*************************************************************
```

Figure 11.1 Sample code to explain procedure calls

indicates that the address in hex). The machine code generated is given in the second column. The third column gives the assembler translation of the source instruction given in the fourth column. For example, `li $v0,0` is translated as `ori $2,$0,0`.

The procedure call instruction in the `main` procedure

```
jal    sum
```

is encoded as `0x0c100022`. The most significant 6 bits represent the opcode and the remaining 26 bits give the offset as shown below:

Opcode	Offset
0000 11	00 0001 0000 0000 0000 0010 0010

Multiplying this offset by four (equivalent to left-shifting by two bit positions), we get the 28-bit value `0400088`. By adding the most significant 4 bits from the PC, we get the target address as `00400088`, which is the address of the `sum` procedure. The same encoding is used to call `sum` in the `avg` procedure.

The `jal` instruction in the `sum` procedure

```
jal    avg
```

is encoded as `0x0c10002c`, which consists of `000011` as the opcode and `0x010002c` as the offset value as shown below:

Opcode	Offset
0000 11	00 0001 0000 0000 0000 0010 1100

Following the target computation process described before, we get `04000b0` by multiplying the 26-bit offset `10002c` by 4. Adding the 4 most significant PC bits, we get the target address of `avg` as `004000b0`.

Returning from a Procedure

To return from a procedure, we use

```
jr      $ra
```

which reads the return address from the `$ra` register and transfers control to this address. In the MIPS32 architecture, the instruction following the `jr` instruction, which is in the branch delay slot, is executed before transferring control. However, see the following SPIM note.

SPIM note	Because the SPIM simulator does not simulate the delayed branch, the control is transferred to the address in the `$ra` register.

Note that this instruction is a special case of the general `jr` instruction. In this instruction, you can specify a register that contains the target address of the jump and has the following format.

```
jr      rs
```

This instruction is encoded as follows.

Opcode	Offset			
0000 00	rs (5 bits)	00 0000 0000	hint (5 bits)	00 1000

In release 1 of the MIPS architecture, only 0 is defined as the valid hint value. This is the value SPIM uses in encoding the `jr` instruction. For the `rs` we can substitute the number of the source register. To return from a procedure, we use `$ra`, which is `r31`. Thus, substituting 31 for the `rs` field, we get the encoding `0x03e00008` for the `jr $ra` instruction.

Parameter Passing

Parameter passing in assembly language is different and more complicated than that used in high-level languages. In assembly language, the calling procedure first places all the parameters needed by the called procedure in a mutually accessible storage area (usually registers or memory). Only then can the procedure be invoked.

There are two common methods depending on the type of storage area used to pass parameters: the *register method* or *stack method*. As their names imply, the register method uses general registers to pass parameters, and the stack is used in the other method. We look at the register method in this section. Stack-based parameter passing is discussed later.

Recall from our discussion in Chapter 4 that registers `$v0` and `$v1` are used to return results from a procedure. Registers `$a0` to `$a3` are used to pass the first four parameters to procedures. The remaining parameters are passed via the stack.

We can divide procedures into two major types: leaf procedures and nonleaf procedures. Leaf procedures do not call other procedures whereas nonleaf procedures do. Simple leaf procedures do not have to use the stack if its local variables can fit the caller-save registers `$t0` to `$t9`. If this is not the case, a leaf procedure will have to use the stack. Nonleaf procedures must use the stack, at least to store the return address. We say more about these procedures later on.

Our First Program

This is a simple program to compute the sum of three integers (see Program 11.1). Our main goal is to explain the basics of the procedures in the MIPS assembly language. The main program requests three integers and passes them to the `find_sum` procedure. The procedure returns the sum. Registers are used for parameter passing as well as to return the result. Registers `$a0`, `$a1`, and `$a2` are used to pass the three integers. The procedure returns the sum in `$v0`.

Program 11.1 Our first procedure example

```
1:  # Find the sum of three numbers          SUM.ASM
2:  #
3:  # Objective: Finds the sum of three integers.
4:  #            To demonstrate register-based
5:  #            parameter passing.
6:  #      Input: Requests three numbers from the user.
7:  #     Output: Outputs the sum.
```

```
 8:  #
 9:  #     $a0, $a1, $a2 - three numbers are passed via
10:  #                        these registers
11:  #              $v0 - returns sum
12:  #
13:  ################## Data segment ##################
14:         .data
15:  prompt:
16:         .asciiz     "Please enter three numbers: \n"
17:  sum_msg:
18:         .asciiz     "The sum is: "
19:  newline:
20:         .asciiz     "\n"
21:
22:  ################## Code segment ##################
23:         .text
24:         .globl main
25:  main:
26:         la    $a0,prompt      # prompt user for input
27:         li    $v0,4
28:         syscall
29:
30:         li    $v0,5           # read 1st number into $a0
31:         syscall
32:         move  $a0,$v0
33:
34:         li    $v0,5           # read 2nd number into $a1
35:         syscall
36:         move  $a1,$v0
37:
38:         li    $v0,5           # read 3rd number into $a2
39:         syscall
40:         move  $a2,$v0
41:
42:         jal   find_sum
43:         move  $t0,$v0
44:
45:         la    $a0,sum_msg     # write sum message
46:         li    $v0,4
47:         syscall
48:
49:         move  $a0,$t0         # output sum
50:         li    $v0,1
51:         syscall
52:
53:         la    $a0,newline     # write newline
54:         li    $v0,4
```

```
55:          syscall
56:
57:          li    $v0,10          # exit
58:          syscall
59:
60:   #-----------------------------------------------
61:   # FIND_SUM receives three integers in $a0, $a1,
62:   # and $a2 and returns their sum in $v0
63:   #-----------------------------------------------
64:   find_sum:
65:          move  $v0,$a0
66:          addu  $v0,$v0,$a1
67:          addu  $v0,$v0,$a2
68:          jr    $ra
```

To invoke the procedure, we use `jal` as shown on line 42. The body of the procedure is simple and straightforward to understand. When the procedure is done, a `jr` instruction returns control back to the main program (see line 68). Because we use `addu`, there will not be any overflow exception. If you want the overflow exception, use `add` instead of `addu` on lines 66 and 67.

Pros and Cons of the Register Method

The register method has its advantages and disadvantages. These are summarized here.

Advantages

1. The register method is convenient and easier for passing a small number of parameters. For example, MIPS conventionally uses `$a0` to `a3` to pass the first four parameters.

2. This method is also faster because all the parameters are available in registers, as opposed to in memory.

Disadvantages

1. The main disadvantage is that the register-based method is not useful as a general mechanism for parameter passing. For example, only a few parameters can be passed by using registers, as there are a limited number of them available. Later on we look at another example that passes a variable number of parameters. This example requires the use of the stack. Chapter 16, which discusses recursive procedures, also demonstrates the need for the stack in procedures.

2. Another problem is that the registers are often used by the calling procedure for some other purpose. Thus, it is necessary to temporarily save the contents of these registers on the stack to free them for use in parameter passing before calling a

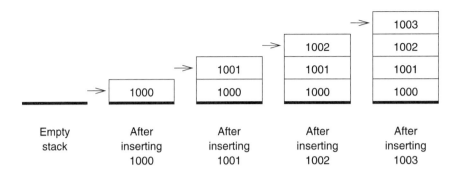

Figure 11.2 An example showing stack growth: numbers 1000 through 1003 are inserted in ascending order. The arrow points to the top-of-stack.

procedure, and restore them after returning from the called procedure. Because we use the stack to save these registers, it is difficult to realize the second advantage listed above, as the stack operations involve memory access.

For these reasons, the stack is used with procedures. Next we look at these details.

Stack Implementation in MIPS

What Is a Stack

Conceptually, a stack is a last-in-first-out (LIFO) data structure. The operation of a stack is analogous to the stack of trays you find in cafeterias. The first tray removed from the stack would be the last tray that had been placed on the stack. There are two operations associated with a stack: insertion and deletion. If we view the stack as a linear array of elements, stack insertion and deletion operations are restricted to one end of the array. Thus, the only element that is directly accessible is the element at the top-of-stack (TOS). In the stack terminology, insert and delete operations are referred to as *push* and *pop* operations, respectively.

There is another related data structure, the *queue*. A queue can be considered as a linear array with insertions done at one end of the array and deletions at the other end. Thus, a queue is a First-In-First-Out (FIFO) data structure.

As an example of a stack, let us assume that we are inserting numbers 1000 through 1003 into a stack in ascending order. The state of the stack can be visualized as shown in Figure 11.2. The arrow points to the top-of-stack. When the numbers are deleted from the stack, the numbers will come out in the reverse order of insertion. That is, 1003 is removed first, then 1002, and so on. After the deletion of the last number, the stack is said to be in the empty state (see Figure 11.3).

In contrast, a queue maintains the order. Suppose that the numbers 1000 through 1003 are inserted into a queue as in the stack example. When removing the numbers from the

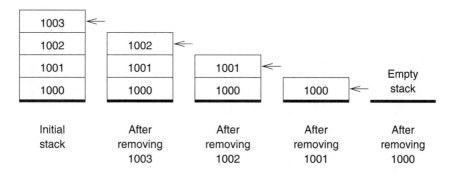

Figure 11.3 Deletion of data items from the stack: the arrow points to the top-of-stack.

queue, the first number to enter the queue would be the one to come out first. Thus, the numbers deleted from the queue would maintain their insertion order.

Stack Implementation

MIPS does not provide any special support to implement the stack. The memory space reserved in the stack segment is used to implement the stack. The MIPS memory layout is shown in Figure 4.3, which is reproduced here for convenience as Figure 11.4. As shown in this figure, the memory from 0x10000000 to 0x7FFFFFFF is used for the data and stack segments.

The stack segment begins at the top end of this memory section (i.e., at address 0x7FFFFFFF) and grows downward. On the other hand, the dynamic data area grows upward. This is an efficient way of sharing the unused memory between the stack and data segments. As a result, we should remember that as we push more data onto the stack, the memory address decreases.

The stack is a LIFO data structure, therefore we just need to maintain a pointer to the top of the stack. In some architectures, a special register is provided to point to the top of the stack. For example, in the Intel architecture the esp register serves this purpose. In the MIPS architecture, however, there is no special register. We can use any general register for this purpose. By convention, the register r29 is used to point to the top of the stack. This register is referred to as the stack pointer register ($sp). Note that TOS points to the last item pushed onto the stack.

Stack Operations

The MIPS architecture does not explicitly support stack operations. In contrast, the Intel architecture provides instructions such as push and pop to facilitate the stack operations. In MIPS, we have to manipulate the stack pointer register to implement the stack.

Memory addresses
(in hex)

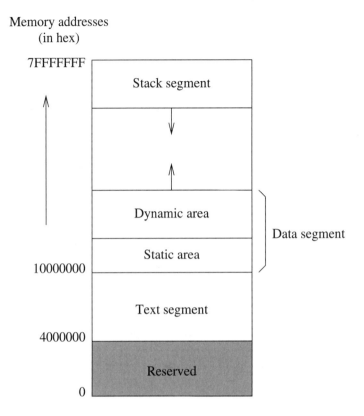

Figure 11.4 Typical memory layout used by operating systems.

PUSH operation   As discussed before, we have to decrement $sp to make room for the value being pushed onto the stack. For example, if we want to push the contents of $a0, we have to reserve four bytes of stack space and use the sw instruction to push the value as shown below:

```
sub     $sp,$sp,4       # reserve 4 bytes of stack
sw      $a0,0($sp)      # save the register
```

POP operation   The operation can be implemented by using the load and add instructions. For example, to restore the value of $a0 from the stack, we use the lw instruction to copy the value and increment $sp by 4 as shown below:

```
lw      $a0,0($sp)      # restore the two registers
addu    $sp,$sp,4       # clear 4 bytes of stack
```

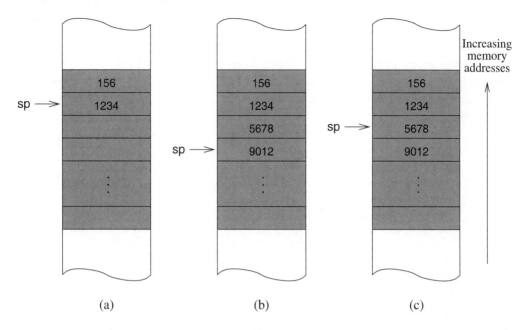

Figure 11.5 Stack implementation in MIPS: (a) initial stack state (sp points to the top-of-stack); (b) stack state after pushing 5678 and 9012; (c) stack state after removing 9012.

A Stack Example

In this example, let us consider 32-bit data even though the stack can be used for other data types. The initial state of the stack is shown in Figure 11.5a. When we push the contents of $a0 (5678) and $a1 (9012) onto this stack, the $sp is decremented by 8 to reserve eight bytes of stack space. Then the values 5678 and 9012 are stored in the stack using the code shown below:

```
sub     $sp,$sp,8       # reserve 8 bytes of stack
sw      $a1,0($sp)      # save registers
sw      $a0,4($sp)
```

The resulting stack state is shown in Figure 11.5b. Suppose we want to pop the stack into $t0. We can do this by the following code fragment.

```
lw      $t0,0($sp)
add     $sp,$sp,4
```

The resulting stack state is shown in Figure 11.5c.

Uses of the Stack

The stack is used for three main purposes: as a scratchpad to temporarily store data, for transfer of program control, and for passing parameters during a procedure call.

Temporary Storage of Data   The stack can be used as a scratchpad to store data on a temporary basis. For example, suppose that a procedure (say, `main`) calls another procedure `test`, which uses some of the callee-save registers (say, `$s0`, `$s1`, and `$s2`). Before using these registers, `test` must save the contents of these registers so that it can restore them before returning control to `main`. The stack can be used for this purpose as shown below:

```
test:
      #save $s0, $s1, and $s2 registers on the stack
      sub    $sp,$sp,12   # reserve 12 bytes of stack
      sw     $s0,0($sp)   # save registers
      sw     $s1,4($sp)
      sw     $s2,8($sp)
      # now these three registers can be used
          . . .
          . . .
      #restore $s0, $s1, and $s2 registers from the stack
      lw     $s0,0($sp)
      lw     $s1,4($sp)
      lw     $s2,8($sp)
      add    $sp,$sp,12
```

As demonstrated in this example, the stack is frequently used as a scratchpad to save and restore registers. The necessity often arises when we need to free up a set of registers so they can be used by the current code. This is often the case with nonleaf procedures as our later examples show.

Transfer of Control   The previous discussion concentrated on how we, as programmers, can use the stack to store data temporarily. The stack is also used to transfer control. In particular, when a nonleaf procedure is called, the return address of the instruction is stored on the stack so that the control can be transferred back to the calling program. We give an example of a nonleaf procedure later (see Example 11.2 on page 202). Also see Chapter 16 for a related discussion.

Parameter Passing   Another important use of the stack is to act as a medium to pass parameters to the called procedure. The stack is extensively used by high-level languages to pass parameters. This is what we discuss next with an example.

Parameter Passing via the Stack

To demonstrate how we can use the stack to pass parameters, we redo the sum example discussed before (see page 189). But this time, we pass the three integers via the stack. The program computes the sum of three integers. The main procedure requests three integers from the user and passes them to the `find_sum` procedure via the stack. As in the previous sum procedure, it returns the sum in `$v0`.

The input numbers are requested using a read loop consisting of lines 27–33 (see Program 11.2). We use $t0 to maintain the loop count. Because we are reading three integers, we initialize $t0 to 3 (line 26). The system call on line 29 places the input number in $v0. The instructions on lines 30 and 31 push this value onto the stack. Then, we decrement the loop count (line 32) and jump back to read more if the loop count is not zero. The remainder of the main procedure is similar to that in Program 11.1.

Program 11.2 The sum procedure uses stack-based parameter passing

```
 1:   # Find the sum of three numbers          SUM_STACK.ASM
 2:   #
 3:   # Objective: Finds the sum of three integers.
 4:   #            To demonstrate stack-based
 5:   #            parameter passing.
 6:   #     Input: Requests three numbers from the user.
 7:   #    Output: Outputs the sum.
 8:   #
 9:   ################## Data segment ##################
10:         .data
11:   prompt:
12:         .asciiz     "Please enter three numbers: \n"
13:   sum_msg:
14:         .asciiz     "The sum is: "
15:   newline:
16:         .asciiz     "\n"
17:
18:   ################## Code segment ##################
19:         .text
20:         .globl main
21:   main:
22:         la    $a0,prompt      # prompt user for input
23:         li    $v0,4
24:         syscall
25:
26:         li    $t0,3           # loop count = 3
27:   read_more:
28:         li    $v0,5           # read 1st number into $a1
29:         syscall               # number is in $v0
30:         sub   $sp,$sp,4       # reserve 4 bytes on stack
31:         sw    $v0,($sp)       # store the number on stack
32:         sub   $t0,$t0,1       # decrement loop count
33:         bnez  $t0,read_more   # if not zero, read more
34:
35:         jal   find_sum
36:         move  $t0,$v0
37:
```

```
38:             la    $a0,sum_msg      # write sum message
39:             li    $v0,4
40:             syscall
41:
42:             move  $a0,$t0          # output sum
43:             li    $v0,1
44:             syscall
45:
46:             la    $a0,newline      # write newline
47:             li    $v0,4
48:             syscall
49:
50:             li    $v0,10           # exit
51:             syscall
52:
53:     #-------------------------------------------------
54:     # FIND_SUM procedure receives three integers
55:     # via the stack and returns their sum in $v0.
56:     #-------------------------------------------------
57:     find_sum:
58:             li    $v0,0            # $v0 = 0 (sum in $v0)
59:             li    $t0,3            # loop iteration count
60:     sum_loop:
61:             lw    $t1,($sp)        # pop into $t1
62:             add   $sp,$sp,4        #
63:             add   $v0,$v0,$t1
64:             sub   $t0,$t0,1
65:             bnez  $t0,sum_loop
66:             jr    $ra
```

We also use a loop to add the numbers. This sum loop consists of lines 60–65. Because we want to return the sum in $v0, we use this register to keep the sum. It is initialized to zero on line 58. As in the main procedure, we use $t0 for the loop count. The two instructions on lines 61 and 62 implement the stack pop operation. The value in $t1 is added to our sum in $v0. At the end of the loop, the final sum is in $v0 as in the previous sum example. Notice that at the end of the sum loop, the stack is cleared of the three values passed onto the procedure.

One main difference between this program and the previous one is that we can use a loop to read the numbers and to add them up. When we use registers, this is not possible. To understand the flexibility of the stack-based parameter passing, consider adding 20 numbers instead of 3. In the stack version, all we have to do is change the loop count initialization from 3 to 20 (on lines 26 and 59).

Preserving Calling Procedure State

It is important to preserve the contents of the registers across a procedure call. The necessity for this is illustrated by the following code.

```
                · · ·
            li      $s0,50
    repeat:
            call    compute
                · · ·
            subu    $s0,$s0,1
            bnez    $s0,repeat
                · · ·
```

The code invokes the `compute` procedure 50 times. The `$s0` register maintains the number of remaining iterations. Now suppose that the `compute` procedure uses `$s0` during its execution. Then, when `compute` returns control to the calling program, `$s0` would have changed, and the program logic would be incorrect. To preserve the contents of `$s0`, it should be saved. Of course, we use the stack for this purpose.

Which Registers Should Be Saved?

The answer to this question is simple: save those registers that are used by the calling procedure but changed by the called procedure. This leads to the following question. Which procedure, the calling or the called, should save the registers?

If the calling procedure is to save the necessary registers, it needs to know the registers used by the called procedure. This causes two serious difficulties:

1. Program maintenance would be difficult because, if the called procedure were modified later on and a different set of registers used, every procedure that calls this procedure would have to be modified.
2. Programs tend to be longer because if a procedure is called several times, we have to include the instructions to save and restore the registers each time the procedure is called.

For these reasons, we prefer to make the called procedure responsible for saving the registers that it uses and restoring them before returning to the calling procedure. This also conforms to modular program design principles.

This strategy works fine from the logical standpoint but may not be the most efficient one. To see why this might be the case, assume that the called procedure uses 10 registers. However, none of these registers is used by the calling procedure. In this case, we would be wasting resources and time in saving and restoring these 10 registers. To solve this problem, MIPS divides the registers into two groups:

1. *Caller-save registers:* As the name implies, these registers are saved by the caller. In MIPS, `$t0` to `$t9` registers are used as caller-save registers. These registers

can be overwritten by the called procedure without any concern. If the caller keeps something useful in these registers, it has to take care of preserving their contents across procedure calls.

2. *Callee-save registers:* These registers are saved by the called procedure. In MIPS, registers $s0 to $s8 are used as callee-save registers. These registers, if used by the called procedure, must be preserved by the called procedure. This is often done by pushing these registers onto the stack and restoring them before returning from the procedure.

Illustrative Examples

We have looked at some simple procedure examples. Now we give some more examples to further illustrate the concepts discussed here.

Example 11.1 *Compute Fibonacci function.*
The Fibonacci sequence of numbers is defined as

$$\text{fib}(1) = 1,$$
$$\text{fib}(2) = 1,$$
$$\text{fib}(n) = \text{fib}(n-1) + \text{fib}(n-2) \text{ for } n > 2.$$

In other words, the first two numbers in the Fibonacci sequence are 1. The subsequent numbers are obtained by adding the previous two numbers in the sequence. Thus,

$$1, 1, 2, 3, 5, 8, 13, 21, 34, \ldots$$

is the Fibonacci sequence of numbers.

The program shown in Program 11.3 requests a number $n > 0$ and outputs fib(n). For example, if $n = 9$, the program outputs 34. If $n \leq 0$, an error message is displayed and the user is requested to enter another valid number (lines 33–37). Thus, we always call the Fibonacci procedure with $n > 0$.

Program 11.3 An example to compute Fibonacci number

```
 1:   # Computes Fibonacci number                    FIB_LOOP.ASM
 2:   #
 3:   # Objective: Computes the Fibonacci number.
 4:   #            Uses iteration.
 5:   #    Input: Requests a number n.
 6:   #   Output: Outputs Fibonacci number fib(n).
 7:   #
 8:   #    $a0 - number n is passed via this register
 9:   #    $v0 - fib(n) is returned
10:   #
```

```
11:    ################# Data segment #################
12:           .data
13:    prompt:
14:           .asciiz      "Please enter a number n>0: \n"
15:    error_prompt:
16:           .asciiz      "Not a valid number!\n"
17:    out_msg:
18:           .asciiz      "Fib(n) = "
19:    newline:
20:           .asciiz      "\n"
21:
22:    ################# Code segment #################
23:           .text
24:           .globl main
25:    main:
26:           la    $a0,prompt        # prompt user for input
27:           li    $v0,4
28:           syscall
29:
30:           li    $v0,5             # read n into $v0
31:           syscall
32:
33:           bgtz  $v0,number_OK     # number is OK if n>0
34:           la    $a0,error_prompt  # output error message
35:           li    $v0,4
36:           syscall
37:           b     main
38:
39:    number_OK:
40:           move  $a0,$v0
41:           jal   find_fib          # fib(n) returned in $v0
42:           move  $t0,$v0
43:
44:           la    $a0,out_msg       # write output message
45:           li    $v0,4
46:           syscall
47:
48:           move  $a0,$t0           # output fib(n)
49:           li    $v0,1
50:           syscall
51:
52:           la    $a0,newline       # write newline
53:           li    $v0,4
54:           syscall
55:
56:           li    $v0,10            # exit
57:           syscall
```

```
58:
59:    #----------------------------------------------------
60:    # FIND_FIB receives an integer n>0 in $a0
61:    # and returns fib(n) in $v0
62:    #      $t0: holds the second last fib value
63:    #      $v0: holds the last fib value
64:    #      $t1: used to compute the next fib value
65:    #----------------------------------------------------
66:    find_fib:
67:          li    $v0,1              # if n = 1 or n = 2
68:          ble   $a0,2,fib_done # return 1
69:
70:          # last fib value is in $v0
71:          li    $t0,1              # $t0 = second last fib value
72:
73:    loop1:
74:          add   $t1,$t0,$v0       # compute the next fib value
75:          move  $t0,$v0           # shift the last & 2nd last
76:          move  $v0,$t1           #       fib numbers
77:          sub   $a0,$a0,1         # n = n-1
78:          bgt   $a0,2,loop1       # loop if n>2
79:
80:    fib_done:
81:          jr    $ra
```

The find_fib procedure returns 1 for $n \leq 2$. For higher n values, it computes the Fibonacci number using the loop (lines 73–78). Notice that we use add, rather than addu, so that for large n, arithmetic overflow can be generated. For example, if $n = 50$, we see the following error message from SPIM.

```
Exception 12   [Arithmetic overflow]   occurred and ignored
```

In this example, we have used a loop to compute fib(n). In Chapter 16, we rewrite this example using recursion.

Example 11.2 *Finds the range of three numbers.*

This is a simple program to explain the basics of nonleaf procedures in the MIPS assembly language. The objective is to find the range of three numbers. For example, if the three numbers are 5, 10, and 12, the range is computed as $12 - 5 = 7$.

The main program requests three integers and passes them to find_range procedure. It in turn calls two procedures: find_min and find_max. Each procedure returns a value: minimum or maximum. Registers are used for parameter passing as well as to return the result. Registers $a1, $a2, and $a3 are used to pass the three integers. Each procedure returns its result in $v0.

It is important to notice the difference between `find_range` and `find_max` or `find_min` procedures. Because the `find_range` procedure is a nonleaf procedure, we need to save the return address in $ra before invoking other procedures. We do this on lines 63 and 64. We restore the $ra register on lines 71 and 72. The two leaf procedures are simple and straightforward to understand.

Program 11.4 A simple nonleaf procedure example

```
 1:   # Finds the range of three numbers              RANGE.ASM
 2:   #
 3:   # Objective: Finds the range of three integers. To
 4:   #           demonstrate writing nonleaf procedures.
 5:   #    Input: Requests three numbers.
 6:   #   Output: Outputs the range.
 7:   #
 8:   #     $a0, $a1, $a2 - three numbers are passed
 9:   #     $v0 - range is returned
10:   #
11:   ################# Data segment #####################
12:         .data
13:   prompt:
14:         .asciiz     "Please enter three numbers: \n"
15:   range_msg:
16:         .asciiz     "The range is: "
17:   newline:
18:         .asciiz     "\n"
19:
20:   ################# Code segment #####################
21:         .text
22:         .globl main
23:   main:
24:         la    $a0,prompt        # prompt user for input
25:         li    $v0,4
26:         syscall
27:
28:         li    $v0,5             # read 1st number into $a0
29:         syscall
30:         move  $a0,$v0
31:
32:         li    $v0,5             # read 2nd number into $a1
33:         syscall
34:         move  $a1,$v0
35:
36:         li    $v0,5             # read 3rd number into $a2
37:         syscall
38:         move  $a2,$v0
```

```
39:
40:         jal    find_range
41:         move   $t0,$v0
42:
43:         la     $a0,range_msg      # write range message
44:         li     $v0,4
45:         syscall
46:
47:         move   $a0,$t0            # output range
48:         li     $v0,1
49:         syscall
50:
51:         la     $a0,newline        # write newline
52:         li     $v0,4
53:         syscall
54:
55:         li     $v0,10             # exit
56:         syscall
57:
58: #-----------------------------------------------------------
59: # FIND_RANGE receives three integers in $a0, $a1, and $a2
60: # and returns the range in $v0
61: #-----------------------------------------------------------
62: find_range:
63:         sub    $sp,$sp,4          # save $ra
64:         sw     $ra,0($sp)
65:
66:         jal    find_min
67:         move   $t0,$v0
68:         jal    find_max
69:         sub    $v0,$v0,$t0
70:
71:         lw     $ra,0($sp)         # restore $ra
72:         add    $sp,$sp,4
73:         jr     $ra
74:
75: #-----------------------------------------------------------
76: # FIND_MIN receives three integers in $a0, $a1, and $a2
77: # and returns the minimum of the three in $v0
78: #-----------------------------------------------------------
79: find_min:
80:         move   $v0,$a0
81:         ble    $v0,$a1,min_skip_a1
82:         move   $v0,$a1
83: min_skip_a1:
84:         ble    $v0,$a2,min_skip_a2
85:         move   $v0,$a2
```

```
 86:  min_skip_a2:
 87:          jr      $ra
 88:
 89:  #------------------------------------------------------------
 90:  # FIND_MAX receives three integers in $a0, $a1, and $a2
 91:  # and returns the maximum of the three in $v0
 92:  #------------------------------------------------------------
 93:  find_max:
 94:          move    $v0,$a0
 95:          bge     $v0,$a1,max_skip_a1
 96:          move    $v0,$a1
 97:  max_skip_a1:
 98:          bge     $v0,$a2,max_skip_a2
 99:          move    $v0,$a2
100:  max_skip_a2:
101:          jr      $ra
```

Example 11.3 *Reverses a given string.*

This example performs string reversal. For example, if the input string is `pals`, it gives `slap` as the output string. We do this reversal in place (i.e., within the input string array). The algorithm is simple: we maintain two pointers `front` and `back`. Initially `front` and `back` point to the first and last characters of the string, respectively. After exchanging these two characters, `front` is advanced by one character and `back` is decremented by one to point to the previous character. We exchange the characters pointed to by these pointers. We repeat this process until `front` $\geq$ `back`. The algorithm is summarized below:

```
string_reverse(string)
    front := 0
    back := 0
    while ((string[back] ≠ linefeed) AND (string[back] ≠ NULL))
        back := back + 1
    end while
    back := back − 1
    while (front < back)
        string[front] ⟺ string[back]    {Exchange the two characters}
    end while
end string_reverse
```

Program 11.5 uses this algorithm to reverse a string. The main program prompts the user for a string and passes it to the `string_reverse` procedure. After returning from the string reverse procedure, it prints the reversed string.

Program 11.5 A string reverse example

```
 1:    # Reverses a string                        STRING_REVERSE.ASM
 2:    #
 3:    # Objective: Reverses a given string.
 4:    #      Input: Requests a string from the user.
 5:    #     Output: Outputs the reversed string.
 6:    #
 7:    #    $a0 - string pointer
 8:    #
 9:    ################# Data segment #####################
10:          .data
11:    prompt:
12:          .asciiz      "Please enter a string: \n"
13:    out_msg:
14:          .asciiz      "The reversed string is: "
15:    in_string:
16:          .space       31
17:
18:    ################# Code segment #####################
19:          .text
20:          .globl main
21:    main:
22:          la    $a0,prompt           # prompt user for input
23:          li    $v0,4
24:          syscall
25:
26:          la    $a0,in_string        # read input string
27:          li    $a1,31               # buffer length in $a1
28:          li    $v0,8
29:          syscall
30:
31:          la    $a0,in_string
32:          jal   string_reverse
33:
34:          la    $a0,out_msg          # write output message
35:          li    $v0,4
36:          syscall
37:
38:          la    $a0,in_string        # output reversed string
39:          li    $v0,4
40:          syscall
41:
42:          li    $v0,10               # exit
43:          syscall
44:
45:    #------------------------------------------------------
```

```
46:    # STRING_REVERSE receives a pointer to a string in $a0
47:    # and reverses the string
48:    #       $a0 - front pointer
49:    #       $t1 - back pointer
50:    #       $t2, $t3 - used as temporaries
51:    #-------------------------------------------------------
52:    string_reverse:
53:          move  $t1,$a0            # init $t1 to front pointer
54:    loop1:
55:          lbu   $t2,($t1)
56:          beq   $t2,0xA,done1      # if linefeed
57:          beqz  $t2,done1          # or NULL, we are done
58:          addu  $t1,$t1,1
59:          b     loop1
60:    done1:
61:          sub   $t1,$t1,1          # $t1 = back pointer
62:
63:    reverse_loop:
64:          bleu  $t1,$a0,done       # if back <= front, done
65:          lbu   $t2,($a0)          #
66:          lbu   $t3,($t1)          # exchange values
67:          sb    $t2,($t1)          # at front & back
68:          sb    $t3,($a0)          #
69:          addu  $a0,$a0,1          # update front
70:          subu  $t1,$t1,1          # and back
71:          b     reverse_loop
72:    done:
73:          jr    $ra
```

The string reverse procedure uses the $a0 and $t1 registers for front and back pointers, respectively. The first while loop is implemented on lines 54–59. The second while loop condition is implemented on line 64. The two characters, pointed to by front and back, are exchanged on lines 65–68. The two pointers are updated on lines 69 and 70. Because this is a leaf procedure, we can leave the return address in the $ra register.

Passing Variable Number of Parameters

Procedures in C can be defined to accept a variable number of parameters. The input and output functions, scanf and printf, are the two common procedures that take a variable number of parameters. In this case, the called procedure does not know the number of parameters passed onto it. Usually, the first parameter in the parameter list specifies the number of parameters passed.

In assembly language procedures, a variable number of parameters can be easily handled by the stack method of parameter passing. Only the stack size imposes a limit on the number of parameters that can be passed. The next example illustrates the use of the stack to pass a variable number of parameters in the MIPS assembly language programs.

Example 11.4 *Passing a variable number of parameters via the stack.*

The objective of this example is to show how easy it is to pass a variable number of parameters using the stack. The program, shown in Program 11.6, reads a number of integers and outputs their sum.

The procedure sum receives a variable number of integers via the stack. The parameter count is passed via $a0.

Program 11.6 Passing a variable number of parameters to a procedure

```
 1:  # Sum of variable number of integers              VAR_PARA.ASM
 2:  #
 3:  # Objective: Finds sum of variable number of integers.
 4:  #            Passes variable number of integers via stack.
 5:  #     Input: Requests integers from the user; input can be
 6:  #            terminated by entering a zero.
 7:  #    Output: Outputs the sum of input numbers.
 8:  #
 9:  #     $a0 - number of integers passed via the stack
10:  #     $v0 - sum is returned via this register
11:  #
12:  ################### Data segment #######################
13:        .data
14:  prompt:
15:        .ascii     "Please enter integers. \n"
16:        .asciiz    "Entering zero terminates the input. \n"
17:  sum_msg:
18:        .asciiz    "The sum is: "
19:  newline:
20:        .asciiz    "\n"
21:
22:  ################### Code segment #######################
23:        .text
24:        .globl main
25:  main:
26:        la    $a0,prompt          # prompt user for input
27:        li    $v0,4
28:        syscall
29:
30:        li    $a0,0
31:  read_more:
32:        li    $v0,5               # read a number
```

```
33:             syscall
34:             beqz  $v0,exit_read
35:             subu  $sp,$sp,4            # reserve 4 bytes on stack
36:             sw    $v0,($sp)            # store the number on stack
37:             addu  $a0,$a0,1
38:             b     read_more
39:   exit_read:
40:             jal   sum                  # sum is returned in $v0
41:             move  $t0,$v0
42:
43:             la    $a0,sum_msg          # write output message
44:             li    $v0,4
45:             syscall
46:
47:             move  $a0,$t0              # output sum
48:             li    $v0,1
49:             syscall
50:
51:             la    $a0,newline          # write newline
52:             li    $v0,4
53:             syscall
54:
55:             li    $v0,10               # exit
56:             syscall
57:
58:   #-----------------------------------------------------
59:   # SUM receives the number of integers passed in $a0
60:   # and the actual numbers via the stack. It returns
61:   # the sum in $v0.
62:   #-----------------------------------------------------
63:   sum:
64:             li    $v0,0                 # init sum = 0
65:   sum_loop:
66:             beqz  $a0,done
67:             lw    $t0,($sp)             # pop the top value
68:             addu  $sp,$sp,4             # into $t0
69:             addu  $v0,$v0,$t0
70:             subu  $a0,$a0,1
71:             b     sum_loop
72:   done:
73:             jr    $ra
```

The main program reads a sequence of integers from the input. Entering a zero terminates the input. Each number read from the input is pushed directly onto the stack (lines 35 and 36). Because $sp always points to the last item pushed onto the stack, we can pass this value to the procedure. Thus, a simple procedure call (line 40) is sufficient to pass the parameter count and the actual values.

The procedure sum reads the numbers from the stack. As it reads, it decreases the stack size (i.e., $sp increases). The loop in the sum procedure terminates when $a0 is zero (line 66). When the loop terminates, the stack is also cleared of all the arguments.

Summary

We have introduced procedures and discussed how procedures are implemented in the MIPS assembly language. We can divide procedures into leaf and nonleaf categories. A leaf procedure does not call another procedure whereas a nonleaf procedure invokes another procedure. In the MIPS architecture, leaf procedures can be written using internal registers. As part of procedure invocation, the return address is stored in the $ra register. This value is used to transfer control back to the caller after executing the procedure. Nonleaf procedures, however, need to use the stack.

The stack is a last-in-first-out data structure that plays an important role in nonleaf procedure invocation and execution. The stack supports two operations: push and pop. Only the element at the top-of-stack is directly accessible through these operations. The $sp register points to the top of the stack. It is important to note that the stack grows downward (i.e., towards lower memory addresses). Because the MIPS architecture does not explicitly support stack operations, we need to manipulate the stack pointer ($sp) register to implement the stack push and pop operations.

When writing procedures in assembly language, parameter passing has to be explicitly handled. Parameter passing can be done via registers or the stack. Although the register method is efficient, the stack-based method is more general and flexible. Also, when the stack is used for parameter passing, passing a variable number of parameters is straightforward. We have demonstrated this by means of an example.

In this chapter we discussed direct procedure calls in which the target instruction address is directly specified. The MIPS architecture also supports indirect procedure calls. In these calls, the target is specified indirectly through a register. Even though we haven't used this mechanism to invoke a procedure, we have used it to return from a procedure. We discuss indirect procedure calls in Chapter 14.

12

Addressing Modes

MIPS supports several ways to specify the location of the operands required by an instruction. These are called addressing modes. Most instructions expect their operands in the registers. However, load and store instructions are special in the sense that they interface with memory. These instructions require a memory address, which can be specified in several ways. This chapter gives details on the addressing modes we can use in writing MIPS assembly language programs.

Introduction

As discussed in Chapter 3, RISC processors use simple addressing modes. In contrast, CISC processors provide complex addressing modes. In this chapter, we look at the MIPS addressing modes in detail. SPIM simulates the MIPS R2000 processor, therefore our focus is on the assembly language of this processor.

As mentioned before, MIPS uses the load/store architecture. In this architecture, only the load and store instructions move data between memory and processor registers. All other instructions expect their operands in registers. Thus, they use the register addressing mode. The load and store instructions, however, need a memory address. A variety of addressing modes is available to specify the address of operands located in memory. The MIPS architecture supports the following addressing modes.

- Register addressing mode
- Immediate addressing mode
- Memory addressing mode

We look at these three addressing modes in the next three sections. Following this description, we give details on accessing and organizing arrays. We consider both one-dimensional and multidimensional arrays. We give several examples to illustrate the use the addressing modes presented here. We conclude the chapter with a summary.

Addressing Modes

In this section, we briefly look at the three addressing modes. Later sections give examples that use these addressing modes.

Register Addressing Mode

This is the commonly used addressing mode. In this addressing mode, the operands are located in the registers. For example, in the instruction

```
add     $t2,$t1,$t0
```

the two source operands are in $t1 and $t0. The result of the operation is also stored in a register ($t2 in this example). Most instructions, excluding the load and store, use this addressing mode. These instructions are encoded using the R-type format shown in Figure 4.2 on page 52.

Immediate Addressing Mode

In immediate addressing mode, the operand is stored in the instruction itself. This addressing mode is used for constants as shown in the following example.

```
addi    $t0,$t0,4
```

This instruction is encoded using the I-type instruction format (see Figure 4.2). As you can see from this format, the immediate value is limited to 16 bits. As a consequence, the constant is limited to a signed 16-bit value. The advantage of this addressing mode is that the immediate operand is fetched along with the instruction; it does not require a separate memory access.

Memory Addressing Modes

As discussed in Chapter 4, the bare machine provides only a single memory addressing mode, disp(Rx), where displacement disp is a signed, 16-bit immediate value. The address is computed by adding disp to the contents of register Rx. The virtual machine supported by the assembler provides additional addressing modes for load and store instructions to help in assembly language programming. Table 12.1 shows the addressing modes supported by the virtual machine. Like the immediate addressing mode, the I-type instruction format is used to encode this addressing mode (see Figure 4.2).

Next we look at some examples of the memory addressing modes. The following instruction

```
lw      $t0,($t1)
```

loads the 32-data at the address given by the $t1 register. In the following examples, we assume that the array is declared as

Table 12.1 Addressing modes

Format	Address computed as
(Rx)	Contents of register Rx
imm	Immediate value imm
imm(Rx)	imm + contents of Rx
symbol	Address of symbol
symbol± imm	Address of symbol ±imm
symbol± imm(Rx)	Address of symbol ±(imm + contents of Rx)

```
array:
     .word        15,16,17,18,19,20
```

We use the load instruction to illustrate the various memory addressing modes. We can also specify the address by using array as in the following example.

```
lw    $t1,array
```

This instruction loads the first word (i.e., value 15) into the $t1 register. We can specify an immediate constant as in the following example.

```
lw    $t1,4($t0)
```

If $t0 contains the address of array, this instruction loads the second element (i.e., value 16) into the $t1 register. Of course, we can do the same thing using the following instruction.

```
lw    $t1,array+4
```

In our next example, we look at the last addressing mode given in Table 12.1. In this addressing mode, the address is computed from three components: symbol±imm(Rx). Here is an example that uses these three components:

```
lw    $t2,array+4($t0)
sw    $t2,array+0($t0)
```

This two-instruction sequence copies the second element into the first element, assuming that $t0 contains 0. We use this instruction sequence in an example later (see Example 12.1 on page 219).

Note that most load and store instructions operate only on aligned data. The MIPS, however, provides some instructions for manipulating unaligned data.

Processing Arrays

Arrays are useful in organizing a collection of related data items, such as test marks of a class, salaries of employees, and so on. We have used arrays of characters to represent strings. Such arrays are one-dimensional: only a single subscript is necessary to access a character in the array. Next we discuss one-dimensional arrays. High-level languages support multidimensional arrays, which are discussed towards the end of this chapter.

One-Dimensional Arrays

A one-dimensional array of test marks can be declared in C as

```
int    test_marks [10];
```

In C, the subscript always starts at zero. Thus, the mark of the first student is given by `test_marks[0]` and that of the last student by `test_marks[9]`.

Array declaration in high-level languages specifies the five attributes:

- Name of the array (`test_marks`),
- Number of the elements (10),
- Element size (4 bytes),
- Type of element (integer), and
- Index range (0 to 9).

From this information, the amount of storage space required for the array can be easily calculated. Storage space in bytes is given by

$$\text{Storage space} = \text{number of elements} * \text{element size in bytes}.$$

In our example, it is equal to $10 * 4 = 40$ bytes. In assembly language, arrays are implemented by allocating the required amount of storage space. For example, we can declare the `test_marks` array as

```
test_marks:    .space    40
```

An array name can be assigned to this storage space. But that is all the support you get in assembly language! It is up to you as a programmer to "properly" access the array taking into account the element size and the range of subscripts.

You need to know how the array is stored in memory in order to access its elements. For one-dimensional arrays, representation of the array in memory is rather direct: array elements are stored linearly in the same order, as shown in Figure 12.1. In the remainder of this section, we use the convention used for arrays in C (i.e., subscripts are assumed to begin with 0).

To access an element we need to know its displacement in bytes relative to the beginning of the array. Because we know the element size in bytes, it is rather straightforward to compute the displacement from the subscript:

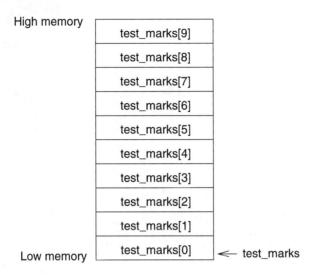

Figure 12.1 One-dimensional array storage representation.

$$\text{displacement} = \text{subscript} * \text{element size in bytes}.$$

For example, to access the sixth student's mark (i.e., subscript is 5), you have to use $5 * 4 = 20$ as the displacement into the `test_marks` array. Later we present an example that computes the sum of a one-dimensional integer array.

Multidimensional Arrays

Programs often require arrays of more than one dimension. For example, we need a two-dimensional array of size 50×3 to store test marks of a class of 50 students taking three tests during a semester. In this section, we discuss how two-dimensional arrays are represented and manipulated in the assembly language. Our discussion can be generalized to higher-dimensional arrays.

For example, a 5×3 array to store test marks can be declared in C as

```
int    class_marks[5][3];    /* 5 rows and 3 columns */
```

Storage representation of such arrays is not as direct as that for one-dimensional arrays. Because the memory is one-dimensional (i.e., linear array of bytes), we need to transform the two-dimensional structure to a one-dimensional structure. This transformation can be done in one of two common ways:

- Order the array elements row-by-row, starting with the first row,
- Order the array elements column-by-column, starting with the first column.

The first method, called the *row-major ordering*, is shown in Figure 12.2a. Row-major ordering is used in most high-level languages including C. The other method, called the

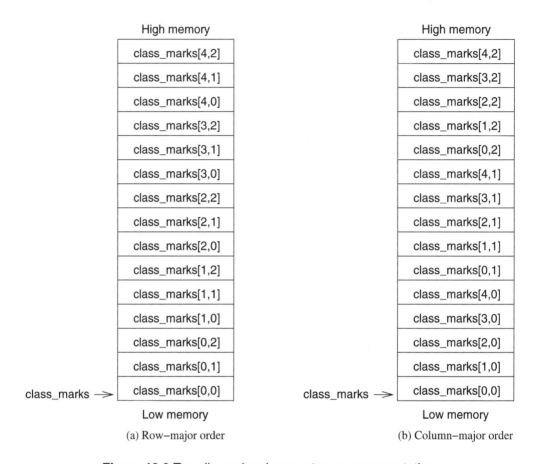

Figure 12.2 Two-dimensional array storage representation.

column-major ordering, is shown in Figure 12.2b. Column-major ordering is used in FORTRAN. In the remainder of this section, we focus on the row-major ordering scheme.

Why do we need to know the underlying storage representation? When we use a high-level language, we really do not have to bother about the storage representation. Access to arrays is provided by subscripts: one subscript for each dimension of the array. However, when using the assembly language, we need to know the storage representation in order to access individual elements of the array for reasons discussed next.

In assembly language, we can allocate storage space for the class_marks array as

```
class_marks:    .space    60
```

This statement simply allocates the 60 bytes required to store the array. Now we need a formula to translate row and column subscripts to the corresponding displacement. In C, which uses the row-major ordering with subscripts starting from zero, we can express displacement of an element at row i and column j as

$$\text{displacement} = (i \ast \text{COLUMNS} + j) \ast \text{ELEMENT\_SIZE},$$

where COLUMNS is the number of columns in the array and ELEMENT_SIZE is the number of bytes required to store an element. For example, we can compute the displacement of `class_marks[3,1]` as $(3 \ast 3 + 1) \ast 4 = 40$. Later we give an example to illustrate how two-dimensional arrays are manipulated.

Our First Program

This example shows how one-dimensional arrays can be manipulated. Program 12.1 finds the sum of the `test_marks` array and displays the result. The array is declared on lines 20 and 21. Each integer takes four bytes, therefore we use the `.space` directive to allocate 160 bytes of space for the array. The `.align` statement on line 19 aligns the array on a word boundary.

The main program prompts the user and reads the input values into the array. The read loop consists of lines 34–41. The input can be terminated either by entering a zero or by entering 40 values. These two conditions are tested on lines 40 and 41. The `$t1` register keeps track of the number of values entered. It is initialized to the array size (40 in our example) and decremented each time a value is entered. The read loop is terminated if this register is zero (line 41).

Notice the different addressing modes used in this loop. For example, the immediate addressing mode is on lines 38 and 39 to specify constants 4 and 1, respectively. The memory addressing mode is used on line 37. The register addressing mode is used in several instructions including lines 38, 39, and 46. The instructions on lines 38 and 39 use mixed-mode addressing: they use both register and immediate addressing mode. In contrast, the instruction on line 46 uses only the register-addressing mode.

Once the read loop is terminated, we compute the number of values entered by subtracting the value in `$t1` from 39 (see lines 45 and 46). This array size value is passed to the array sum procedure in `$a1`. The array pointer is passed via the `$a0` register (line 44). After returning from the procedure, the main program displays the sum with an appropriate message.

Program 12.1 A one-dimensional array sum example

```
1:  # Find the sum of an array              ARRAYSUM.ASM
2:  #
3:  # Objective: Finds the sum of an integer array.
4:  #      Input: Requests the array values.
5:  #     Output: Outputs the sum.
6:  #
7:  #     $a0 - array pointer
8:  #     $a1 - array size
9:  #     $v0 - array sum is returned
```

```
10:    #
11:    ################## Data segment ##################
12:          .data
13:    prompt:
14:          .asciiz      "Please enter the numbers: \n"
15:    sum_msg:
16:          .asciiz      "The sum is: "
17:    newline:
18:          .asciiz      "\n"
19:    .align 2
20:    test_marks:
21:          .space       160       # space for 40 integers
22:
23:    ################## Code segment ##################
24:          .text
25:          .globl main
26:    main:
27:          la   $a0,prompt       # prompt user for input
28:          li   $v0,4
29:          syscall
30:
31:          la   $t0,test_marks  # $t0 = array pointer
32:          li   $t1,40          # $t1 = array size
33:
34:    read_loop:
35:          li   $v0,5           # read the input number
36:          syscall
37:          sw   $v0,0($t0)
38:          addu $t0,$t0,4       # update array pointer
39:          subu $t1,$t1,1       # decrement loop count
40:          beqz $v0,exit_loop   # if number = 0, exit loop
41:          bnez $t1,read_loop   # if loop count is not 0,
42:                               # read more
43:    exit_loop:
44:          la   $a0,test_marks  # $a0 = array pointer
45:          li   $a1,39
46:          subu $a1,$a1,$t1     # $a1 = array size
47:          jal  array_sum
48:          move $s0,$v0
49:
50:          la   $a0,sum_msg     # write sum message
51:          li   $v0,4
52:          syscall
53:
54:          move $a0,$s0         # output sum
55:          li   $v0,1
56:          syscall
```

```
57:
58:          la    $a0,newline      # write newline
59:          li    $v0,4
60:          syscall
61:
62:          li    $v0,10           # exit
63:          syscall
64:
65:    #----------------------------------------------------
66:    # ARRAY_SUM receives the array pointer in $a0
67:    # and its size $a1 and returns their sum in $v0
68:    #      $t0 = used as a temporary
69:    #----------------------------------------------------
70:    array_sum:
71:          li    $v0,0            # sum = 0
72:    add_loop:
73:          beqz  $a1,exit_add_loop
74:          lw    $t0,($a0)
75:          add   $v0,$v0,$t0
76:          addu  $a0,$a0,4
77:          subu  $a1,$a1,1
78:          b     add_loop
79:    exit_add_loop:
80:          jr    $ra
```

The array_sum procedure is very similar to the read loop in the main program. Because we return the sum in $v0, we initialized it to zero using the li instruction (line 71). The sum loop on lines 72 to 78 is very similar to the read loop of the main program. It uses $a1 as the loop count and $t2 to read the array elements from the memory.

Illustrative Examples

This section gives two more examples to illustrate the application of the addressing modes described here. Both examples deal with processing arrays. The first example uses a one-dimensional array and the second one uses a two-dimensional array.

Example 12.1 *Cyclic permutation of an array.*

In this example, we permute a given sequence by one element. For example, if the given sequence is

    1,2,3,4,5,6,7,8,9

its cyclic permutation is defined to be

```
2,3,4,5,6,7,8,9,1
```

The program listing is given in Program 12.2. As in the last program, we declare an array of words using the .space directive on lines 16 and 17. The main program prompts the user for the input sequence. This input sequence is read into the array using the read loop on lines 30–37. It is very similar to the read loop we used in Program 12.1. The array size is computed as in the last program.

Program 12.2 A program to perform cyclic permutation of a sequence

```
 1:   # Performs cyclic permutation      CYCLIC_PERMUTE.ASM
 2:   #
 3:   # Objective: Performs cyclic permutation of an array.
 4:   #     Input: Requests array input (minimum 2 integers).
 5:   #     Output: Outputs permuted array.
 6:   #
 7:   ################## Data segment ##################
 8:         .data
 9:   prompt:
10:         .asciiz     "Please enter the numbers: \n"
11:   sum_msg:
12:         .asciiz     "The permuted array is: \n"
13:   newline:
14:         .asciiz     "\n"
15:   .align 2
16:   array:
17:         .space      160     # space for 40 integers
18:
19:   ################## Code segment ##################
20:         .text
21:         .globl main
22:   main:
23:         la   $a0,prompt     # prompt user for input
24:         li   $v0,4
25:         syscall
26:
27:         la   $t0,array      # $t0 = array pointer
28:         li   $t1,40         # $t1 = array size
29:
30:   read_loop:
31:         li   $v0,5          # read the input number
32:         syscall
33:         beqz $v0,exit_loop  # if number = 0, exit loop
34:         sw   $v0,0($t0)
35:         addu $t0,$t0,4      # update array pointer
36:         subu $t1,$t1,1      # decrement loop count
37:         bnez $t1,read_loop  # if loop count is not 0,
```

```
38:                                 # read more
39:   exit_loop:
40:           li    $t3,39
41:           subu  $t3,$t3,$t1    # $t3 = array size
42:
43:           li    $t0,0
44:           lw    $t1,array+0($t0)  # $t1 = first element
45:   permute:
46:           lw    $t2,array+4($t0)
47:           sw    $t2,array+0($t0)
48:           addu  $t0,$t0,4
49:           subu  $t3,$t3,1
50:           bnez  $t3,permute
51:
52:           sw    $t1,array($t0) # last element = first element
53:
54:           la    $a0,sum_msg     # write sum message
55:           li    $v0,4
56:           syscall
57:
58:           li    $t0,0           # $t0 = array byte index
59:
60:   write_loop:
61:           lw    $a0,array($t0)
62:           beqz  $a0,write_done
63:           li    $v0,1           # write the number
64:           syscall
65:           la    $a0,newline     # write newline
66:           li    $v0,4
67:           syscall
68:           addu  $t0,$t0,4       # update array byte index
69:           bne   $t0,160,write_loop
70:
71:   write_done:
72:           la    $a0,newline     # write newline
73:           li    $v0,4
74:           syscall
75:
76:           li    $v0,10          # exit
77:           syscall
```

The permutation is done using the loop on lines 45–50. We use $t0 to keep the offset in the array. It is initialized to zero on line 43. We copy the first element of the array into $t1 on line 44. After exiting the loop, we copy this value into the last element's place. We use the load instruction on line 46 to read an element, which is written into its previous position using the store instruction on line 47. Notice that we use an immediate value to specify the element we want to process. After copying, we update the offset in t0 by four to point to the next element (line 48). The loop index is decremented on line 49.

Once the permutation loop terminates, all the elements except the first element are permuted. All we have to do now is to store the first element we saved in $t1 at the end of the array. This is done on line 52. The permuted array is output by the write loop on lines 60–69.

Example 12.2 *Finding the sum of a column in a two-dimensional array.*

Consider the class_marks array representing the test scores of a class. For simplicity, assume that there are only 10 students in the class. Also, assume that the class is given 4 tests. As we discussed before, we can use a 10 × 4 array to store the marks. Each row represents the 4 test marks of a student in the class. The first column represents the marks of the first test; the second column represents the marks of the second test, and so on. The objective of this example is to find the sum of test marks specified by the user. The program listing is given in Program 12.3.

Program 12.3 A program to find the sum of a column in a two-dimensional array

```
 1:  # Find sum of a column in a 2-D array      COL_SUM.ASM
 2:  #
 3:  # Objective: Finds the sum of a column in a 2-D array.
 4:  #      Input: Requests the column number to be added.
 5:  #     Output: Outputs the sum of the column.
 6:  #
 7:  ################# Data segment #################
 8:          .data
 9:  try_again:
10:          .asciiz     "Invalid column number!\n"
11:  prompt:
12:          .asciiz     "Enter the column to add (1-4): \n"
13:  sum_msg:
14:          .asciiz     "The sum of the column is: "
15:  newline:
16:          .asciiz     "\n"
17:  class_marks:        # 10X4 matrix
18:          .word       10,11,12,13
19:          .word       20,21,22,23
20:          .word       30,31,32,33
21:          .word       40,41,42,43
22:          .word       50,51,52,53
23:          .word       60,61,62,63
24:          .word       70,71,72,73
25:          .word       80,81,82,83
26:          .word       90,91,92,93
27:          .word       95,96,97,98
```

```
28:
29:    ################## Code segment ##################
30:           .text
31:           .globl main
32:    main:
33:           la    $a0,prompt      # prompt user for input
34:           li    $v0,4
35:           syscall
36:
37:           li    $v0,5           # read the column number
38:           syscall
39:
40:           blez  $v0,invalid     # validate column number
41:           ble   $v0,4,valid
42:    invalid:
43:           la    $a0,try_again   # error message
44:           li    $v0,4
45:           syscall
46:           b     main
47:
48:    valid:
49:           subu  $t2,$v0,1
50:           sll   $t2,$t2,2       # column number * 4
51:           li    $t3,10          # number of rows
52:           li    $t0,0           # sum = 0
53:    add_loop:
54:           lw    $t1,class_marks($t2)
55:           add   $t0,$t0,$t1     # update sum
56:           addu  $t2,$t2,16      # add number of bytes in a row
57:           subu  $t3,$t3,1       # decrement loop index
58:           bnez  $t3,add_loop
59:
60:           la    $a0,sum_msg     # write sum message
61:           li    $v0,4
62:           syscall
63:
64:           move  $a0,$t0         # output sum
65:           li    $v0,1
66:           syscall
67:
68:           la    $a0,newline     # write newline
69:           li    $v0,4
70:           syscall
71:
72:           li    $v0,10          # exit
73:           syscall
```

The two-dimensional array (10 × 4) is declared and initialized on lines 17–27. The user is prompted to enter the test number (i.e., the column number) for which the sum is to be computed. This is done by using the `read_int` system call (see lines 37 and 38). The input column number is validated on lines 40 and 41. For a valid column number, it should be between 1 and 4. If an invalid test number is given, the user is prompted again after reporting the error (lines 43–46).

The column number is converted into column index by decrementing it on line 49. Thus the valid column index ranges from 0 to 3. The column index is converted to the byte displacement by multiplying the column number by 4. This done by shifting left by two bit positions rather than by multiplication on line 50. The test sum is maintained in `$t0`, which is initialized to zero on line 52.

The add loop is similar to the add loop we used in Program 12.1. The one major difference, due to the two-dimensional array, is the constant added to move the pointer to the next element. Because we are interested in adding the column, each successive element that we want to add is separated by 16 bytes, equivalent to the number of bytes in a row, as shown on line 56. The rest of the program is straightforward to follow.

Summary

We have described the addressing modes that we can use to write the assembly language programs. Some of these modes are provided by the assembler, not by the processor. We have also discussed how arrays are represented and manipulated in the assembly language. We looked at one-dimensional and two-dimensional arrays. However, our discussion can easily be extended to higher-dimensional arrays.

We have presented several examples to illustrate the use of these addressing modes. These examples have shown how the memory addressing modes are used in writing the assembly language programs. However, MIPS being a RISC processor supports only a limited number of memory addressing modes compared to CISC processors. The last example brings out the drawback of providing simple addressing modes. To access elements of an array, we have to work with byte displacement. In contrast, CISC processors such as Pentium provide support to access arrays using indices.

13

Arithmetic Instructions

This chapter describes the arithmetic instructions of the MIPS instruction set in detail. We have introduced some of the basic arithmetic operations such as add and subtract in Chapter 10. Here we provide a thorough discussion of the arithmetic instructions, including the pseudoinstructions supported by the assembler. We then give several examples to illustrate their use in assembly language programs. We conclude the chapter with a summary.

Introduction

The MIPS instruction set supports the four basic arithmetic operations: addition, subtraction, multiplication, and division. We have already introduced the basic add and subtract instructions. These instructions can potentially cause overflow/underflow problems. The MIPS architecture deals with them by generating an exception.

In addition to the add and subtract instructions, two pseudoinstructions are provided for signed integers. One computes the absolute value and the other reverses the sign of a number (i.e., a positive number is converted into a negative number and vice versa).

Multiplication is more complicated than addition or subtraction for these reasons: (i) it produces a result that is double the size of the input operands. For example, multiplying two 32-bit numbers produces a 64-bit result. (ii) We need two separate instructions to operate signed and unsigned numbers. In contrast, the add instruction can be used with both signed and unsigned numbers. We give details on how the MIPS instruction set handles these complications.

The division operation is even more complicated than multiplication for the following reasons: (i) it produces two results: a quotient and a remainder. For example, dividing 200 by 15 results in a quotient of 13 and remainder of 5. (ii) In multiplication, there is no overflow problem. The result always fits the 64-bit destination. In the division operation, there is a potential overflow problem that needs to be handled. For example, divide by zero leads to such a situation. In fact, it need not be zero; any number that is small enough to produce a quotient that is bigger than the destination can cause the overflow problem. Of course, as with multiplication, we need two separate instructions to operate on signed and unsigned numbers.

As shown in Figure 4.1, two special registers—LO and HI—are used to meet the specific requirements of the multiply and divide instructions. Each of these two special registers is 32 bits long. In the multiplication instruction, these two registers together hold the 64-bit result. In the division instructions, the quotient is placed in the LO register and remainder in the HI register.

In the following sections, we describe these four arithmetic instruction groups in detail. Following this discussion, we give several examples to show how these arithmetic instructions are used in assembly language programs.

Addition

The basic addition instruction

        add   Rdest,Rsrc1,Rsrc2

adds the contents of `Rsrc1` and `Rsrc2` and stores the result in `Rdest`. The numbers are treated as signed integers. In the case of an overflow, an overflow exception is generated. We can use `addu` if no overflow exception is needed. Except for this, there is no difference between the `add` and `addu` instructions.

The second operand can be specified as an immediate 16-bit number. The format is

        addi   Rdest,Rsrc1,imm

The 16-bit value is sign-extended to 32 bits and added to the contents of `Rsrc1`. As in the `add` instruction, an overflow exception is generated; use `addiu` if the overflow exception is not needed.

For convenience, assembler provides a pseudoinstruction that can take a register or an immediate value as the second source operand. The format is

        add[†]   Rdest,Rsrc1,Src2

where `Src2` can be either a 16-bit immediate value or a register. We can use `addu`[†] if the overflow exception is not needed.

Subtraction

The subtract instruction

        sub   Rdest,Rsrc1,Rsrc2

subtracts the contents of `Rsrc2` from `Rsrc1` (i.e., `Rsrc1 − Rsrc2`). The result is stored in `Rdest`. The contents of the two source registers are treated as signed numbers and an integer overflow exception is generated. We use `subu` if this exception is not required.

There is no immediate version of the subtract instruction. It is not really needed as we can treat subtraction as an addition of a negative number. However, we can use the assembler pseudoinstruction to operate on immediate values. The format is

```
sub†     Rdest,Rsrc1,Src2
```

where `Src2` can be a 16-bit immediate value or a register. If `Src2` is an immediate value, it uses the add instruction. For example, the pseudoinstruction

```
sub     $t0,$t1,15
```

is translated as

```
addi    $8,$9,-15
```

Note that `$t0` and `$t1` map to the `$8` and `$9` registers, respectively.

To negate a value, we can use the assembler pseudoinstruction `neg` for signed numbers. The instruction

```
neg†     Rdest,Rsrc
```

negates the contents of `Rsrc` and stores the result in `Rdest`. An overflow exception is generated if the value is -2^{31}. Negation without the overflow exception (`negu†`) is also available.

As noted, `neg` is not a processor instruction; the SPIM assembler translates the negate instruction using `sub` as

```
sub     Rdest,$0,Rsrc
```

`abs` is another pseudoinstruction that is useful to get the absolute value. The format is

```
abs†     Rdest,Rsrc
```

This pseudoinstruction is implemented as

```
bgez     Rsrc,skip
sub      Rdest,$0,Rsrc
skip:
```

The `bgez` instruction compares the value in `Rsrc` with zero. If it is greater than or equal to zero, it skips the `sub` instruction; otherwise, it subtracts the number in `Rsrc` from zero to reverse the sign. In the translation, the `bgez` instruction actually uses an offset of 8 to affect the jump as shown below:

```
bgez     Rsrc,8
```

We give a detailed discussion of the branch instructions in the next chapter.

Multiplication

MIPS provides two multiply instructions: one for signed numbers (`mult`) and the other for unsigned numbers (`multu`). The instruction

```
mult    Rsrc1,Rsrc2
```

multiplies the contents of `Rsrc1` with the contents of `Rsrc2`. The numbers are treated as signed numbers. The 64-bit result is placed in two special registers LO and HI. The LO register receives the lower-order word and the higher-order word is placed in the HI register. No integer overflow exception is generated. The `multu` instruction has the same format but treats the source operands as unsigned numbers.

There are instructions to move data between these special LO/HI registers and general registers. The instruction `mfhi` (move from HI)

```
mfhi    Rdest
```

moves the contents of the HI register to the general register `Rdest`. Use `mflo` to move data from the LO register. For movement of data into these special registers, use `mthi` (move to HI) or `mtlo` (move to LO). For example,

```
mtlo    Rsrc
```

copies the value in the `Rsrc` register into the LO register.

The assembler multiply pseudoinstruction can be used to place the result directly in a destination register. A limitation of the pseudoinstruction is that it stores only the 32-bit result, not the 64-bit value. Note that multiplication of two 32-bit numbers can produce a 64-bit result. We can use these pseudoinstructions if we know that the result can fit in 32 bits. The instruction

```
mul†    Rdest,Rsrc1,Src2
```

places the 32-bit result of the product of `Rsrc1` and `Src2` in `Rdest`. The `Src2` operand can be a register or an immediate value. This instruction does not generate an overflow exception. If an overflow exception is required, use the `mulo` instruction. Both these instructions treat the numbers as signed. To multiply two unsigned numbers, use the `mulou` instruction (multiply with overflow unsigned).

The `mul` pseudoinstruction is translated as

```
mult    Rsrc1,Src2
mflo    Rdest
```

when `Src2` is a register. If `Src2` is an immediate value, it uses an additional `ori` instruction. For example, the pseudoinstruction

```
mul     $a0,$a1,32
```

is translated into

```
ori    $1,$0,32
mult   $5,$1
mflo   $4
```

Remember that $a0 maps to $4, $a1 to $5, and $at to $1. This example shows how the assembler uses the $at register to translate pseudoinstructions.

Division

As with the multiply instructions, we can use div and divu instructions to divide signed and unsigned numbers, respectively. The instruction

```
div    Rsrc1,Rsrc2
```

divides the contents of Rsrc1 by the contents of Rsrc2 (i.e., Rsrc1/Rsrc2). The contents of both source registers are treated as signed numbers. The result of the division is placed in LO and HI registers. The LO register receives the quotient and the HI register receives the remainder. No integer overflow exception is generated.

The result of the operation is undefined if the divisor is zero. Thus, a check for a zero divisor should precede this instruction.

Assembler provides three-operand divide pseudoinstructions similar to the multiply instructions. The instruction

```
div†    Rdest,Rsrc1,Src2
```

places the quotient of the division Rsrc1/Src2 in Rdest. The two numbers are treated as signed integers. As in the other instructions, Src2 can be a register or an immediate value. For unsigned numbers, use the divu† pseudoinstruction. The quotient is rounded towards zero. Overflow is signalled when dividing -2^{31} by -1 as the quotient is greater than $2^{31} - 1$. To see how the assembler implements this pseudoinstruction, let's look at the following.

```
div  $t0,$t1,$t2
```

This pseudoinstruction is translated as

```
bne    $10, $0, 8
break  $0
div    $9, $10
mflo   $8
```

The first instruction compares the divisor in $t2 (mapped to register $10) with zero. If it is equal to zero, it causes exception 0 using the break instruction. If it is not equal to zero, the bne instruction transfers control to the div instruction using offset 8. Because the div instruction leaves the quotient in the LO register, the last instruction moves this to the destination register $t0, which is mapped to register $8.

Assembler generates the real div instruction if we use

```
div     $0,Rsrc1,Src2.
```

To get the remainder instead of the quotient, use

```
rem†    Rdest,Rsrc1,Src2
```

for signed numbers. This pseudoinstruction is implemented like the `div` pseudoinstruction except that it uses `mfhi` instead of the `mflo` instruction.

Our First Program

As our first example of the chapter, let us write a program to compute a factorial using iteration. The factorial of n (represented by $n!$) is defined as follows.

$$\text{Fact}(0) = 1$$
$$\text{Fact}(n) = \prod_{i=1}^{n} i \quad \text{for } n > 0$$

For example, Fact(5) is

$$5! = 1 \times 2 \times 3 \times 4 \times 5 = 120.$$

This leads us to an iterative algorithm in which a single loop can compute the factorial. There is also a recursive version that we discuss in Chapter 16.

Program 13.1 shows the listing of the factorial program that receives a positive integer and outputs its factorial. The main program prompts the user for a positive integer on lines 26–28. The input number is read using the `read_integer` function on lines 31–33. We use the `bgez` instruction to check if the input number is greater than or equal to zero (line 35).

Once the number is validated, it calls the factorial procedure `fact1`. This procedure returns the factorial value in `$v0`, which is saved in `$t0` as `$v0` is needed for `syscalls`. This value is output with an appropriate message.

Program 13.1 A program to compute factorial (iterative version)

```
 1:  # Finds factorial of a number                    FACTORIAL1.ASM
 2:  #
 3:  # Objective: Computes factorial of an integer.
 4:  #            Uses iteration.
 5:  #     Input: Requests an integer n.
 6:  #    Output: Outputs n!
 7:  #
 8:  #      $a0 - used to pass n
 9:  #      $v0 - used to return result
10:  #
11:  ################## Data segment ######################
12:         .data
```

```
13:   prompt:
14:         .asciiz       "Please enter a positive integer: \n"
15:   out_msg:
16:         .asciiz       "The factorial is: "
17:   error_msg:
18:         .asciiz       "Not a positive number. Try again.\n "
19:   newline:
20:         .asciiz       "\n"
21:
22:   ################## Code segment ######################
23:         .text
24:         .globl main
25:   main:
26:         la    $a0,prompt          # prompt user for input
27:         li    $v0,4
28:         syscall
29:
30:   try_again:
31:         li    $v0,5                # read number into $a0
32:         syscall
33:         move  $a0,$v0
34:
35:         bgez  $a0,num_OK
36:         la    $a0,error_msg        # write error message
37:         li    $v0,4
38:         syscall
39:         b     try_again
40:
41:   num_OK:
42:         jal   fact1
43:         move  $t0,$v0
44:
45:         la    $a0,out_msg          # write output message
46:         li    $v0,4
47:         syscall
48:
49:         move  $a0,$t0              # output factorial
50:         li    $v0,1
51:         syscall
52:
53:         la    $a0,newline          # write newline
54:         li    $v0,4
55:         syscall
56:
57:         li    $v0,10               # exit
58:         syscall
59:
```

```
60:     #------------------------------------------------------
61:     # FACT1 receives n in $a0 and returns n! in $v0.
62:     # It uses iteration to compute n!.
63:     #------------------------------------------------------
64:     fact1:
65:             li      $v0,1
66:             ble     $a0,1,fact_done
67:     loop:
68:             mulou $v0,$a0,$v0           # $v0 = $a0*$v0
69:             subu    $a0,$a0,1           # n = n-1
70:             bgt     $a0,1,loop          # loop back if n>1
71:     fact_done:
72:             jr      $ra
```

The fact1 procedure receives n in the $a0 register and returns $n!$ in the $v0 register. The latter register is initialized to 1 on line 65. If $n \leq 1$, the procedure is terminated as $v0 contains the result; otherwise, the loop on lines 67–70 computes $n!$. We use the mulou to multiply two unsigned numbers (line 68).

Illustrative Examples

In this section we present three examples to further illustrate the application of the arithmetic instructions discussed in this chapter.

Example 13.1 *Add individual digits of a number.*

This example shows how individual digits of an integer can be added. For example, if the input is 123456, it outputs $1 + 2 + 3 + 4 + 5 + 6 = 21$. We have done another version of this example in Example 10.1 on page 174. In that example, we read the input as a string, not as a number. Here we read the input as a number. In this case, to perform this addition, we need to separate individual digits. This can be done by successively dividing the number by 10 as shown here:

		Quotient	Remainder
123456/10	=	12345	6
12345/10	=	1234	5
1234/10	=	123	4
123/10	=	12	3
12/10	=	1	2
1/10	=	0	1

As shown in this example, we divide the number by 10 to separate the least significant digit. The quotient is repeatedly divided until it is zero. Then we can add the remainders to get the sum we want. Our implementation essentially follows this algorithm.

Program 13.2 A program to add individual digits of an integer

```
 1:   # Add individual digits of a number        ADDIGITS2.ASM
 2:   #
 3:   # Objective: To add individual digits of an integer.
 4:   #            To use the arithmetic instructions.
 5:   #     Input: Requests a number from the user.
 6:   #    Output: Outputs the sum.
 7:   #
 8:   #      t0 - holds the quotient
 9:   #      t1 - holds constant 10
10:   #      t2 - maintains the running sum
11:   #      t3 - holds the remainder
12:   #
13:   ################## Data segment ###################
14:
15:          .data
16:   number_prompt:
17:          .asciiz   "Please enter an integer: \n"
18:   out_msg:
19:          .asciiz   "The sum of individual digits is: "
20:   newline:
21:          .asciiz       "\n"
22:
23:   ################## Code segment ###################
24:          .text
25:          .globl main
26:   main:
27:          la    $a0,number_prompt  # prompt user for input
28:          li    $v0,4
29:          syscall
30:
31:          li    $v0,5             # read input as an integer
32:          syscall                 # into $t0
33:          move  $t0,$v0
34:
35:          abs   $t0,$t0           # get absolute value
36:
37:          la    $a0,out_msg       # write output message
38:          li    $v0,4
39:          syscall
40:
41:          li    $t1,10            # $t1 holds divisor 10
42:          li    $t2,0             # init sum to zero
43:   loop:
44:          divu  $t0,$t1           # $t0/$t1
45:          # leaves quotient in LO and remainder in HI
```

```
46:          mflo   $t0              # move quotient to $t0
47:          mfhi   $t3              # move remainder to $t3
48:          addu   $t2,$t2,$t3      # add remainder to total
49:          beqz   $t0,exit_loop    # exit loop if quotient is 0
50:          b      loop
51: exit_loop:
52:          move   $a0,$t2          # output sum
53:          li     $v0,1
54:          syscall
55:
56:          la     $a0,newline      # write newline
57:          li     $v0,4
58:          syscall
59:
60:          li     $v0,10           # exit
61:          syscall
```

The main program, shown in Program 13.2, prompts for the input number and reads it into the $t0 register. It then uses the abs instruction to convert this into a positive number (line 35).

The sum is computed using the loop on lines 43–50. Before entering the loop, we initialize $t1 to 10 (line 41) and $t2, which holds the sum, to 0 (line 42). The divide instruction on line 44 leaves the quotient in LO and remainder in HI registers. We use mflo and mfhi instructions to move the quotient and remainder to the $t0 and $t3 registers, respectively (lines 46 and 47). After adding the remainder to the sum (line 48), we check if the quotient is zero (line 49). We exit the loop if it is zero. After exiting the loop, the program prints the sum in the $t2 register.

Example 13.2 *String-to-number conversion to read an integer.*

In this example, we show how integers are read from the input. Note that the input value is given as a sequence of characters. For example, the number 158 is given as three characters "1", "5", and "8". To convert this to an integer, we need to first convert each character to its numeric equivalent. Then we add this value to a running sum after multiplying it by 10. The conversion process is illustrated here for 158:

Input digit	Numeric value	Number = Number * 10 + Numeric value
Initial value	—	0
"1" (0x31)	1	$0 * 10 + 1 = 1$
"5" (0x35)	5	$1 * 10 + 5 = 15$
"8" (0x38)	8	$15 * 10 + 8 = 158$

The pseudocode for the conversion process is given below:

```
convert_int (numString)
    index := 0
    number := 0
    while (TRUE)
        char := numString[index]
        if ((char ≠ linefeed) AND (char ≠ NULL))
        then
            number := number * 10 + (char AND 0xF)
        else
            goto convert_done
        end if
        index := index + 1
    end while
convert_done:
    return
end convert_int
```

The `convert_int` procedure implements this algorithm as shown in Program 13.3. The main program simply requests a number and reads it as a string using the `read_string` system call (lines 29–32). A pointer to this string is passed to the `convert_int` procedure via `$a0`.

Program 13.3 A program to read integers

```
 1: # Converts a digit string to integer          GETINT.ASM
 2: #
 3: # Objective: Converts a string of digits into integer.
 4: #      Input: Requests an integer. Reads it as a string.
 5: #     Output: Outputs the integer.
 6: #
 7: #      $a0 - used to pass the string pointer
 8: #      $v0 - used to return the result
 9: #
10: ################### Data segment ######################
11:         .data
12: prompt:
13:         .asciiz     "Please enter a positive integer: \n"
14: out_msg:
15:         .asciiz     "The number is: "
16: newline:
17:         .asciiz     "\n"
18: in_number:
```

```
19:          .space      11
20:
21:  ################## Code segment ######################
22:          .text
23:          .globl main
24:  main:
25:          la    $a0,prompt          # prompt user for input
26:          li    $v0,4
27:          syscall
28:
29:          la    $a0,in_number       # read input string
30:          li    $a1,11              # buffer length in $a1
31:          li    $v0,8
32:          syscall
33:
34:          la    $a0,in_number
35:          jal   convert_int
36:          move  $t0,$v0
37:
38:          la    $a0,out_msg         # write output message
39:          li    $v0,4
40:          syscall
41:
42:          move  $a0,$t0             # output integer
43:          li    $v0,1
44:          syscall
45:
46:          la    $a0,newline         # write newline
47:          li    $v0,4
48:          syscall
49:
50:          li    $v0,10              # exit
51:          syscall
52:
53:  #----------------------------------------------------
54:  # CONVERT_INT receives a pointer to a string in $a0
55:  # and returns the number in $v0.
56:  #     $t1 - used as a temporary
57:  #----------------------------------------------------
58:  convert_int:
59:          li    $v0,0               # number = 0
60:  loop:
61:          lbu   $t1,($a0)
62:          beq   $t1,0xA,done        # if linefeed or
63:          beqz  $t1,done            # NULL, we are done
64:          and   $t1,$t1,0xF         # mask off upper bits
65:          mulou $v0,$v0,10          # number = number * 10
```

```
66:           addu    $v0,$v0,$t1       # add the current digit
67:           addu    $a0,$a0,1         # update pointer
68:           b       loop
69:   done:
70:           jr      $ra
```

The convert_int procedure uses $v0 to keep the number. It is initialized to zero on line 59. The conversion loop consists of lines 60–68. Each character from the input string is read into $t1 (line 61). Note that the input string, read by the read_string syscall, may consist of the linefeed (0xA) character if the number of characters entered is less than the buffer length. On the other hand, if 10 digits are entered, there will not be a linefeed character. In both cases, the string is terminated by a NULL character. Thus, the end-of-string test should check for a linefeed or NULL character. These two conditions are tested on lines 62 and 63. If either of them is true, the conversion process is done.

The character in $t1 is converted to its numeric equivalent by masking the upper four bits (line 64). The required multiplication (by 10) is done on line 65 and the numeric value of the current digit (in $t1) is added on line 66. The index is updated on line 67. When the loop is terminated, we simply return as the value is in the $v0 register.

Example 13.3 *Number-to-string conversion to display an integer.*

Our objective here is to write a procedure that displays a signed 32-bit integer. In order to do this, we have to separate individual digits of the number to be displayed and convert each digit to its ASCII representation. The steps involved are illustrated by the following example, which assumes that the number is 108.

separate 1 → convert to ASCII → 0x31 → display
separate 0 → convert to ASCII → 0x30 → display
separate 8 → convert to ASCII → 0x38 → display

Separating individual digits is the heart of the procedure. This step is surprisingly simple! All we have to do is repeatedly divide the number by 10, as shown here:

		Quotient	Remainder
108/10	=	10	8
10/10	=	1	0
1/10	=	0	1

The only problem with this step is that the digits come out in the reverse order of display. Therefore, we need to buffer the digits and reverse them before displaying. The pseudocode for the process_int procedure is shown below:

```
process_int (number, Buffer)
    index := 0
    if (number is negative)
    then
        Buffer[index] := '−'
        index := index + 1
        number := ABS(number)        {get absolute value}
    end if
    repeat
        quotient := number/10        {integer division}
        remainder := number % 10   {% is modulo operator}
        {save the ASCII character equivalent of remainder}
        Buffer[index] := remainder OR 0x30
        index := index + 1
        number := quotient
    until (number = 0)
    string_reverse (Buffer)
    return
end process_int
```

The program listing is given in Program 13.4. As in the other programs, the main program handles the user interface. It reads the input number using the read_int system call (lines 29–31). It passes the integer in $a1 and a buffer pointer in $a0 to the process_int procedure.

Program 13.4 A program to output 32-bit integers

```
 1:  # Converts an integer to a digit string        PUTINT.ASM
 2:  #
 3:  # Objective: Converts an integer into a string of digits.
 4:  #      Input: Requests an integer.
 5:  #     Output: Outputs the digit string.
 6:  #
 7:  #     $a0 - used to pass the string pointer
 8:  #     $a1 - used to pass the number
 9:  #
10:  ################## Data segment #####################
11:          .data
12:  prompt:
13:          .asciiz     "Please enter a positive integer: \n"
14:  out_msg:
15:          .asciiz     "The number is: "
16:  newline:
17:          .asciiz     "\n"
```

```
18:   out_number:
19:         .space      11
20:
21:   ################## Code segment #####################
22:         .text
23:         .globl main
24:   main:
25:         la    $a0,prompt          # prompt user for input
26:         li    $v0,4
27:         syscall
28:
29:         li    $v0,5               # read number into $a1
30:         syscall
31:         move  $a1,$v0
32:
33:         la    $a0,out_number      # $a0 = string pointer
34:         jal   process_int
35:
36:         la    $a0,out_msg         # write output message
37:         li    $v0,4
38:         syscall
39:
40:         la    $a0,out_number      # output number
41:         li    $v0,4
42:         syscall
43:
44:         la    $a0,newline         # write newline
45:         li    $v0,4
46:         syscall
47:
48:         li    $v0,10              # exit
49:         syscall
50:
51:   #--------------------------------------------------------
52:   # PROCESS_INT receives a pointer to a string and an
53:   # integer. It converts the number to string form and
54:   # returns it in the string.
55:   #     $a0 - string pointer
56:   #     $a1 - integer to be converted (also quotient)
57:   #     $t0 - pointer to string for string reverse
58:   #     $t1 - remainder
59:   #--------------------------------------------------------
60:   process_int:
61:         sub   $sp,$sp,4           # save $ra
62:         sw    $ra,0($sp)
63:
64:         # $t0 keeps string pointer (for string reverse)
```

```
65:          # if the number is +ve, this is the value passed
66:          # if -ve, $t0 is advanced past the -ve sign
67:          move  $t0,$a0
68:
69:          bgez  $a1,positive
70:          abs   $a1,$a1
71:          li    $t0,'-'            # $t0 is used as a temp
72:          sb    $t0,($a0)
73:          addu  $a0,$a0,1
74:          # save this position for string reverse
75:          move  $t0,$a0
76:
77: positive:
78:          li    $t2,10             # $t2 = divisor
79: loop:
80:          divu  $a1,$t2
81:          # div leaves quotient in LO and remainder in HI
82:          mflo  $a1
83:          mfhi  $t1
84:          or    $t1,$t1,0x30       # convert digit to char.
85:          sb    $t1,($a0)
86:          addu  $a0,$a0,1
87:          bnez  $a1,loop           # if quotient is not 0,
88:                                   # loop
89:          sb    $a1,($a0)          # append NULL ($a1=0)
90:
91:          # now reverse the string (excluding the -ve sign)
92:          move  $a0,$t0
93:          jal   string_reverse
94:
95:          lw    $ra,0($sp)         # restore $ra
96:          add   $sp,$sp,4
97:          jr    $ra
98:
99:  #-----------------------------------------------------------
100: # STRING_REVERSE receives a pointer to a string in $a0
101: # and reverses the string
102: #-----------------------------------------------------------
103: string_reverse:
104:          move  $t1,$a0            # $t1 points to string
105: loop1:
106:          lbu   $t2,($t1)
107:          beqz  $t2,done           # if NULL, we are done
108:          addu  $t1,$t1,1
109:          b     loop1
110: done:
111:          sub   $t1,$t1,1          # $t1 = end of string
```

```
112:   reverse_loop:
113:          bleu   $t1,$a0,done_reverse
114:          lbu    $t2,($a0)             #
115:          lbu    $t3,($t1)             # exchange
116:          sb     $t2,($t1)             # characters
117:          sb     $t3,($a0)             #
118:          addu   $a0,$a0,1
119:          subu   $t1,$t1,1
120:          b      reverse_loop
121:   done_reverse:
122:          jr     $ra
```

The process_int procedure follows the logic of the pseudocode. The code on lines 70–75 is executed if the number is negative. This test is done by bgez on line 69. The repeat loop is implemented on lines 79–87. Because the divide instruction (on line 80) leaves the quotient and remainder in the LO and HI registers, we use mflo and mfhi to move these values to general registers (lines 82 and 83). The loop termination condition (i.e., quotient = 0) is tested on line 87. After exiting the loop, it calls the string_reverse procedure to reverse the string for output.

The string_reverse procedure follows the pseudocode shown below:

> string_reverse (Buffer)
>   left := 0
>   right := 0
>   {Move right to the end of string}
>   **while** (Buffer[right] $\neq$ NULL)
>   right := right + 1
>   **end while**
>   right := right $-$ 1 {back up to point to the end of string}
>   **while** (left < right)
>   Buffer[left] $\Leftrightarrow$ Buffer[right]   {exchange}
>   left := left + 1
>   right := right $-$ 1
>   **end while**
>   return
> end string_reverse

The left index is initialized to point to the left-hand side of the string. The right index is moved to the last digit in the string by the first while loop. Once the left and right are pointing to the beginning and end of the string, we exchange the values. Then the indexes left and right are updated (left is incremented and right is decremented). We repeat this process as long as left is less than right (the continuation condition for the second while loop). The string_reverse procedure implements this algorithm in a straightforward way. The first `while` loop is implemented on lines 105–109 and the second `while` loop on lines 112–120.

Summary

We have presented details on the arithmetic instructions. The MIPS instruction set supports the basic add, subtract, multiply, and divide operations. The multiply and divide instructions place the result in special HI and LO registers. The instruction set provides instructions that move data between these registers and the general registers. Although add and subtract instructions work on both signed and unsigned numbers, multiply and divide operations have separate instructions to work on signed and unsigned numbers. We have used several examples to illustrate the application of these instructions.

14

Conditional Execution

Conditional execution is important to alter the control flow from the default sequential execution. The MIPS architecture provides several instructions to facilitate conditional execution. We have already seen some of these instructions including the unconditional and conditional branch instructions. In addition, procedure invocation and return also alter control flow. We briefly introduced some of these instructions in previous chapters. This chapter gives a complete discussion of these instructions.

The target address of these flow-altering instructions can be specified either directly in the instruction or indirectly via a register. In previous chapters, we used direct specification for jumps and procedure calls. However, we used indirect specification to return from a procedure. Most jumps and procedure calls use the direct specification. However, sometimes it is useful to specify the target address indirectly via a register. We discuss such indirect jumps and procedure calls toward the end of the chapter. We conclude the chapter with a summary.

Introduction

Modern high-level languages provide a variety of decision structures. These structures include selection structures such as `if-then-else` and iterative structures such as `while` and `for` loops. Assembly language, being a low-level language, does not provide these structures directly. However, assembly language provides several basic instructions that could be used to construct these high-level language selection and iteration structures. For example, the following code

```
        li      $t2,50
loop:
        addu    $t0,$t0,$t1
        sub     $t2,$t2,1
        bnez    $t2,loop
```

implements a loop that iterates 50 times.

In this example, we implemented the loop using a conditional branch instruction. Some instruction architectures provide loop instructions to implement the iterative construct. For example, the Intel IA-32 architecture provides a loop instruction that decrements the loop index and jumps to the target if it is not zero. Thus, the loop instruction essentially is equivalent to the two-instruction sequence sub/bnez in our code. In fact, on Pentium, the two-instruction sequence is faster than the single loop instruction. As a result, the loop instruction is not used to optimize the code. This example reinforces the reasons we discussed in Chapter 3 for not using complex instructions.

The MIPS assembly language provides instructions for unconditional and conditional jumps, procedure calls, and so on. We briefly introduced some of these instructions in Chapters 10 and 11. Our discussion in this chapter complements that discussion.

There are two distinct ways by which the target address of an instruction such as branch can be specified: *direct* and *indirect*. In direct specification, the target address is specified directly as part of the instruction. For example, the conditional branch instruction (bnez) in the previous code fragment is encoded as

```
bne     $10,$0,−8
```

where −8 is the relative offset of the branch instruction. In indirect target specification, the address is given via a register. We have used indirect jumps to return from a procedure. For example, we used the instruction

```
jr      $ra
```

to return from a procedure where the return address is in the $ra register. In general, we can use any register for indirect jumps. Similarly, procedures can also be invoked via indirect target specification. We look at this topic towards the end of the chapter.

The MIPS assembly language also provides several compare instructions. These instructions are discussed next.

Comparison Instructions

Several comparison pseudoinstructions are available. All these instructions compare the contents of two registers and if the specified condition such as "less than" is true, the destination register is set to 1; otherwise, it is cleared to zero. For example, the instruction slt (Set on Less Than)

```
slt†     Rdest,Rsrc1,Rsrc2
```

sets Rdest to one if the contents of Rsrc1 are less than the contents of Rsrc2; otherwise, Rdest is set to zero. This instruction treats the contents of Rsrc1 and Rsrc2 as signed numbers. To test for the "less than" relationship, slt subtracts contents of Rsrc2 from the contents of Rsrc1.

Table 14.1 MIPS comparison instructions

Instruction	Description
seq[†] Rdest,Rsrc1,Src2	Rdest is set to one if contents of Rsrc1 and Src2 are equal; otherwise, Rdest is set to zero.
sgt[†] Rdest,Rsrc1,Src2	Rdest is set to one if contents of Rsrc1 are greater than Src2; otherwise, Rdest is set to zero. Source operands are treated as signed numbers.
sgtu[†] Rdest,Rsrc1,Src2	Same as sgt except that the source operands are treated as unsigned numbers.
sge[†] Rdest,Rsrc1,Src2	Rdest is set to one if contents of Rsrc1 are greater than or equal to Src2; otherwise, Rdest is set to zero. Source operands are treated as signed numbers.
sgeu[†] Rdest,Rsrc1,Src2	Same as sge except that the source operands are treated as unsigned numbers.
slt[†] Rdest,Rsrc1,Src2	Rdest is set to one if contents of Rsrc1 are less than Src2; otherwise, Rdest is set to zero. Source operands are treated as signed numbers.
sltu[†] Rdest,Rsrc1,Src2	Same as slt except that the source operands are treated as unsigned numbers.
sle[†] Rdest,Rsrc1,Src2	Rdest is set to one if contents of Rsrc1 are less than or equal to Src2; otherwise, Rdest is set to zero. Source operands are treated as signed numbers.
sleu[†] Rdest,Rsrc1, Src2	Same as sle except that the source operands are treated as unsigned numbers.
sne[†] Rdest,Rsrc1,Src2	Rdest is set to one if contents of Rsrc1 and Src2 are not equal; otherwise, Rdest is set to zero.

The second operand can be a 16-bit immediate value. In this case, use slti (set on less than immediate) as shown below:

```
slti[†]    Rdest,Rsrc1,imm
```

For unsigned numbers, use sltu for the register version and sltiu for the immediate-operand version. As a convenience, the assembler allows us to use slt and sltu for both register and immediate-operand versions.

The assembler provides several comparison instructions to test for equal, not equal, greater than, greater than or equal, and less than or equal relationships. Table 14.1 summarizes the comparison instructions provided by the assembler. Notice that all comparison instructions in Table 14.1 are pseudoinstructions. For example, the pseudoinstruction

```
seq     $a0,$a1,$a2
```

is translated as

```
        beq     $6,$5,skip1
        ori     $4,$0,0
        beq     $0,$0,skip2
skip1:
        ori     $4,$0,1
skip2:
            . . .
```

Note that $a0, $a1, and $a2 represent registers $4, $5, and $6, respectively. The branch instructions are discussed next.

Unconditional Branch Instructions

Unconditional transfer of control is implemented by jump and branch instructions. Let us first look at the basic jump instruction. The jump instruction

```
j       target
```

transfers control to the target address. As discussed before, this is a direct jump instruction in which the target address is given as part of the instruction. In the MIPS32 architecture, the control is transferred to target after executing the delay slot instruction. However, see the following SPIM note.

SPIM note	Because SPIM does not simulate delayed branch, it does not execute the delay slot instruction.

There are other types of jump instructions that are useful as procedure calls. We have already discussed some of these instructions in Chapter 11. For example, we use the jal instruction to invoke a procedure. Similarly, the jr instruction is used to return from a procedure.

Branch instructions provide a more flexible test and jump execution. MIPS supports several branch instructions. We describe some of these instructions in this section.

The unconditional branch instruction

```
b†      target
```

transfers control to target unconditionally. Semantically, it is very similar to the jump instruction. The main difference is that the b instruction uses a 16-bit relative address whereas the j instruction uses a 26-bit absolute address. Thus, the jump instruction has a larger range than the branch instruction. But the branch is more convenient because it uses relative address.

An Example To illustate the difference between jump and branch instructions, let us look at the following code fragment.

```
                    loop_back:
[0x00400048]            addu    $t0,$t0,$t1
[0x0040004c]            j       loop_back
```

The numbers in the square brackets are the addresses of the instructions. For example, the addu instruction is at address 0x00400048. The SPIM assembler translates the jump (j) instruction in this code as

```
j    0x00400048
```

by replacing the label loop_back by its address 0x00400048. As you can see from this example, the absolute value is used to specify the target address. However, as we have seen in Chapter 11, the instruction encoding is slightly different. The instruction encoding follows the explanation given in the example on page 186. If you have read that explanation on how the jal instruction is encoded, you will see that the j instruction follows similar encoding.

As in the jal instruction, this instruction uses the J-type encoding shown in Figure 4.2 on page 52. This jump instruction is encoded as 0x08100012. The target address is specified using 26 bits as shown below:

Opcode	Offset
0000 10	00 0001 0000 0000 0000 0001 0010

Because all instructions are aligned on word boundaries, the least significant 2 bits are always zero. As a result, these 2 bits are not explicitly stored in the instruction. By appending these 2 zeros, we get the 28-bit offset value as 0x0400048. By adding the most significant 4 bits from the PC, we get the target address as 0x00400048, which is the address of the addu instruction at loop_back.

Now we replace the jump instruction by the branch instruction as shown below:

```
                    loop_back:
[0x00400048]            addu    $t0,$t0,$t1
[0x0040004c]            b       loop_back
```

The unconditional branch instruction (b) is encoded as

```
bgez    $0,-4
```

This example gives the following information about the encoding of the b instruction:

- Because the branch instruction is actually a pseudoinstruction, it is encoded using the conditional branch instruction bgez. How can this instruction implement an unconditional branch? Well, we compare register $0 to zero and jump to target if the register has a value greater than or equal to zero. Register $0 is hardwired to zero, therefore the test is always true, causing the jump to always take place.
- The offset used is a PC-relative value, not the absolute value as in the j instruction. In our example, the relative offset is −4.

Conditional Branch Instructions

Now we look at the conditional branch instructions. These instructions compare the contents of two registers and jump to the target if the specified condition is true. For example, the branch instruction

```
beq     Rsrc1,Rsrc2,target
```

compares the contents of Rsrc1 and Rsrc2 and transfers control to target if they are equal.

Branch instructions to test "less than" and "greater than" are also supported. As an example, the instruction

```
bgt     Rsrc1,Rsrc2,target
```

branches to the target location when the contents of Rsrc1 are greater than Rsrc2. When comparing, the contents of Rsrc1 and Rsrc2 are treated as signed numbers. For unsigned numbers, we have to use the bgtu instruction.

Branch instructions to test combinations such as "greater than or equal to" are also available. Table 14.2 summarizes some of the branch instructions provided by the MIPS assembler.

Very often, we need to compare a value with zero and transfer control to the target based on this comparison. This is often the case in constructing loops. For example, look at the code given at the beginning of this chapter. For this reason, MIPS supports conditional branch instructions that compare with zero. To illustrate the format of these instructions, we use the beqz instruction. The format is

```
beqz    Rsrc,target
```

This instruction transfers control to target if the value of Rsrc is equal to zero. Table 14.3 summarizes these instructions.

Table 14.2 MIPS branch instructions (based on register comparison)

Instruction		Description
b[†]	`target`	Branches unconditionally to `target`.
`beq`	`Rsrc1,Rsrc2,target`	Branches to `target` if the contents of `Rsrc1` and `Rsrc2` are equal.
`bne`	`Rsrc1,Rsrc2,target`	Branches to `target` if the contents of `Rsrc1` and `Rsrc2` are not equal.
`blt`	`Rsrc1,Rsrc2,target`	Branches to `target` if the value of `Rsrc1` is less than the value of `Rsrc2`. The source operands are considered as signed numbers.
`bltu`	`Rsrc1,Rsrc2,target`	Same as `blt` except that the source operands are treated as unsigned numbers.
`bgt`	`Rsrc1,Rsrc2,target`	Branches to `target` if the value of `Rsrc1` is greater than the value of `Rsrc2`. The source operands are treated as signed numbers.
`bgtu`	`Rsrc1,Rsrc2,target`	Same as `bgt` except that the source operands are treated as unsigned numbers.
`ble`	`Rsrc1,Rsrc2,target`	Branches to `target` if the value of `Rsrc1` is less than or equal to the value of `Rsrc2`. The source operands are treated as signed numbers.
`bleu`	`Rsrc1,Rsrc2,target`	Same as `ble` except that the source operands are treated as unsigned numbers.
`bge`	`Rsrc1,Rsrc2,target`	Branches to `target` if the value of `Rsrc1` is greater than or equal to the value of `Rsrc2`. The source operands are treated as signed numbers.
`bgeu`	`Rsrc1,Rsrc2,target`	Same as `bge` except that the source operands are considered as unsigned numbers.

Our First Program

As our first example of the chapter, we look at counting the number of uppercase letters in a given string. The program listing is given in Program 14.1. The main program prompts the user for a string and passes it on to the `count` procedure via the `$a0` register. The `count` procedure returns the uppercase count in `$v0`. The procedure follows the algorithm given below:

Table 14.3 MIPS branch instructions (based on comparison to zero)

Instruction	Description
`beqz   Rsrc,target`	Branches to `target` if the value of `Rsrc` is equal to zero.
`bnez   Rsrc,target`	Branches to `target` if the value of `Rsrc` is not equal to zero.
`bltz   Rsrc,target`	Branches to `target` if the value of `Rsrc` is less than zero.
`bgtz   Rsrc,target`	Branches to `target` if the value of `Rsrc` is greater than zero.
`blez   Rsrc,target`	Branches to `target` if the value of `Rsrc` is less than or equal to zero.
`bgez   Rsrc,target`	Branches to `target` if the value of `Rsrc` is greater than or equal to zero.

```
count(string)
    uppercase_count := 0
    i := 0
    while (string[i] ≠ NULL)
        if ((string[i] ≥ 'A') AND (string[i] ≤ 'Z'))
            uppercase_count := uppercase_count + 1
        end if
        i := i + 1
    end while
    return (uppercase_count)
end count
```

The `if` condition is tested on lines 63 and 64. If the condition is true, the uppercase count (in `$v0`) is incremented on line 65. The `count` loop index (in `$t0`) is incremented on line 67. The `while` loop condition is tested on line 62. If the loop condition is not true, the loop is terminated by the `beqz` instruction on line 62.

Program 14.1 A program to count the number of uppercase letters in a string

```
1:  # Counts the uppercase letters           UPPER_COUNT.ASM
2:  #
3:  # Objective: Counts uppercase letters in a string.
4:  #     Input: Requests a string from the user.
```

```
 5:    #      Output: Outputs the uppercase letter count.
 6:    #
 7:    #      $a0 - string pointer
 8:    #      $v0 - returns the uppercase letter count
 9:    #
10:    ################# Data segment #####################
11:          .data
12:    prompt:
13:          .asciiz     "Please enter a string: \n"
14:    out_msg:
15:          .asciiz     "The number of uppercase letters is: "
16:    newline:
17:          .asciiz     "\n"
18:    in_string:
19:          .space      31
20:
21:    ################# Code segment #####################
22:          .text
23:          .globl main
24:    main:
25:          la    $a0,prompt          # prompt user for input
26:          li    $v0,4
27:          syscall
28:
29:          la    $a0,in_string       # read input string
30:          li    $a1,31              # buffer length in $a1
31:          li    $v0,8
32:          syscall
33:
34:          la    $a0,in_string       # call the count proc.
35:          jal   count
36:          move  $t0,$v0             # count is in $v0
37:
38:          la    $a0,out_msg         # write output message
39:          li    $v0,4
40:          syscall
41:
42:          move  $a0,$t0             # output the count
43:          li    $v0,1
44:          syscall
45:
46:          la    $a0,newline         # write newline
47:          li    $v0,4
48:          syscall
49:
50:          li    $v0,10              # exit
51:          syscall
```

```
52:
53:    #------------------------------------------------------------
54:    # COUNT receives a pointer to a string in $a0 and
55:    # returns the number of uppercase letters in $v0.
56:    #     $t0 - temporary
57:    #------------------------------------------------------------
58:    count:
59:          li    $v0,0                    # count = 0
60:    count_loop:
61:          lbu   $t0,($a0)
62:          beqz  $t0,count_done           # if NULL, we are done
63:          bgtu  $t0,'Z',skip_count
64:          bltu  $t0,'A',skip_count
65:          addu  $v0,$v0,1                # update count
66:    skip_count:
67:          addu  $a0,$a0,1
68:          b     count_loop
69:    count_done:
70:          jr    $ra
```

Illustrative Examples

We give two examples to further illustrate the instructions discussed in this chapter.

Example 14.1 *Sorting of an integer array using selection sort.*
The main program, shown in Program 14.2, prompts the user for the array values. The read loop on lines 33–39 reads the values entered by the user. This loop is terminated when a zero is entered. This is not a safe loop as it is possible to exceed the array bounds (which in our example can take 50 elements). You can make this loop safe by adding another termination condition that takes care of the array boundary.

The main program copies the array pointer into $a0 (line 42) and its size in $a1 (line 43 and 44). Notice that we use the shift right instruction (srl) on line 44 to divide the byte count by 4 to get the array size. The selection sort procedure is invoked on line 45. After the array has been sorted, the main program displays the sorted array using the loop on lines 52–61.

Program 14.2 Selection sort program

```
1:    # Selection sort                        SEL_SORT.ASM
2:    #
3:    # Objective: Sorts an array using selection sort.
4:    #     Input: Requests integers from the user;
```

```
 5:    #              terminated by entering a zero.
 6:    #      Output: Outputs the sorted integer array.
 7:    #
 8:    #      $a0 - array pointer
 9:    #      $a1 - array size
10:    #
11:    ################### Data segment #######################
12:          .data
13:    prompt:
14:          .ascii     "Please enter integers (at least two).\n"
15:          .asciiz    "Entering zero terminates the input.\n"
16:    output_msg:
17:          .asciiz    "The sorted array is:\n"
18:    newline:
19:          .asciiz    "\n"
20:    .align 2
21:    array:
22:          .space      200         # space for 50 integers
23:
24:    ################### Code segment #######################
25:          .text
26:          .globl main
27:    main:
28:          la    $a0,prompt        # prompt user for input
29:          li    $v0,4
30:          syscall
31:
32:          la    $t0,array
33:    read_more:
34:          li    $v0,5             # read a number
35:          syscall
36:          sw    $v0,($t0)         # store it in the array
37:          beqz  $v0,exit_read
38:          addu  $t0,$t0,4
39:          b     read_more
40:    exit_read:
41:          # prepare arguments for procedure call
42:          la    $a0,array         # $a0 = array pointer
43:          subu  $a1,$t0,$a0       # $a1 = array size in bytes
44:          srl   $a1,$a1,2         # $a1 = $a1/4
45:          jal   sel_sort
46:
47:          la    $a0,output_msg    # write output message
48:          li    $v0,4
49:          syscall
50:
51:          la    $t0,array
```

```
52:   write_more:
53:         lw    $a0,($t0)              # output sorted array
54:         beqz  $a0,exit_write
55:         li    $v0,1
56:         syscall
57:         la    $a0,newline           # write newline
58:         li    $v0,4
59:         syscall
60:         addu  $t0,$t0,4
61:         b     write_more
62:   exit_write:
63:
64:         li    $v0,10                 # exit
65:         syscall
66:
67:   #------------------------------------------------------------
68:   # SEL_SORT receives a pointer to the array in $a0 and
69:   # its size in $a1. It sorts the array in ascending order
70:   # using the selection sort algorithm.
71:   #    $t1 - array[j] pointer
72:   #    $t2 - min_value
73:   #    $t3 - array[min_position] pointer
74:   #    $t4 - used as a temporary
75:   #    $a0 - array[position] pointer
76:   #    $a1 - array[size-1] pointer
77:   #------------------------------------------------------------
78:   sel_sort:
79:         # computes array[size-1] pointer (i.e., &A[size-1])
80:         subu  $a1,$a1,1
81:         sll   $a1,$a1,2
82:         addu  $a1,$a1,$a0
83:
84:         ########## outer for loop ###########
85:   outer_for:
86:         lw    $t2,($a0)    # min_value = A[position]
87:         move  $t3,$a0      # &A[min_position] = &A[position]
88:
89:         # inner for loop
90:         addu  $t1,$a0,4             # &A[j] = &A[position+1]
91:   inner_for:
92:         lw    $t4,($t1)             # 1st if condition
93:         bgeu  $t4,$t2,skip_1st_if   #
94:
95:         # 1st if statement
96:         move  $t2,$t4              # min_value = A[j]
97:         move  $t3,$t1              # &A[min_pos] = &A[j]
98:         # end of 1st if statement
```

```
 99:
100:   skip_1st_if:
101:          addu  $t1,$t1,4              # $t1 = &A[j+1]
102:          bleu  $t1,$a1,inner_for
103:          # end of inner for loop
104:
105:          beq   $a0,$t3,skip_2nd_if   # 2nd if condition
106:   second_if:
107:          # 2nd if statement
108:          lw    $t4,($a0)
109:          sw    $t4,($t3)
110:          sw    $t2,($a0)
111:          # end of 2nd if statement
112:
113:   skip_2nd_if:
114:          addu  $a0,$a0,4              # $a0 = &A[position+1]
115:          bltu  $a0,$a1,outer_for
116:          # end of outer for loop
117:
118:          jr    $ra
```

The sort procedure receives a pointer to the array to be sorted in $a0 and its size in $a1. It uses the selection sort algorithm to sort the array in ascending order. The basic idea is as follows.

1. Search the array for the smallest element;
2. Move the smallest element to the first position by exchanging values of the first and smallest element positions;
3. Search the array for the smallest element from the second position of the array;
4. Move this element to the second position by exchanging values as in Step 2;
5. Continue this process until the array is sorted.

The selection sort procedure implements the following pseudocode.

```
selection_sort (array, size)
    for (position = 0 to size−2)
         min_value := array[position]
         min_position := position
         for (j = position+1 to size−1)
             if (array[j] < min_value)
             then
                  min_value := array[j]
                  min_position := j
             end if
```

end for
if (position ≠ min_position)
then
      array[min_position] := array[position]
      array[position] := min_value
end if
end for
end selection_sort

The selection sort procedure, shown in Program 14.2, implements this pseudocode. The code on lines 80 and 81 converts the array size into bytes. The addu instruction on line 82 adds the array pointer in $a0 to this byte count to get the array-end pointer.

The first if statement is implemented on lines 92 and 93. The body of this if statement is on lines 96 and 97. The inner for loop condition is tested on line 102. The inner for loop body consists of lines 91–102.

The second if statement condition is tested on line 105. This if statement's body is implemented on lines 108–110. The outer for loop condition is tested on line 115. The outer for loop consists of lines 86–115.

Example 14.2 *Linear search of an integer array.*

In this example, the user is asked to input an array of nonzero integers and then queries whether a given number is in the array. The program uses a procedure that implements the linear search to locate a given number in an unsorted array.

The program listing is given in Program 14.3. The main program is very similar to the one in the last example. Before calling the linear search procedure, it passes the array pointer (in $a0), its size (in $a1), and the number to be searched (in $a2).

The linear search procedure returns the status of the search (found or not-found) in $v0. If found, the position of the number in the array is returned in $v1. The main program outputs the appropriate message depending on the status returned by the linear search procedure.

Program 14.3 Linear search of an array

```
 1:   # Linear search                          LINEAR_SEARCH.ASM
 2:   #
 3:   # Objective: Searches for an integer using linear search.
 4:   #     Input: Requests array input and the number
 5:   #              to be searched;
 6:   #    Output: Outputs the position of the number, if found.
 7:   #
 8:   #     $a0 - array pointer
 9:   #     $a1 - array size
10:   #     $a2 - number to be searched
```

```
11:     #
12:     ################### Data segment ######################
13:         .data
14:     array_prompt:
15:         .ascii      "Please enter integers.\n"
16:         .asciiz     "Entering zero terminates the input.\n"
17:     number_prompt:
18:         .asciiz     "Enter the number to be searched:\n"
19:     found_msg:
20:         .asciiz     "The number is at position\n"
21:     not_found_msg:
22:         .asciiz     "The number is not in the array!\n"
23:     newline:
24:         .asciiz     "\n"
25:     .align 2
26:     array:
27:         .space      200             # space for 50 integers
28:
29:     ################### Code segment ######################
30:         .text
31:         .globl main
32:     main:
33:         la      $a0,array_prompt    # prompt user for input
34:         li      $v0,4
35:         syscall
36:
37:         la      $t0,array
38:     read_more:
39:         li      $v0,5               # read a number
40:         syscall
41:         sw      $v0,($t0)           # store it in the array
42:         beqz    $v0,exit_read
43:         addu    $t0,$t0,4
44:         b       read_more
45:     exit_read:
46:         la      $a0,number_prompt   # prompt user for number
47:         li      $v0,4
48:         syscall
49:         li      $v0,5               # read a number
50:         syscall                     # number in $v0
51:
52:         # prepare arguments for procedure call
53:         la      $a0,array           # $a0 = array pointer
54:         subu    $a1,$t0,$a0         # $a1 = array size in bytes
55:         srl     $a1,$a1,2           # $a1 = $a1/4
56:         move    $a2,$v0             # $a2 = given number
57:         jal     lin_search
```

```
58:
59:          beqz   $v0,not_found
60:          la     $a0,found_msg        # write found message
61:          li     $v0,4
62:          syscall
63:          move   $a0,$v1              # write position
64:          li     $v0,1
65:          syscall
66:          la     $a0,newline          # write newline
67:          li     $v0,4
68:          syscall
69:          b      done
70:
71:  not_found:
72:          la     $a0,not_found_msg   # write not found message
73:          li     $v0,4
74:          syscall
75:  done:
76:          li     $v0,10               # exit
77:          syscall
78:
79:  #-----------------------------------------------------------
80:  # LIN_SEARCH receives a pointer to the array in $a0,
81:  # its size in $a1, and the number to be searched in $a2.
82:  # It uses linear search algorithm.
83:  #    $t0 - array pointer
84:  #    $t1 - array value
85:  #    $a1 - pointer to the last element
86:  #    $v0 - status (0 = not found, 1 = found)
87:  #    $v1 - position if found
88:  #-----------------------------------------------------------
89:  lin_search:
90:          # computes the address of the last element
91:          subu   $a1,$a1,1        # last element index
92:          sll    $a1,$a1,2        # convert to bytes ($a1 * 4)
93:          addu   $a1,$a1,$a0      # $a1 = pointer to last element
94:
95:          move   $t0,$a0                  # $t0 =  array pointer
96:  loop:
97:          lw     $t1,($t0)                # array value in $t1
98:          beq    $t1,$a2,num_found
99:          addu   $t0,$t0,4                # point to the next element
100:         bleu   $t0,$a1,loop
101:
102:         # number not found
103:         li     $v0,0                    # status = not found
104:         b      search_done
```

```
105:
106:   num_found:
107:          li     $v0,1                    # status = found
108:          # compute the position
109:          subu   $v1,$t0,$a0
110:          srl    $v1,$v1,2
111:          addu   $v1,$v1,1
112:   search_done:
113:          jr     $ra
```

The linear search procedure receives a pointer to the array, its size, and the number to be searched. The search process starts at the first element of the array and proceeds until either the element is located or the array is exhausted. First we have to convert the array size into number of bytes (lines 91 and 92). As in the selection sort procedure, we use `sll` to multiply the size by 4 (line 92). To compute the address of the last element, we add the array pointer to this byte count (line 93).

The search loop consists of lines 96–100. The loop iteration condition is tested on line 100 and the comparison to the number is done on line 98. If the number is not found in the array, the `$v0` is cleared to zero (line 103) to indicate the not-found status. On the other hand, if the number is found, `$v0` is set to 1 (line 107). In this case, we have to compute the position of the number in the array, which is done on lines 109–111. We use the `srl` instruction on line 110 to divide the byte count by 4.

Indirect Jumps

So far, we have used only the direct jump instructions. We now look at indirect jumps. In an indirect jump, the target address is specified indirectly. The MIPS architecture provides a register-based indirect jump instruction. As we have seen before, the format of this instruction is

```
jr     rs
```

where `rs` is a register. We have already discussed this instruction in Chapter 11 (see page 188). The next example shows how indirect jumps can be used with a jump table stored in memory.

Example 14.3 *An example with an indirect jump.*
The objective here is to show how we can use the indirect jump instruction. To this end, we show a simple program that reads a digit from the user and prints the corresponding choice represented by the input. The listing is shown in Program 14.4. An input between 0 and 9 is valid. If a nondigit input is given to the program, it displays an error message and requests a valid digit input. If the input is 0, 1, or 2, it displays a simple message to indicate the class selection. Other digits terminate the program.

Program 14.4 A simple program to illustrate indirect jumps

```
 1:  # Indirect jump program      INDIRECT_JUMP.ASM
 2:  #
 3:  # Objective: To demonstrate indirect jumps.
 4:  #     Input: Requests a digit.
 5:  #    Output: Outputs the class selected.
 6:  #
 7:  ################## Data segment ##################
 8:        .data
 9:  prompt:
10:        .asciiz    "Please enter a digit: "
11:  try_prompt:
12:        .asciiz    "Not a digit! Try again: \n"
13:  msg0:
14:        .asciiz    "Economy class selected.\n"
15:  msg1:
16:        .asciiz    "Business class selected.\n"
17:  msg2:
18:        .asciiz    "First class selected.\n"
19:  default_msg:
20:        .asciiz    "Not a valid selection!\n"
21:  newline:
22:        .asciiz    "\n"
23:
24:  input_digit:
25:        .space     2
26:
27:  jump_table:
28:        .word      code_for_0
29:        .word      code_for_1
30:        .word      code_for_2
31:        .word      default_code
32:        .word      default_code
33:        .word      default_code
34:        .word      default_code
35:        .word      default_code
36:        .word      default_code
37:        .word      default_code
38:
39:  ################## Code segment ##################
40:        .text
41:        .globl main
42:  main:
43:        la    $a0,prompt          # prompt user for input
44:        li    $v0,4
45:        syscall
```

```
46:
47:         la      $a0,input_digit     # read input
48:         li      $a1,2
49:         li      $v0,8
50:         syscall
51:         la      $a0,newline
52:         li      $v0,4
53:         syscall
54:
55:         lbu     $t0,input_digit
56:         sub     $t0,$t0,'0'         # $t0 = input - '0'
57:         bgtu    $t0,9,not_digit     # if >9, not a digit
58:         bltz    $t0,not_digit       # if <0, not a digit
59:
60:         sll     $t0,$t0,2           # $t0 = $t0*4
61:
62:         # we have to jump to the pointer in jump_table
63:         la      $t1,jump_table
64:         add     $t1,$t1,$t0
65:         lw      $t2,($t1)
66:         jr      $t2
67:
68:  not_digit:                         # input is not a digit
69:         la      $a0,try_prompt      # ask user to try again
70:         li      $v0,4
71:         syscall
72:         b       main
73:
74:  code_for_0:
75:         la      $a0,msg0            # write message 0
76:         li      $v0,4
77:         syscall
78:         b       done
79:
80:  code_for_1:
81:         la      $a0,msg1            # write message 1
82:         li      $v0,4
83:         syscall
84:         b       done
85:
86:  code_for_2:
87:         la      $a0,msg2            # write message 2
88:         li      $v0,4
89:         syscall
90:         b       done
91:
92:  default_code:
```

```
93:              la    $a0,default_msg    # write default message
94:              li    $v0,4
95:              syscall
96:
97:   done:
98:              li    $v0,10             # exit
99:              syscall
```

In order to use the indirect jump, we have to build a jump table of pointers (see lines 27–37). The input is tested for its validity on lines 56–58. If the input is a digit, it is converted to act as an index into the jump table (line 60). This value is used in the indirect jump instruction (lines 63–66). The rest of the program is straightforward to follow.

Indirect Procedures

In this section we look at indirect procedure calls. The mechanism is very similar to that used for the indirect jumps in the last example. However, we cannot use the jr instruction for procedure calls. For this purpose the MIPS architecture provides a separate jump and link instruction. The format of this instruction is similar to the jr instruction, as shown here:

```
jalr    rs
```

where rs is a register. This instruction works as does the jal instruction but takes the contents of rs as the target address. The next example illustrates how we can use this instruction to effect indirect procedure calls.

Example 14.4 *An example with an indirect procedure call.*

The objective here is to show how we can use the jalr instruction. The main program prompts the user for a string and a digit between 0 and 3 to select an option on how the string should be processed. The available choices are:

    0 — convert to uppercase
    1 — convert to lowercase
    2 — flip the case
    3 — reverse the string

These four functions are implemented as procedures, as shown in Program 14.5. To invoke the appropriate procedure based on the user choice, we use the jalr instruction. To facilitate this, we build the jump table as in the last example (lines 26–30). Once this value is loaded into $t2, we can specify this register in the jalr instruction on line 60.

Program 14.5 An example to illustrate indirect procedure calls

```
 1:   # Indirect jump program         INDIRECT_PROCS.ASM
 2:   #
 3:   # Objective: To demonstrate indirect procedures.
 4:   #      Input: Requests a string and a digit.
 5:   #     Output: Outputs the processed string.
 6:   #
 7:   ################## Data segment ##################
 8:           .data
 9:   string_prompt:
10:           .asciiz     "Please enter a string (<80 chars): "
11:   digit_prompt:
12:           .ascii      "Please enter a digit: \n"
13:           .ascii      "  0 - to convert to upper case\n"
14:           .ascii      "  1 - to convert to lower case\n"
15:           .ascii      "  2 - to flip case\n"
16:           .ascii      "  3 - to reverse string\n"
17:           .asciiz     "  Other numbers are invalid.\n"
18:   try_prompt:
19:           .asciiz     "Not a valid selection! Try again:\n"
20:   out_msg:
21:           .asciiz     "The output string is: "
22:
23:   input_string:
24:           .space      82
25:
26:   jump_table:
27:           .word       to_upper_case
28:           .word       to_lower_case
29:           .word       to_flip_case
30:           .word       string_reverse
31:
32:   ################## Code segment ##################
33:           .text
34:           .globl main
35:   main:
36:           la    $a0,string_prompt  # prompt for string
37:           li    $v0,4
38:           syscall
39:           la    $a0,input_string   # read input
40:           li    $a1,82
41:           li    $v0,8
42:           syscall
43:
44:   digit_again:
45:           la    $a0,digit_prompt   # prompt for digit
```

```
46:         li    $v0,4
47:         syscall
48:         li    $v0,5              # read input
49:         syscall
50:
51:         bgtu  $v0,3,not_valid    # if >3, not valid
52:
53:         sll   $v0,$v0,2          # $v0 = $v0*4
54:
55:         # we have to jump to the pointer in jump_table
56:         la    $t1,jump_table
57:         add   $t1,$t1,$v0
58:         lw    $t2,($t1)
59:         la    $a0,input_string   # string address in $a0
60:         jalr  $t2
61:
62:         la    $a0,out_msg        # display output message
63:         li    $v0,4
64:         syscall
65:         la    $a0,input_string   # display output string
66:         li    $v0,4
67:         syscall
68:         b     done
69:
70: not_valid:                       # input is not a digit
71:         la    $a0,try_prompt     # ask user to try again
72:         li    $v0,4
73:         syscall
74:         b     digit_again
75:
76: done:
77:         li    $v0,10             # exit
78:         syscall
79:
80: #----------------------------------------------------------
81: # STRING_REVERSE receives a pointer to a string in $a0
82: # and reverses the string
83: #----------------------------------------------------------
84: string_reverse:
85:         move $t1,$a0             # $t1 points to string
86: loop1:
87:         lbu   $t2,($t1)
88:         beq   $t2,0xA,done1      # if linefeed
89:         beqz  $t2,done1          # or NULL, we are done
90:         addu  $t1,$t1,1
91:         b     loop1
92: done1:
```

```
 93:         sub   $t1,$t1,1     # $t1 points to end of string
 94:  reverse_loop:
 95:         bleu  $t1,$a0,done_reverse
 96:         lbu   $t2,($a0)
 97:         lbu   $t3,($t1)
 98:         sb    $t2,($t1)
 99:         sb    $t3,($a0)
100:         addu  $a0,$a0,1
101:         subu  $t1,$t1,1
102:         b     reverse_loop
103:  done_reverse:
104:         jr    $ra
105:
106:  #------------------------------------------------------------
107:  # TO_UPPER_CASE receives a pointer to a string in $a0
108:  # and returns the string with lowercase letters
109:  # replaced by uppercase letters
110:  #------------------------------------------------------------
111:  to_upper_case:
112:
113:  upper_loop:
114:         lbu   $t1,($a0)
115:         beqz  $t1,done_upper    # if NULL, we are done
116:         bgtu  $t1,'z',skip_upper
117:         bltu  $t1,'a',skip_upper
118:         subu  $t1,$t1,0x20
119:  skip_upper:
120:         sb    $t1,($a0)
121:         addu  $a0,$a0,1
122:         b     upper_loop
123:  done_upper:
124:         jr    $ra
125:
126:  #------------------------------------------------------------
127:  # TO_LOWER_CASE receives a pointer to a string in $a0
128:  # and returns the string with uppercase letters
129:  # replaced by lowercase letters
130:  #------------------------------------------------------------
131:  to_lower_case:
132:
133:  lower_loop:
134:         lbu   $t1,($a0)
135:         beqz  $t1,done_lower    # if NULL, we are done
136:         bgtu  $t1,'Z',skip_lower
137:         bltu  $t1,'A',skip_lower
138:         addu  $t1,$t1,0x20
139:  skip_lower:
```

```
140:            sb      $t1,($a0)
141:            addu    $a0,$a0,1
142:            b       lower_loop
143:    done_lower:
144:            jr      $ra
145:
146:    #-----------------------------------------------------------
147:    # TO_FLIP_CASE receives a pointer to a string in $a0
148:    # and returns the string with uppercase letters
149:    # replaced by lowercase letters and vice versa
150:    #-----------------------------------------------------------
151:    to_flip_case:
152:
153:    flip_loop:
154:            lbu     $t1,($a0)
155:            beqz    $t1,done_flip        # if NULL, we are done
156:            bgtu    $t1,'z',skip_flip
157:            bgeu    $t1,'a',convert
158:            bgtu    $t1,'Z',skip_flip
159:            bgeu    $t1,'A',convert
160:            b       skip_flip
161:    convert:
162:            xor     $t1,$t1,0x20
163:    skip_flip:
164:            sb      $t1,($a0)
165:            addu    $a0,$a0,1
166:            b       flip_loop
167:    done_flip:
168:            jr      $ra
```

The string reverse procedure we used here is the same as that in Program 13.4 on page 238. The only modification is that we add an additional condition for the termination of the first loop on lines 86–91. This is because, when the string entered is smaller than the buffer length, the read_string system call includes a linefeed (0xA) character. Thus, we terminate the loop if a linefeed (line 88) or NULL (line 89) is encountered.

The procedure to_upper converts all lowercase letters to uppercase. It is based on Program 10.3 (page 178). The lowercase conversion is done by the to_lower procedure. It is very similar to the uppercase conversion procedure with a few minor changes.

The flip case conversion procedure uses exclusive-or (xor) to flip the case. Because the uppercase and lowercase letters differ in the 6th bit from right, we can flip this bit to change the case. For example, the ASCII value for letter "A" is 01000001. The corresponding value for letter "a" is 01100001. Thus, if we use 00100000 as the mask and perform the xor operation, we flip the case. This is what is done in this procedure. Once we check to make sure that the character is a letter (a–z, or A–Z), we use the xor instruction to do the case conversion (line 162).

Summary

We discussed the unconditional and conditional jump instructions as well as compare instructions in detail. These assembly language instructions are useful in implementing high-level language selection and iteration constructs such as if-then-else and while loops. Through detailed examples, we discussed how these high-level decision structures are implemented in the assembly language.

In the previous chapters, we extensively used direct jump and procedure call instructions. In this chapter, we introduced the indirect jumps and procedure calls. In the indirect jump and procedure call instructions, the target of the jump is specified indirectly via a register. By means of examples, we have shown how they are useful in implementing indirect jumps and procedure calls.

15

Logical and Shift Operations

This chapter looks at the logical, shift and rotate instructions provided by MIPS. The MIPS instruction set provides four logical instructions: and, or, xor, *and* nor. *There is no* not *instruction. This operation can be synthesized from the* nor *operation. We have introduced some of these instructions in Chapter 10. The logical instructions are useful to implement high-level language logical expressions. In addition, they can be used for bit manipulation. The shift and rotate instructions are useful in bit shift operations. We give several examples to illustrate the use of these instructions. We end the chapter with a summary.*

Introduction

As we have seen in the last chapter, high-level languages provide several conditional and loop constructs. These constructs require Boolean or logical expressions to specify conditions. In principle, only a single bit is needed to represent the Boolean data. However, such a representation, although compact, is not convenient, as testing a variable involves isolating the corresponding bit.

Most high-level languages use a byte to represent the Boolean data. If the byte is zero, it represents false; otherwise, true. Note that any value other than 0 can be used to represent true. In C, which does not provide an explicit Boolean data type, any data variable can be used in a logical expression to represent Boolean data. The rules mentioned above apply.

Assembly language provides several logical instructions, which are useful in implementing logical expressions of high-level languages. For example, C provides the following logical operators.

C operator	Meaning
||	logical OR
&&	logical AND
!	logical NOT

The logical instructions are also useful in implementing bitwise logical operations. For example, the following four bitwise logical operators are available in C.

C operator	Meaning
|	Bitwise-OR
&	Bitwise-AND
^	Bitwise-XOR
~	Bitwise-NOT

The MIPS architecture also provides several shift instructions. These instructions are useful in implementing bitwise shift operations. For example, C provides the following two shift operators.

C operator	Meaning
>>	Right-shift
<<	Left-shift

In addition to the shift instructions, two rotate instructions are also available. These are actually pseudoinstructions supported by the assembler.

We have discussed some of these instructions in Chapter 10. This chapter complements the material presented on the logical and shift instructions in that chapter. We begin our discussion with the logical instructions.

Logical Instructions

Logical instructions manipulate logical data just as the arithmetic instructions manipulate arithmetic data (e.g., integers) with operations such as addition and subtraction. The logical data can take one of two possible values: `true` or `false`.

Assembly language provides logical operators in the logical family of instructions. MIPS supports four logical operations: `and`, `or`, `nor`, and `xor`. We have already seen the `and` and `or` instructions in Chapter 10. The truth tables for the remaining two operatiors are given in Table 15.1.

Notice that the MIPS instruction set does not have a `not` instruction. This missing operation is supported by a pseudoinstruction, which can be easily implemented using the `nor` instruction as

Table 15.1 Truth tables for the `xor` and `nor` logical operations

xor operation			nor operation		
Input bits		Output bit	Input bits		Output bit
source1	source2	destination	source1	source2	destination
0	0	0	0	0	1
0	1	1	0	1	0
1	0	1	1	0	0
1	1	0	1	1	0

```
nor     Rdest,Rsrc,$0
```

A summary of these instructions is given in Table 15.2. All operations, except `not`, take two source operands and a destination operand. The `not` instruction takes one source operand and one destination operand. As with most instructions, all operands must be in registers. However, `and`, `or`, and `xor` instructions can take one immediate operand.

Assembler pseudoinstructions use the same mnemonics for the logical operations `and`, `or`, and `xor` but allow the second source operand to be either a register or a 16-bit immediate value. Next we look at some typical uses for the logical operators.

The `and` Instruction

The `and` instruction is useful mainly in these situations:

1. To support compound logical expressions and bitwise `and` operations of high-level languages;
2. To clear one or more bits;
3. To isolate one or more bits.

The use of the `and` instruction to express compound logical expressions and to implement bitwise `and` operations is discussed later using examples. Here we concentrate on how `and` can be used to clear or isolate selected bits of an operand.

Clearing Bits   If you look at the truth table of the `and` operation (see Table 10.4 on page 170), you will notice that source1 acts as a *masking* bit: if the masking bit is 0, the output is 0, no matter what the other input bit is; if the masking bit is 1, the other input bit is passed to the output. Consider the following example.

```
$t0 = 10010011 00001111 01110010 11010110   ← operand
$t1 = 11111111 11111111 11111111 11111100   ← mask
$t2 = 10010011 00001111 01110010 11010100
```

Table 15.2 MIPS logical instructions

Instruction		Description
and	Rdest,Rsrc1,Rsrc2	Bitwise AND of Rsrc1 and Rsrc2 is stored in Rdest.
andi	Rdest,Rsrc1,imm16	Bitwise AND of Rsrc1 and a 16-bit imm16 is stored in Rdest. The 16-bit imm16 is zero-extended.
or	Rdest,Rsrc1,Rsrc2	Bitwise OR of Rsrc1 and Rsrc2 is stored in Rdest.
ori	Rdest,Rsrc1,imm16	Bitwise OR of Rsrc1 and a 16-bit imm16 is stored in Rdest. The 16-bit imm16 is zero-extended.
not[†]	Rdest,Rsrc	Bitwise NOT of Rsrc is stored in Rdest.
xor	Rdest,Rsrc1,Rsrc2	Bitwise XOR of Rsrc1 and Rsrc2 is stored in Rdest.
xori	Rdest,Rsrc1,imm16	Bitwise XOR of Rsrc1 and a 16-bit imm16 is stored in Rdest. The 16-bit imm16 is zero-extended.
nor	Rdest,Rsrc1,Rsrc2	Bitwise NOR of Rsrc1 and Rsrc2 is stored in Rdest.

Here, $t0 contains the operand to be modified and $t1 contains a set of masking bits. Let us say that we want to force the least significant two bits to 0 without altering any of the remaining 30 bits. We select our mask in $t1 such that it contains 0s in those two bit positions and 1s in the remainder of the bit positions. With this mask, we use the following instruction to get the desired result in $t2.

```
and    $t2,$t1,$t0
```

Here is an example that utilizes the bit clearing capability of the and instruction.

Example 15.1 *Even-parity generation (partial code).*
Let us consider generation of even parity. Assume that the most significant bit of a byte represents the parity bit; the rest of the byte stores the data bits. The parity bit can be set or cleared so as to make the number of 1s in the whole byte even.

If the number of 1s in the least significant seven bits is even, the parity bit should be 0. Assuming that the byte to be parity-encoded is in the $t0 register, the statement

```
and    $t0,$t0,0x7F
```

clears the parity bit without altering the remaining bits.   □

Isolating Bits Another typical use of the and instruction is to isolate selected bits for testing. This is done by masking all the other bits, as shown in the next example.

Example 15.2 *Determining odd or even number.*
In this example, we want to find out if the unsigned number in the $t0 register is an odd or even number. A simple test to determine this is to check the least significant bit of the number: if this bit is 1, it is an odd number; otherwise, an even number.

Here is the code to perform this test using the and instruction.

```
            and    $t1,$t0,1    ; mask = 0...000001
            beqz   $t1,even_number
    odd_number:
            .  .  .
            <code for processing odd number>
            .  .  .
    even_number:
            .  .  .
            <code for processing even number>
            .  .  .
```

If $t0 has an even number, the least significant bit of $t0 is 0. Therefore,

```
    and    $t1,$t0,1
```

would produce a zero result in $t1. The beqz instruction is then used to test the result in $t1 and to selectively execute the appropriate code fragment. This example shows the use of and to isolate a bit, the least significant bit in this case. We use this test later in a programming example. □

The or Instruction

Like the and instruction, the or instruction is useful in several situations:

1. To support compound logical expressions and bitwise or operations of high-level languages;
2. To set one or more bits;
3. To load a constant into a register.

The use of the or instruction to express compound logical expressions and to implement bitwise or operations is discussed later using examples. We now discuss how the or instruction can be used to set a given set of bits and to load a constant.

Setting Bits As you can see from the truth table for the or operation (see Table 10.4 on page 170), when source1 is 0, the other input is passed on to the output; when source1 is 1, the output is forced to take a value of 1 irrespective of the other input. This property is used to set bits in the output. This is illustrated in the following example.

```
$t0 = 11110000 01010101 00110011 11010110B    ← operand
$t1 = 00000000 00000000 00000000 00000011B    ← mask
$t2 = 11110000 01010101 00110011 11010111B
```

The value in $t2 is produced by the instruction:

```
or      $t2,$t1,$t0
```

The mask value in $t1 causes the least significant two bits to change to 1. Here is an example that illustrates the use of the or instruction.

Example 15.3 *Even-parity encoding (partial code).*
Consider the even-parity encoding discussed in Example 15.1. If the number of 1s in the least significant 7 bits is odd, we have to make the parity bit 1 so that the total number of 1s is even. This is done by

```
or      $t0,$t0,0x80
```

assuming that the byte to be parity-encoded is in the $t0 register. The or operation forces the parity bit to 1 without altering the remaining bits.   □

Loading a Register   MIPS does not provide instructions to move data into registers. As we have seen in Chapter 10, the li pseudoinstruction can be used for this purpose. This pseudoinstruction is implemented by using the or instruction. As an example, look at the following li instruction.

```
li      $t0,0x30
```

This instruction is implemented as

```
ori     $8,$0,50
```

Note that $t0 maps to $8 and register $0 is hardwired to zero.

Cutting and Pasting Bits   The and and or instructions together can be used to "cut and paste" bits from two or more operands. We have already seen how the and can be used to isolate selected bits, analogous to the "cut" operation. The or instruction can be used to "paste" the bits. For example, the following code creates a new byte in $t2 by combining odd bits from $t0 and even bits from $t1 registers.

```
and     $t0,$t0,0x55    ; cut odd bits
and     $t1,$t1,0xAA    ; cut even bits
or      $t2,$t1,$t0     ; paste them together
```

The first and instruction selects only the odd bits from the $t0 register by forcing all even bits to 0. The second and instruction selects the even bits by using the mask 0xAA. The or instruction simply pastes these two bytes together to produce the desired byte in the $t2 register.

The xor Instruction

The xor instruction is useful mainly in these situations:

1. To support compound logical expressions of high-level languages;
2. To toggle one or more bits.

The use of the xor instruction to express compound logical expressions is similar to the and or operations. Here we focus on the use of xor to toggle bits.

Toggling Bits   Using the xor instruction, we can toggle a specific set of bits. To do this, the mask should have 1 in the bit positions that are to be flipped. The following example illustrates this application.

Example 15.4 *Parity conversion.*

Suppose we want to change the parity encoding of incoming data: if even parity, change to odd parity and vice versa. To accomplish this change, all we have to do is flip the parity bit, which can be done by

```
xor     $t0,$t0,0x80
```

Thus, an even-parity encoded ASCII character A in $t0—01000001—is transformed into odd-parity encoding, as shown below:

```
        01000001   ← even-parity encoded ASCII character A
xor     10000000   ← mask
        11000001   ← odd-parity encoded ASCII character A
```

In the above example, we have shown only the least significant byte of $t0. Notice that if we perform the same xor operation on odd-parity encoding of A, we get back the even-parity encoding! This is an interesting property of the xor operation: xoring twice gives back the original value. This is not hard to understand, as xor behaves as the not operation does by selectively flipping bits. This property is used in the following example to encrypt a byte.   □

Example 15.5 *Encryption of data.*

Data encryption is useful in applications that deal with sensitive data. We can write a simple encryption program by using the xor instruction. The idea is that we use the encryption key as the mask byte of the xor instruction as shown below. Assume that the byte to be encrypted is in the $t0 register and the encryption key is 0x26.

```
; read a data byte into $t0
xor     $t0,$t0,0x26
; write the data byte back from $t0
```

Suppose we have received character B, whose ASCII code is 01000010B. After encryption, the character becomes d in ASCII, as shown below.

```
01000010  ← ASCII character B
00100110  ← encryption key (mask)
01100100  ← ASCII character d
```

An encrypted data file can be transformed back into normal form by running the encrypted data through the same encryption process again. To continue with our example, if the above encrypted character code 64H (representing d) is passed through the encryption procedure, we get 42H, which is the ASCII code for character B. □

The `nor` Instruction

The `nor` instruction is needed to implement `not`, as MIPS does not provide it. Its main use is in supporting logical expressions of high-level languages. Furthermore, in languages such as C, it can also be used to implement the bitwise `not` operation.

Another possible use for the `not` instruction is to compute negative numbers in the 1's complement representation. Recall that the 1's complement of a number is simply the complement of the number. However, most systems use the 2's complement representation. The `not` instruction is not particularly useful for generating 2's complement representation. A simple example illustrates this point clearly. In the 2's complement representation, to negate the value in $t0, we have to use

```
not    $t0,$t0
add    $t0,$t0,1
```

However, we can do better than this by using a single `sub` instruction as shown here:

```
sub    $t0,$0,$t0
```

This is precisely what the `neg` pseudoinstruction does.

Shift Instructions

As we have seen in Chapter 10, MIPS supports both left- and right-shift instructions to facilitate bit operations. We have already described the basic shift operations in Chapter 10, therefore we look at the remaining shift instructions in this section.

The number of bit positions to be shifted (i.e., shift count) can be specified as an immediate 5-bit value or via a register. If a register is used, only the least significant five bits are used as the shift count. In the basic left-shift instruction `sll`, the shift count is given as a 5-bit immediate value (see page 170).

The `sllv` (shift left logical variable) instruction

```
sllv   Rdest,Rsrc1,Rsrc2
```

is similar to the `sll` instruction except that the shift count is in the `Rsrc2` register.

There are two types of right-shift operations: logical or arithmetic. The reason for this is that when we shift right, we have the option of filling the vacated left bits by zeros (called logical shift) or copying the sign bit (arithmetic shift).

The logical right-shift instructions—shift right logical (`srl`) and shift right logical variable (`srlv`)—have a format similar to their left-shift cousins. As mentioned, the vacated bits on the left are filled with zeros (see our discussion on page 170).

The arithmetic shift right instructions follow a similar format; however, shifted bit positions on the left are filled with the sign bit (i.e., sign extended), as shown below:

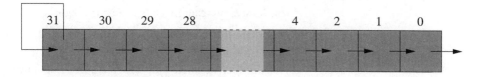

The shift instructions are summarized in Table 15.3. Next we look at the usage of these instructions.

Logical Shift Instructions

Because we discussed the logical shift instructions in Chapter 10, we discuss their usage here. These instructions are useful mainly in these situations:

1. To manipulate bits;
2. To multiply and divide unsigned numbers by a power of 2.

Bit Manipulation The shift operations provide flexibility to manipulate bits as illustrated by the following example.

Example 15.6 *Another encryption example.*

Consider Example 15.5 discussed earlier. In this example, we use the following encryption algorithm: encrypting a byte involves exchanging the upper and lower nibbles (i.e., 4 bits). This algorithm also allows the recovery of the original data by applying the encryption twice, as in Example 15.5.

Assuming that the byte to be encrypted is in the `$t0` register, the following code implements this algorithm.

```
; $t0 contains the byte to be encrypted
move    $t1,$t0
sll     $t0,$t0,4      ; move lower nibble to upper
srl     $t1,$t1,4      ; move upper nibble to lower
or      $t1,$t1,$t0    ; paste them together
; $t1 has the encrypted byte
```

Note that we use the `or` instruction to combine the two nibbles in `$t0` and `$t1`.   □

Table 15.3 MIPS shift instructions

Instruction	Description
sll Rdest,Rsrc,count	Left-shifts Rsrc by count bit positions and stores the result in Rdest. Vacated bits are filled with zeros. count is an immediate value between 0 and 31. If count is outside this range, it uses count MOD 32 as the number of bit positions to be shifted (i.e., takes only the least significant five bits of count).
sllv Rdest,Rsrc1,Rsrc2	Similar to sll except that the count is taken from the least significant five bits of Rsrc2 register.
srl Rdest,Rsrc,count	Right-shifts Rsrc by count bit positions and stores the result in Rdest. This is a logical right-shift (i.e., vacated bits are filled with zeros). count is an immediate value between 0 and 31.
srlv Rdest,Rsrc1,Rsrc2	Similar to srl except that the count is taken from the least significant five bits of Rsrc2 register.
sra Rdest,Rsrc,count	Right-shifts Rsrc by count bit positions and stores the result in Rdest. This is an arithmetic right-shift (i.e., vacated bits are filled with the sign bit). count is an immediate value between 0 and 31.
srav Rdest,Rsrc1,Rsrc2	Similar to sra except that the count is taken from the least significant five bits of the Rsrc2 register.

Multiplication and Division   Shift operations are very effective in performing doubling or halving of unsigned binary numbers. More generally, they can be used to multiply or divide binary numbers by a power of 2. Let us first look at unsigned numbers.

In the decimal number system, we can easily perform multiplication and division by a power of 10. For example, if we want to multiply 254 by 10, we simply append a 0 at the right (analogous to shifting left by a digit with the vacated digit receiving a 0). Similarly, division of 750 by 10 can be accomplished by throwing away the 0 on the right (analogous to right-shift by a digit).

Computers use the binary number system, therefore they can perform multiplication and division by a power of 2. This point is further clarified in Table 15.4. The first half of this table shows how shifting a binary number to the left by one bit position results in multiplying it by 2. Note that the vacated bits are replaced by 0s. This is exactly what the sll instruction does. Therefore, if we want to multiply a number by 8 (i.e., 2^3), we can do so by shifting the number left by three bit positions.

Table 15.4 Doubling and halving of unsigned numbers

Binary number	Decimal value
00011100	28
00111000	56
01110000	112
11100000	224
10101000	168
01010100	84
00101010	42
00010101	21

Table 15.5 Doubling of signed numbers

Signed binary number	Decimal value
00001011	+11
00010110	+22
00101100	+44
01011000	+88
11110101	−11
11101010	−22
11010100	−44
10101000	−88

Similarly, as shown in the second half of the table, shifting right by one bit position is equivalent to dividing by 2. Thus, we can use the `srl` instruction to perform division by a power of 2. For example, to divide a number by 32 (i.e., 2^5), we right-shift the number by five bit positions. Remember that this division process corresponds to integer division, which discards any fractional part of the result.

Doubling Signed Numbers
Doubling a signed number by shifting it left by one bit position may appear to cause problems because the leftmost bit represents the sign. It turns out that this is not a problem at all. Take a look at the examples presented in Table 15.5 to develop your intuition.

The first group presents the doubling effect on positive numbers and the second group shows the doubling effect on negative numbers. In both cases, a 0 replaces the vacated bit. Why isn't shifting out the sign bit causing problems? The reason is that signed numbers are sign-extended to fit a larger-than-required number of bits. For example, if we want to represent numbers in the range of +3 and −4, 3 bits are sufficient. If we use a byte to represent the same range, the number is sign-extended by copying the sign bit into the higher-order five bits, as shown below:

Table 15.6 Division of signed numbers by 2

Signed binary number	Decimal value
01011000	+88
00101100	+44
00010110	+22
00001011	+11
10101000	−88
11010100	−44
11101010	−22
11110101	−11

$$+3 = \overbrace{00000}^{\substack{\textit{sign bit}\\\textit{copied}}}011\text{B}$$

$$-3 = \overbrace{11111}^{\substack{\textit{sign bit}\\\textit{copied}}}101\text{B}$$

Clearly, doubling a signed number is no different than doubling an unsigned number. Thus, no special shift left instruction is needed for signed numbers.

Halving Signed Numbers
Can we also forget about treating the signed numbers differently in halving a number? Unfortunately, we cannot! When we are right-shifting a signed number, the vacated left bit should be replaced by a copy of the sign bit. This rules out the use of shr for signed numbers. See the examples presented in Table 15.6. The sra instruction precisely does this: the sign bit is copied into the vacated bit on the left.

Why use shifts for multiplication and division? The main reason is that shifts are more efficient to execute than the corresponding multiplication or division instructions.

Rotate Instructions

A problem with the shift instructions is that the shifted-out bits are lost. Rotate instructions allow us to capture these bits. The processor does not support rotate instructions. However, assembler provides two rotate pseudoinstructions: rotate left (rol) and rotate right (ror).

In rotate left, the bits shifted out at the left (i.e., the sign-bit side) are inserted on the right-hand side, as shown below:

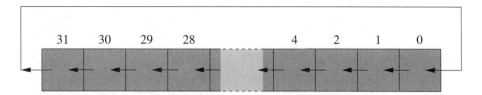

In rotate right, bits falling off the right side are inserted on the sign-bit side, as shown here:

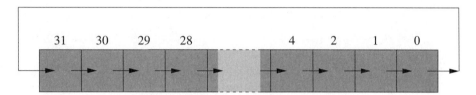

Table 15.7 summarizes the two rotate instructions. As noted, both rotate instructions are pseudoinstructions. For example, the rotate instruction

```
ror†    $t2,$t2,1
```

is translated as

```
sll    $1,$10,31
srl    $10,$10,1
or     $10,$10,$1
```

Note that $t2 maps to the $10 register. This instruction also demonstrates the use of $at, which is the $1 register. You can see from this translation that the assembler uses this register as a temporary register to translate the pseudoinstruction.

Our First Program

The goal of this example is to illustrate how the logical and instruction can be used to test a bit. The main program reads a character from the user and passes this character via $a0 to the print_bin procedure, which outputs the character's ASCII code in binary.

To display the binary value of the input character in $t0, the print_bin procedure tests each bit starting with the most significant (i.e., leftmost) bit. The mask in $t1 is initialized to 0x80, which tests only the value of the most significant bit of the ASCII value. If this bit is 0, the code

```
and    $t2,$t0,$t1
```

sets $t2 to zero. In this case, a 0 is displayed by directing the program flow using the beqz instruction (line 60). Otherwise, a 1 is displayed. The mask is then right-shifted by one bit position (line 69). Thus, we are ready for testing the second most significant bit.

Table 15.7 MIPS rotate instructions

Instruction	Description
rol[†] Rdest,Rsrc,Src2	Rotates contents of Rsrc left by Src2 bit positions and stores the result in Rdest. Src2 can be a register or an immediate value. Bits shifted out on the left are inserted on the right-hand side. Src2 should be a value between 0 and 31. If this value is outside this range, only the least significant five bits of Src2 are used as in the shift instructions.
ror[†] Rdest,Rsrc,Src2	Rotates contents of Rsrc right by Src2 bit positions and stores the result in Rdest. Bits shifted out on the right are inserted on the left-hand side. The Src2 operand is similar to that in the rol instruction.

The process is repeated for each bit of the ASCII value. The pseudocode of the program is as follows:

```
print_bin (char)
    mask := 0x80     {mask is in $t1}
    count := 8    {we don't really use count}
    repeat
        if ((char AND mask) = 0)
        then
            write 0
        else
            write 1
        end if
        mask := mask/2    {done by srl}
        count := count − 1
    until (count = 0)
end print_bin
```

The assembly language program, shown in Program 15.1, follows the pseudocode with one exception. We do not use a count variable to terminate the loop. Instead, we use the fact that, after eight shifts, the mask would have zero as the srl instruction replaces the shifted-out bits by zeros. This is the loop termination condition we use on line 70.

Program 15.1 A program to output binary value of a character

```
 1:   # Outputs binary equivalent of a character     BINCH.ASM
 2:   #
 3:   # Objective: To convert a character to its binary
 4:   #            equivalent.
 5:   #     Input: Requests a character from the user.
 6:   #    Output: Outputs its ASCII value in binary.
 7:   #
 8:   #    $a0 - input character
 9:   #
10:   ################# Data segment #####################
11:         .data
12:   ch_prompt:
13:         .asciiz     "Please enter a character: \n"
14:   out_msg:
15:         .asciiz     "\nThe ASCII value is: "
16:   newline:
17:         .asciiz     "\n"
18:   ch:
19:         .space      2
20:
21:   ################# Code segment #####################
22:         .text
23:         .globl main
24:   main:
25:         la    $a0,ch_prompt      # prompt for a character
26:         li    $v0,4
27:         syscall
28:
29:         la    $a0,ch             # read input character
30:         li    $a1,2
31:         li    $v0,8
32:         syscall
33:
34:         la    $a0,out_msg        # write output message
35:         li    $v0,4
36:         syscall
37:
38:         lb    $a0,ch             # $a0 = input character
39:         jal   print_bin
40:
41:         la    $a0,newline        # output newline
42:         li    $v0,4
43:         syscall
44:
```

```
45:            li      $v0,10              # exit
46:            syscall
47:
48:    #-----------------------------------------------------
49:    # PRINT_BIN receives a character in $a0 and
50:    # prints its binary value.
51:    #    $t0: holds the character
52:    #    $t1: holds the mask byte
53:    #    $t2: temporary
54:    #-----------------------------------------------------
55:    print_bin:
56:            move    $t0,$a0             # char. in $t0
57:            li      $t1,0x80            # mask byte = 0x80
58:    loop:
59:            and     $t2,$t0,$t1
60:            beqz    $t2,zero
61:            li      $a0,1               # print 1
62:            b       skip
63:    zero:
64:            li      $a0,0               # print 0
65:    skip:
66:            li      $v0,1
67:            syscall
68:
69:            srl     $t1,$t1,1           # shift mask byte
70:            bnez    $t1,loop            # exit loop if mask is 0
71:
72:            jr      $ra
```

Illustrative Examples

To further illustrate the application of the logical, shift, and rotate instructions, we give two examples.

Example 15.7 *Binary to octal conversion.*

In this example, we convert a number from its binary representation to the octal system. For example, if the number is -1, it is stored as all 1s in the 2's complement representation (i.e., all 32 bits are 1). Thus, when we express it in the octal number system, we get 37777777777.

The main program is straightforward. It requests a number and passes it on to the print_octal procedure via the $a0 register (lines 35 and 36). This procedure outputs the octal value. Let us look at the logic of this procedure next.

To convert to the octal equivalent, we start with the most significant octal digit. However, because the number of bits (i.e., 32) is not a multiple of 3, the most significant octal digit should be derived using the leftmost two bits of the number. Thus, the most significant digit of the output can be at most 3 as in our example. Once we have converted these two bits, the remaining bits can be processed three bits at a time. The `print_octal` procedure follows the pseudocode shown below:

```
print_octal (number)
    mask := 0xE0000000 {mask is in $t1}
    {Handle the leftmost octal digit—special case}
    temp := number
    shift temp right by 1 bit position
    temp := temp AND mask
    rotate temp left by 3 bit positions
    write temp
    {Handle the remaining 10 octal digits}
    count := 10 {count is in $t3}
    shift number left by 2 bit positions
    repeat
        temp := number AND mask
        rotate temp left by 3 bit positions
        write temp
        shift number left by 3 bit positions
        count := count − 1
    until (count = 0)
end print_octal
```

We set the mask such that the most significant three bits are 1 and the remaining bits are 0. To use the mask, we right-shift the number by one bit position so that the leftmost three bits can be isolated to output the most significant octal digit. However, to print the value of these three bits, we need to move them to the least significant three bit positions. This is done by rotating it three bit positions. To output the remaining 10 octal digits, we use a loop in which we left-shift the number by three bit positions so that we can isolate the next three bits. Once isolated, we rotate left by three bit positions to output the value as explained before.

Program 15.2 A program to convert binary numbers to octal

```
1:  # Integer to octal conversion                      OCTAL.ASM
2:  #
3:  # Objective: To convert a number to its octal
4:  #            equivalent.
5:  #     Input: Requests a number from the user.
6:  #    Output: Outputs its octal value.
7:  #
```

```
 8:    #      $a0 - input number
 9:    #
10:    ################## Data segment #######################
11:          .data
12:    prompt:
13:          .asciiz      "Please enter a number: \n"
14:    out_msg:
15:          .asciiz      "The number in octal is: "
16:    newline:
17:          .asciiz      "\n"
18:
19:    ################## Code segment #######################
20:          .text
21:          .globl main
22:    main:
23:          la    $a0,prompt        # prompt for a character
24:          li    $v0,4
25:          syscall
26:
27:          li    $v0,5             # read input number
28:          syscall
29:          move  $t0,$v0           # save the number in $s0
30:
31:          la    $a0,out_msg       # write output message
32:          li    $v0,4
33:          syscall
34:
35:          move  $a0,$t0           # $a0 = input number
36:          jal   print_octal
37:
38:          la    $a0,newline       # output newline
39:          li    $v0,4
40:          syscall
41:
42:          li    $v0,10            # exit
43:          syscall
44:
45:    #-------------------------------------------------
46:    # PRINT_OCTAL receives a number in $a0 and
47:    # prints its value in octal.
48:    #     $t0: holds the number
49:    #     $t1: holds the mask
50:    #     $t2: used as a temporary
51:    #     $t3: holds the loop count
52:    #-------------------------------------------------
53:    print_octal:
54:          move  $t0,$a0           # copy number to $t0
```

```
55:          li    $t1,0xE0000000      # mask = 0xE0000000
56:
57:          # print the most significant octal digit
58:          srl   $t2,$t0,1
59:          and   $t2,$t2,$t1
60:          rol   $a0,$t2,3
61:          li    $v0,1               # print octal digit
62:          syscall
63:          sll   $t0,$t0,2
64:
65:          li    $t3,10              # loop count = 10
66:
67:  octal_loop:
68:          and   $t2,$t0,$t1
69:          rol   $a0,$t2,3
70:          li    $v0,1               # print octal digit
71:          syscall
72:          sll   $t0,$t0,3           # shift number by 3 bits
73:          sub   $t3,$t3,1
74:          bnez  $t3,octal_loop
75:
76:          jr    $ra
```

The print_octal procedure, shown in Program 15.2, follows the pseudocode with the following mapping. The number is stored in $t0 whereas the mask is in $t1. The $t2 register is used as temp. The loop count is maintained in the $t3 register.

Example 15.8 *Even parity encoding.*

In this example, we parity encode a byte and print its encoded value in the binary form. We use even parity in this example. The most significant bit is used for the parity bit. The idea is simple: if the number of 1s in the remaining 7 bits is even, make the parity bit zero so that the number of 1s, including the parity bit, is even. If the count is odd, we have to make the parity bit a 1 so that the number of 1s is even. We have discussed parity encoding in Examples 15.1 and 15.3.

The main program prompts the user for a character and passes it on to the parity procedure. The parity procedure receives the character via $a0. When it receives the character, the parity bit is zero. Thus, to count the number of 1s, we use all 8 bits. The procedure calls another procedure (count_bits) to count the number of 1s. This function returns the count in $v0. The count_bits procedure is based on the print_bin procedure we used in Program 15.1.

The parity procedure then tests to check if the count is even or odd. This test is done by looking at the least significant bit of the count. We do this by using the and instruction on line 58. If the count is even, we do nothing as the parity bit is zero. If it is odd, we make the parity bit 1 by using the or instruction on line 60.

Program 15.3 Even parity encoding example

```
 1:   # Even parity encoding                          PARITY.ASM
 2:   #
 3:   # Objective: To encode a character using even parity
 4:   #     Input: Requests a character from the user.
 5:   #    Output: Outputs parity encoded byte in binary.
 6:   #
 7:   #    $a0 - input character
 8:   #
 9:   ################### Data segment ######################
10:          .data
11:   ch_prompt:
12:          .asciiz      "Please enter a character: \n"
13:   out_msg:
14:          .asciiz      "\nThe parity encoded value is: "
15:   newline:
16:          .asciiz      "\n"
17:   ch:
18:          .space     2
19:
20:   ################### Code segment ######################
21:          .text
22:          .globl main
23:   main:
24:          la   $a0,ch_prompt      # prompt for a character
25:          li   $v0,4
26:          syscall
27:
28:          la   $a0,ch             # read the input character
29:          li   $a1,2
30:          li   $v0,8
31:          syscall
32:
33:          la   $a0,out_msg        # write output message
34:          li   $v0,4
35:          syscall
36:
37:          lb   $a0,ch             # $a0 = input character
38:          jal  parity
39:
40:          la   $a0,newline        # output newline
41:          li   $v0,4
42:          syscall
43:
44:          li   $v0,10             # exit
45:          syscall
```

```
46:
47:    #-------------------------------------------------
48:    # PARITY receives a character in $a0 and
49:    # prints its binary value.
50:    #     $t0 - temporary
51:    #     $t1 - holds the mask byte
52:    #-------------------------------------------------
53:    parity:
54:          sub    $sp,$sp,4           # save $ra
55:          sw     $ra,0($sp)
56:
57:          jal    count_bits          # returns count in $v0
58:          and    $t0,$v0,1           # count is odd or even?
59:          beqz   $t0,skip_parity     # if even, skip (no action)
60:          or     $a0,$a0,0x80        # else, parity = 1
61:    skip_parity:
62:          jal    print_bin
63:
64:          lw     $ra,0($sp)          # restore $ra
65:          add    $sp,$sp,4
66:          jr     $ra
67:
68:    #-------------------------------------------------
69:    # COUNT_BITS receives a character in $a0 and
70:    # returns the number of 1 bits in $v0.
71:    # Preserves $a0.
72:    #     $t0 - temporary
73:    #     $t1 - holds the mask byte
74:    #-------------------------------------------------
75:    count_bits:
76:          li     $v0,0               # count (in $v0) = 0
77:          li     $t1,0x80            # mask = 0x80
78:    count_loop:
79:          and    $t0,$a0,$t1
80:          beqz   $t0,skip_count
81:          addu   $v0,$v0,1           # increment count
82:    skip_count:
83:          srl    $t1,$t1,1           # shift mask byte
84:          bnez   $t1,count_loop      # exit loop if mask is 0
85:
86:          jr     $ra
87:
88:    #-------------------------------------------------
89:    # PRINT_BIN receives a character in $a0 and
90:    # prints its binary value.
91:    #     $t0 - holds the character
92:    #     $t1 - holds the mask byte
```

```
 93:    #      $t2 - temporary
 94:    #--------------------------------------------------
 95:    print_bin:
 96:            move   $t0,$a0               # char. in $t0
 97:            li     $t1,0x80              # mask = 0x80
 98:    loop:
 99:            and    $t2,$t0,$t1
100:            beqz   $t2,zero
101:            li     $a0,1                 # print 1
102:            b      skip
103:    zero:
104:            li     $a0,0                 # print 0
105:    skip:
106:            li     $v0,1
107:            syscall
108:
109:            srl    $t1,$t1,1             # shift mask byte
110:            bnez   $t1,loop             # exit loop if mask is 0
111:
112:            jr     $ra
```

Once the byte is parity encoded, the parity procedure calls the print_bin procedure to print the parity-encoded byte in binary form. Note that the print_bin procedure is the same as that used in Program 15.1.

Summary

We discussed the logical, shift, and rotate instructions available in the MIPS assembly language. Logical instructions are useful to implement bitwise logical operators and Boolean expressions. However, in some instances Boolean expressions can also be implemented by using conditional jump instructions without using the logical instructions.

Shift and rotate instructions provide flexibility to bit manipulation operations. There are two types of shift instructions: logical shifts work on unsigned data and the arithmetic shifts are meant for signed data.

Shift instructions can be used to multiply or divide by a number that is a power of 2. Shifts for such arithmetic operations are more efficient than the corresponding arithmetic instructions. We have demonstrated the application of these instructions through several examples.

16

Recursion

We can use recursion as an alternative to iteration. Solutions to some problems can be naturally expressed using recursion. We start this chapter with an overview of recursive procedures. Next we give some example recursive procedures in the MIPS assembly language. The advantages and pitfalls associated with a recursive solution as opposed to an iterative solution are discussed towards the end of the chapter.

Introduction

A recursive procedure calls itself, either directly or indirectly through another procedure. In direct recursion, a procedure calls itself directly. In indirect recursion, procedure P makes a call to procedure Q, which in turn calls procedure P. The sequence of calls could be longer before a call is made to procedure P.

Recursion is a powerful tool that allows us to express our solution elegantly. Some solutions can be naturally expressed using recursion. Computing factorials is a classic example. Factorial n, denoted $n!$, is the product of positive integers from 1 to n. For example,

$$5! = 1 \times 2 \times 3 \times 4 \times 5.$$

The factorial function can be formally defined as

factorial(0) = 1
factorial(n) = $n *$ factorial($n - 1$) for $n > 0$.

Recursion shows up in this definition as we define factorial(n) in terms of factorial($n-1$). Every recursive function should have a termination condition to end the recursion. In this example, when $n = 0$, recursion stops. Some other examples include the binary search, quicksort, and Fibonacci function. Towards the end of this chapter, we give examples of quicksort and the Fibonacci function.

How do we express such recursive functions in programming languages? Let us first look at how this function is written in C:

```
int fact(int n)
{
    if (n == 0)
        return(1);
    return(n * fact(n-1));
}
```

This is an example of direct recursion. How is this function implemented? At the conceptual level, its implementation is not any different from implementing other procedures. Once you understand that each procedure call instance is distinct from the others, the fact that a recursive procedure calls itself does not make a big difference.

Each active procedure maintains an activation record, which is stored on the stack. The activation record, which consists of the parameters, return address, local variables, and a frame pointer, comes into existence when a procedure is invoked and disappears when the procedure is terminated. Thus, for each procedure that is not terminated, an activation record that contains the state of that procedure is stored. A stack is used to keep these activation records. The number of activation records, and hence the amount of stack space required to run the program, depend on the depth of recursion.

Figure 16.1 shows the stack activation records for factorial(3). As you can see from this figure, each call to the factorial function creates an activation record. In the next two sections we look at some example recursive procedures in the MIPS assembly language.

Our First Program

In MIPS, we can write procedures without using the stack. For simple leaf procedures, we do not have to use the stack. The availability of a large number of registers allows us to use register-based parameter passing. However, when we write recursive procedures, we have to use the stack because recursive procedures are essentially nonleaf procedures (see our discussion of leaf and nonleaf procedures on page 189).

To understand how we can write a recursive procedure, let us look at the factorial function. We have defined factorial at the beginning of this chapter. We implement a slightly modified definition of factorial, as implemented in Chapter 13 (see the example on page 230 that implements the iterative version).

$$\text{fact}(n) = 1 \text{ for } n \leq 1.$$
$$= n * \text{fact}(n - 1) \text{ for } n \geq 2.$$

Program 16.1 requests an integer n from the user and passes this on to the factorial procedure (`fact`) via the $a0 register. After returning from the procedure, it outputs fact(n).

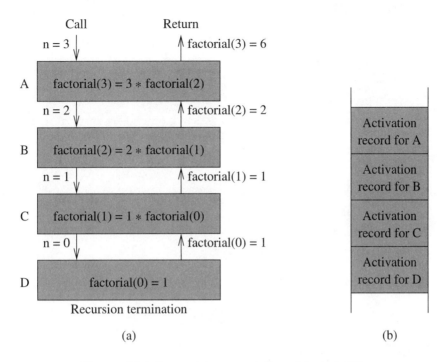

Call   Return
n = 3   ↑ factorial(3) = 6

A   factorial(3) = 3 * factorial(2)

n = 2   ↑ factorial(2) = 2

B   factorial(2) = 2 * factorial(1)

n = 1   ↑ factorial(1) = 1

C   factorial(1) = 1 * factorial(0)

n = 0   ↑ factorial(0) = 1

D   factorial(0) = 1

Recursion termination

(a)

Activation
record for A

Activation
record for B

Activation
record for C

Activation
record for D

(b)

Figure 16.1 Recursive computation of factorial(3).

Program 16.1 Computing factorial—an example recursive function

```
 1:   # Finds factorial of a number                    FACTORIAL.ASM
 2:   #
 3:   # Objective: Computes factorial of an integer.
 4:   #            To demonstrate recursive procedures.
 5:   #     Input: Requests an integer n from the user.
 6:   #    Output: Outputs n!
 7:   #
 8:   #    $a0 - used to pass n
 9:   #    $v0 - used to return result
10:   #
11:   ################# Data segment #####################
12:          .data
13:   prompt:
14:          .asciiz     "Please enter a positive integer: \n"
15:   out_msg:
16:          .asciiz     "The factorial is: "
17:   error_msg:
18:          .asciiz     "Not a positive number. Try again.\n"
19:   newline:
```

```
20:         .asciiz     "\n"
21:
22:  ################## Code segment ######################
23:         .text
24:         .globl main
25:  main:
26:         la    $a0,prompt          # prompt user for input
27:         li    $v0,4
28:         syscall
29:
30:  try_again:
31:         li    $v0,5               # read number into $a0
32:         syscall
33:         move  $a0,$v0
34:
35:         bgez  $a0,num_OK
36:         la    $a0,error_msg       # write error message
37:         li    $v0,4
38:         syscall
39:         b     try_again
40:
41:  num_OK:
42:         jal   fact
43:         move  $s0,$v0
44:
45:         la    $a0,out_msg         # write output message
46:         li    $v0,4
47:         syscall
48:
49:         move  $a0,$s0             # output factorial
50:         li    $v0,1
51:         syscall
52:
53:         la    $a0,newline         # write newline
54:         li    $v0,4
55:         syscall
56:
57:         li    $v0,10              # exit
58:         syscall
59:
60:  #------------------------------------------------------------
61:  # FACT receives n in $a0 and returns the result in $v0.
62:  # It uses recursion to find n!
63:  #------------------------------------------------------------
64:  fact:
65:         subu  $sp,$sp,4           # allocate stack space
66:         sw    $ra,0($sp)          # save return address
```

```
67:
68:           bgt    $a0,1,one_up        # recursion termination
69:           li     $v0,1
70:           b      return
71:
72:   one_up:
73:           subu   $a0,$a0,1           # recursion with (n-1)
74:           jal    fact
75:           addu   $a0,$a0,1
76:           mulou  $v0,$a0,$v0         # $v0 = $a0*$v0
77:
78:   return:
79:           lw     $ra,0($sp)          # restore return address
80:           addu   $sp,$sp,4           # clear stack space
81:           jr     $ra
```

First we have to determine the state information that needs to be saved (i.e., our activation record). In all procedures, we need to store the return address. This is what we did for nonleaf procedures (see Example 11.2 on page 202). In our factorial example, we need to keep track of the current value in $a0. However, we don't really have to save $a0 on the stack as we can restore its value by adding 1, as shown on line 75. Thus, we save just the return address (lines 65 and 66) and restore it on lines 79 and 80. The body of the procedure can be divided into two parts: recursion termination and recursive call. The recursion termination condition is implemented on lines 68–70.

If the value is more than 1, a recursive call is made with $(n-1)$ (lines 73 and 74). After the call is returned, $a0 is incremented to make it n before multiplying it with the values returned for $(n-1)!$ in $v0 (lines 75 and 76).

In this example, each recursive call takes four bytes of stack space. Thus, the amount of stack space required to run the program is $4n$ bytes. In general, the stack space required by recursive procedures is proportional to the number of recursive calls.

Illustrative Examples

In the last section, we introduced a simple program to illustrate how recursion is implemented in the MIPS assembly language. In this section, we present two more examples to further illustrate the concepts introduced in this chapter.

Example 16.1 *Compute the Fibonacci function.*
We have seen an iterative version of this function in Chapter 11 (see page 200). Here we write a recursive procedure to compute fib(n). Recall that the Fibonacci function is defined as follows.

$$\text{fib}(1) = 1,$$
$$\text{fib}(2) = 1,$$
$$\text{fib}(n) = \text{fib}(n - 1) + \text{fib}(n - 2) \text{ for } n > 2.$$

The main program takes care of the user interface. It requests n and invokes the fib procedure and outputs the fib(n) value returned by the procedure. It invokes the procedure on line 32 after copying n into the $a0 register.

The fib procedure stores the return address on the stack as in the last example. In addition, we need to keep two values on the stack: the last and second to last Fibonacci values that are in $v0 and $s0, respectively. Thus, our stack frame consists of three values: $ra, $v0, and $s0 (see lines 57–60). These three registers are restored on lines 80–83. The fib procedure is recursively called on lines 69 and 74 to compute fib($n - 1$) and fib($n - 2$), respectively. The rest of the code is straightforward to follow.

Program 16.2 Fibonacci function using recursion

```
 1:   # Computes Fibonacci number              FIB_RECUR.ASM
 2:   #
 3:   # Objective: Computes the Fibonacci number.
 4:   #            Uses recursion.
 5:   #     Input: Requests a number n.
 6:   #    Output: Outputs Fibonacci number fib(n).
 7:   #
 8:   #     $a0 - number n is passed
 9:   #     $v0 - fib(n) is returned
10:   #
11:   ################## Data segment ##################
12:           .data
13:   prompt:
14:           .asciiz     "Please enter a number n: \n"
15:   out_msg:
16:           .asciiz     "Fib(n) = "
17:   newline:
18:           .asciiz     "\n"
19:
20:   ################## Code segment ##################
21:           .text
22:           .globl main
23:   main:
24:           la     $a0,prompt      # prompt user for input
25:           li     $v0,4
26:           syscall
27:
28:           li     $v0,5           # read number into $a0
```

```
29:          syscall
30:          move   $a0,$v0
31:
32:          jal    fib
33:          move   $s0,$v0
34:
35:          la     $a0,out_msg      # write output message
36:          li     $v0,4
37:          syscall
38:
39:          move   $a0,$s0          # output fib(n)
40:          li     $v0,1
41:          syscall
42:
43:          la     $a0,newline      # write newline
44:          li     $v0,4
45:          syscall
46:
47:          li     $v0,10           # exit
48:          syscall
49:
50:  #-------------------------------------------------
51:  # FIB receives an integer n in $a0 and
52:  # returns fib(n) in $v0 (uses recursion)
53:  #    $s0: holds the second to last fib value
54:  #    $v0: holds the last fib value
55:  #-------------------------------------------------
56:  fib:
57:          sub    $sp,$sp,12       # reserve 12 bytes for
58:          sw     $s0,($sp)        # $ra and local variables
59:          sw     $a0,4($sp)
60:          sw     $ra,8($sp)
61:
62:          bgtu   $a0,2,Nis2plus
63:          li     $v0,1            # if n = 1 or n = 2
64:          b      fib_done         # return 1
65:
66:  Nis2plus:
67:          # compute fib(n-1)
68:          sub    $a0,$a0,1
69:          jal    fib
70:          move   $s0,$v0          # save fib(n-1) in $s0
71:
72:          # compute fib(n-2)
73:          sub    $a0,$a0,1
74:          jal    fib              # fib(n-2) in $v0
75:
```

```
76:          # compute fib(n)= fib(n-1) + fib(n-2)
77:          add    $v0,$s0,$v0
78:
79: fib_done:
80:          lw     $s0,($sp)        # restore and return
81:          lw     $a0,4($sp)
82:          lw     $ra,8($sp)
83:          add    $sp,$sp,12
84:          jr     $ra
```

Unlike the factorial example, the stack space requirement of this example is higher for two reasons. Each procedure call needs 12 bytes on the stack. In addition, each procedure call results in two recursive calls. This further increases the stack space requirement.

Example 16.2 *Another recursion example—quicksort.*

In this example, we implement the quicksort algorithm using recursion. Quicksort is one of the most popular sorting algorithms. Once you understand the basic principle of the quicksort, you will see why recursion naturally expresses it.

At its heart, quicksort uses a divide-and-conquer strategy. The original sort problem is reduced to two smaller sort problems. This is done by selecting a partition element x and partitioning the array into two subarrays: all elements less than x are placed in one subarray and all elements greater than x in the other. Now, we have to sort these two subarrays, which are smaller than the original array. We apply the same procedure to sort these two subarrays. This is where the recursive nature of the algorithm shows up. The quicksort procedure to sort an N-element array is summarized below:

1. Select a partition element x.

2. Assume that we know where this element x should be in the final sorted array. Let it be at array[i]. We give details of this step shortly.

3. Move all elements that are less than x into positions array[0] ⋯ array[i-1]. Similarly, move those elements that are greater than x into positions array[i+1] ⋯ array[N-1]. Note that these two subarrays are not sorted.

4. Now apply the quicksort procedure recursively to sort these two subarrays until the array is sorted.

In Step 2, we assume that we know where x should be in the sorted array. But how do we know x's final position without sorting the array? We really don't have to sort the array; we just need to know the number of elements either before or after it.

To clarify the working of the quicksort algorithm, let us look at an example. In this example, and in our quicksort implementation, we pick the last element as the partition value x. In the following example, we pick 6 as the partition value.

Initial state: 2 9 8 1 3 4 7 6   ⟵   Partition element;
After 1st pass: 2 1 3 4 **6** 7 9 8   Partition element 6 is in its final place.

After 6 has been placed in its final position, we get the following two subarrays:

1st subarray: 2 1 3 4
2nd subarray: 7 9 8

The second pass works on these two subarrays.

Obviously, selection of the partition element influences the performance of the quick-sort algorithm. There are several better ways of selecting the partition value; you can get these details in most textbooks on sorting.

To move the partition element to its final place, we use two pointers i and j. Initially, i points to the first element and j points to the second to last element. Note that we are using the last element as the partition element x. The index i is advanced until it points to an element that is greater than or equal to x. Similarly, j is moved backwards until it points to an element that is less than or equal to x. Then we exchange the two values at i and j. We continue this process until i is greater than or equal to j. In the quicksort pseudocode, shown below, lo and hi identify the low and high bounds of the array to be sorted.

```
quick_sort (array, lo, hi)
    if (hi > lo)
        x := array[hi]
        i := lo
        j := hi
        while (i < j)
            while (array[i] < x)
                i := i + 1
            end while
            while (array[j] > x)
                j := j − 1
            end while
            if (i < j)
                array[i] ⟺ array[j]          /* exchange values */
            end if
        end while
        array[i] ⟺ array[hi]                  /* exchange values */
        quick_sort (array, lo, i−1)
        quick_sort (array, i+1, hi)
    end if
end quick_sort
```

Program 16.3 gives an implementation of the quicksort algorithm in the MIPS assembly language. The main program reads integers from input until terminated by a zero (lines 35–41). We store the zero in the array, as we use it as the sentinel to output the sorted array (see lines 55 and 56). Lines 44–46 prepare the two arguments for the qsort procedure.

Program 16.3 Quicksort—another example recursive program

```
 1:   # Sorting numbers using quicksort            QUICKSORT.ASM
 2:   #
 3:   # Objective: Sorts an array of integers using quicksort.
 4:   #            Uses recursion.
 5:   #     Input: Requests integers from the user;
 6:   #            terminated by entering a zero.
 7:   #    Output: Outputs the sorted integer array.
 8:   #
 9:   #     $a0 - start of array
10:   #     $a1 - beginning of (sub)array (lo pointer)
11:   #     $a2 - end of (sub)array (hi pointer)
12:   #
13:   ################## Data segment ######################
14:          .data
15:   prompt:
16:          .ascii      "Please enter nonzero integers. \n"
17:          .asciiz     "Entering a zero terminates the input.\n"
18:   output_msg:
19:          .asciiz     "The sorted array is: \n"
20:   newline:
21:          .asciiz     "\n"
22:   .align 2
23:   array:
24:          .space      200           # space for 50 integers
25:
26:   ################## Code segment ######################
27:          .text
28:          .globl main
29:   main:
30:          la    $a0,prompt          # prompt user for input
31:          li    $v0,4
32:          syscall
33:
34:          la    $t0,array
35:   read_more:
36:          li    $v0,5               # read a number
37:          syscall
38:          sw    $v0,($t0)           # store it in the array
```

```
39:             beqz  $v0,exit_read
40:             addu  $t0,$t0,4
41:             b     read_more
42:  exit_read:
43:             # prepare arguments for procedure call
44:             la    $a1,array        # $a1 = lo pointer
45:             move  $a2,$t0
46:             subu  $a2,$a2,4        # $a2 = hi pointer
47:             jal   qsort
48:
49:             la    $a0,output_msg   # write output message
50:             li    $v0,4
51:             syscall
52:
53:             la    $t0,array
54:  write_more:
55:             lw    $a0,($t0)        # output sorted array
56:             beqz  $a0,exit_write
57:             li    $v0,1
58:             syscall
59:             la    $a0,newline      # write newline message
60:             li    $v0,4
61:             syscall
62:             addu  $t0,$t0,4
63:             b     write_more
64:  exit_write:
65:
66:             li    $v0,10           # exit
67:             syscall
68:
69:  #-----------------------------------------------------------
70:  # QSORT receives a pointer to the start of (sub)array
71:  # in $a1 and end of (sub)array in $a2.
72:  #-----------------------------------------------------------
73:  qsort:
74:             subu  $sp,$sp,16       # save registers
75:             sw    $a1,0($sp)
76:             sw    $a2,4($sp)
77:             sw    $a3,8($sp)
78:             sw    $ra,12($sp)
79:
80:             ble   $a2,$a1,done     # end recursion
81:                                    # if hi <= lo
82:             move  $t0,$a1
83:             move  $t1,$a2
84:
85:             lw    $t5,($t1)        # $t5 = xsep
```

```
 86:
 87:    lo_loop:                              #
 88:          lw    $t2,($t0)                 #
 89:          bge   $t2,$t5,lo_loop_done      # LO while loop
 90:          addu  $t0,$t0,4                 #
 91:          b     lo_loop                   #
 92:    lo_loop_done:
 93:
 94:          subu  $t1,$t1,4          # hi = hi-1
 95:    hi_loop:
 96:          ble   $t1,$t0,sep_done          #
 97:          lw    $t3,($t1)                 #
 98:          blt   $t3,$t5,hi_loop_done      # HI while loop
 99:          subu  $t1,$t1,4                 #
100:          b     hi_loop                   #
101:    hi_loop_done:
102:
103:          sw    $t2,($t1)                 #
104:          sw    $t3,($t0)                 # x[i]<=>x[j]
105:          b     lo_loop                   #
106:
107:    sep_done:
108:          move  $t1,$a2                   #
109:          lw    $t4,($t0)                 #
110:          lw    $t5,($t1)                 # x[i] <=> x[hi]
111:          sw    $t5,($t0)                 #
112:          sw    $t4,($t1)                 #
113:
114:          move  $a3,$a2             # save HI for second call
115:          move  $a2,$t0                   #
116:          subu  $a2,$a2,4           # set hi as i-1
117:          jal   qsort
118:
119:          move  $a1,$a2                   #
120:          addu  $a1,$a1,8           # set lo as i+1
121:          move  $a2,$a3
122:          jal   qsort
123:    done:
124:          lw    $a1,0($sp)          # restore registers
125:          lw    $a2,4($sp)
126:          lw    $a3,8($sp)
127:          lw    $ra,12($sp)
128:          addu  $sp,$sp,16
129:
130:          jr    $ra
```

The `qsort` recursive procedure stores `$a3` in addition to the `$a1`, `$a2`, and `$ra` registers. This is because we store the end-of-subarray pointer in `$a3`, which is required for the second recursive call (line 122). Because MIPS does not have an addressing mode that allows access to arrays using the index, we have to use pointers to access individual elements. This means updating the index involves adding or subtracting 4 (see lines 90, 94, 99, and 116). The rest of the procedure follows the quicksort algorithm described earlier.

The stack space requirements of this program are similar to the Fibonacci program in that each procedure call generates two recursive calls. For each call, it needs 16 bytes of stack space.

Recursion Versus Iteration

In theory, every recursive function has an iterative counterpart. We have seen two examples: factorial and Fibonacci functions. We have looked at the recursive versions of these two functions in this chapter. The iterative versions are given in previous chapters (see Program 13.1 on page 230 for the factorial function and Program 11.3 on page 200 for the Fibonacci function).

From these examples, it is obvious that the recursive versions reflect the mathematical definition of the functions more directly. Once you get through the initial learning problems with recursion, recursive code is easier to understand for those functions that are defined recursively.

This leads us to the question of when to use recursion. To answer this question, we need to look at the potential problems recursion can cause. There are two main problems with recursion:

- *Inefficiency:* In most cases, recursive versions tend to be inefficient. You can see this point by comparing the recursive and iterative versions of the factorial function. The recursive version induces more overheads to invoke and return from procedure calls. To compute $N!$, we need to call the factorial function about N times. In the iterative version, the loop iterates about N times.

  Recursion could also introduce duplicate computation. For example, to compute the Fibonacci number `fib(5)` a recursive procedure computes `fib(3)` two times, `fib(2)` three times, and so on, as shown in Figure 16.2.

- *Increased Memory Requirement:* Recursion tends to demand more memory. This can be seen from the simple factorial example. For large N, the demand for stack memory can be excessive. The other examples (Fibonacci and quicksort) require even more stack memory. In some applications, the limit on the available stack memory may make the recursive version impractical.

On the positive side, however, recursion leads to better understanding of the code for those naturally recursive problems. In this case, recursion may be useful as it aids in program maintenance.

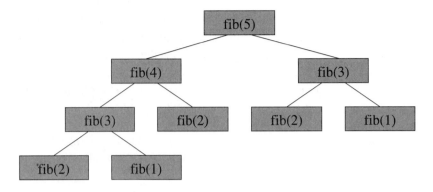

Figure 16.2 Recursive computation of fib(5).

Summary

We can use recursive procedures as an alternative to iterative ones. A procedure that calls itself, whether directly or indirectly, is called a recursive procedure. In direct recursion, a procedure calls itself as in our factorial example. In indirect recursion, a procedure may initiate a sequence of calls that eventually results in calling the procedure itself.

For some applications, we can write an elegant solution because recursion is a natural fit. We illustrated the principles of recursion using three examples: factorial, Fibonacci, and quicksort. We presented recursive versions of these functions in the MIPS assembly language. In the last section we identified the tradeoffs associated with recursion as opposed to iteration.

17

Floating-Point Operations

In this chapter, we look at floating-point instructions. The floating-point unit coprocessor supports several floating-point instructions. We describe the floating-point registers of the floating-point unit. The floating-point instructions include the four basic arithmetic operations on both single-precision and double-precision floating-point numbers. We give several examples to illustrate the application of these instructions. We conclude the chapter with a summary.

Introduction

In the previous chapters, we have looked at arithmetic operations on integers. These operations are supported by the CPU. In the MIPS architecture, the floating-point operations are supported by a separate Floating-Point Unit (FPU), which is coprocessor 1. There are instructions that move data between the processor registers and the FPU registers. The FPU supports the basic arithmetic operations, including addition, subtraction, multiplication, and division. These operations are available for both single-precision and double-precision floating-point numbers.

A single-precision floating-point number takes 32 bits whereas the double-precision number takes 64 bits. These are useful in implementing the floating-point numbers supported by high-level languages. For example, the C `float` data type corresponds to the single-precision number and the `double` to the double-precision floating-point number.

When we have several formats to represent numbers, we need instructions to convert a number from one representation to another. The FPU instruction set includes instructions to do conversions among integers, and single-precision and double-precision floating-point numbers. For example, there are instructions to convert integers to double-precision floating-point numbers and vice versa. Such conversions are often done in high-level languages. Suppose we declared the following variables in C.

```
double    average, sum;
int       count;
```

Then the statement

```
average = sum/count;
```

computes the average. However, because sum is a double and count is an integer, it promotes count to double before the division. As another example, consider the following declaration.

```
double    average;
int       result;
```

Then the statement

```
result = (int *) average;
```

uses the cast operator to convert average to the integer format before assigning it to the result variable. Conversions like these can be done using the conversion instructions supported by the FPU.

Our goal in this chapter is to give an overview of the floating-point instructions. We describe the FPU instruction set along with its registers. For complete details, you should consult the MIPS documentation. We start this chapter with a description of the registers available in the FPU.

FPU Registers

The floating-point unit has 32 floating-point registers. These registers are numbered like the CPU registers. In the floating-point instructions we refer to these registers as $f0, $f1, and so on. Each of these registers is 32 bits wide. Thus, each register can hold one single-precision floating-point number. How can we use these registers to store double-precision floating-point numbers? Because these numbers require 64 bits, register pairs are used to store them. This strategy is implemented by storing double-precision numbers in even-numbered registers. For example, when we store a double-precision number in $f2, it is actually stored in registers $f2 and $f3.

As with the CPU registers, the FPU register usage convention has been established to make programs portable (see Table 17.1). Even though each floating-point register can hold a single-precision number, the numbers are often stored in even registers so that they can be easily upgraded to double-precision values.

The first four registers are used to return values from a procedure. These registers can be used to return two double-precision floating-point numbers. The caller-save temporaries can be used freely by the called procedure. If the caller needs the values in these

Table 17.1 Floating-point register usage convention

$f0 – $f3	Used to return values from a procedure
$f4 – $f11	Used as temporaries (caller saved) The called procedure can overwrite them.
$f12 – $f15	Used for parameter passing These registers are not preserved across procedure calls.
$f16 – $f19	Used as temporaries (caller-saved) The called procedure can overwrite them.
$f20 – $f31	Used as temporaries (callee saved) The called procedure cannot overwrite them.

registers, it is responsible for saving them. The last 12 registers are used as callee-save temporaries. If the called procedure uses these registers, it must restore them before returning from the procedure. The registers $f12 to $f15 are used for parameter passing. For example, these can be used to pass the first two double values. If more need to be passed, we have to use the stack. Later in this chapter we show how parameter passing is done via the stack.

Floating-Point Instructions

The FPU supports several floating-point instructions including the standard four arithmetic operations. Furthermore, as are the processor instructions, several pseudoinstructions are derived from these instructions. We start this section with the data movement instructions.

Move Instructions

There are several instructions to move data between registers. Let us look at some of these instructions next. The move instruction (mov) can be used to move data between two floating-point registers. The size of the operand is specified as shown below:

```
mov.s     FRdest,FRsrc
```

This instruction copies a single-precision floating-point number from the FRsrc to the Frdest register. If we want to copy a double-precision number, use mov.d instead. For example, the instruction

```
mov.d     $f12,$f0
```

copies the double floating-point in $f0 into the $f12 register.

The mov instruction facilitates data transfer between two floating-point registers. However, we also need to move data between the CPU registers and the floating-point registers. This data movement is facilitated by the mtc1 and mfc1 instructions. Note that the 1 in these instructions identifies coprocessor 1. There are also instructions to address other coprocessors (e.g., mtf0 for coprocessor 0, mtf2 for coprocessor 2, and so on) but we focus here only on the FPU, which is coprocessor 1.

The mfc1 (move from coprocessor 1) instruction

```
mfc1    Rdest,FRsrc
```

moves a 32-bit value from the FRsrc floating-point register to the Rdest CPU register. To move the data in the opposite direction, we use the mtc1 (move to coprocessor 1) instruction, which has the following format.

```
mtc1    FRdest,Rsrc
```

This instruction moves a 32-bit value from the Rsrc CPU register to the FRdest FPU register.

These instructions are useful to move single-precision floating-point numbers between CPU and FPU registers. However, if we want to move double-precision values, we have to use two of these instructions. There is a pseudoinstruction that does this job as shown here:

```
mfc1.d    Rdest,FRsrc
```

This pseudoinstruction copies the contents of the two floating-point registers (FRsrc and FRsrc+1) to two CPU registers (Rdest and Rdest+1). For example, the pseudoinstruction

```
mfc1.d    $t0,$f2
```

is translated as

```
mfc1    $8,$2
mfc1    $9,$3
```

Note that the second register number in these two instructions refers to the floating-point register. The first register number refers to a CPU register. As you know, $t0 maps to $8. Thus, we can rewrite this sequence as

```
mfc1    $t0,$f2
mfc1    $t1,$f3
```

This is more readable than the code generated by SPIM.

Load and Store Instructions

The basic load instruction `lwc1` (load a word from memory to an FPU register) has the following format.

```
lwc1    FRdest,address
```

Notice that the instruction includes the coprocessor 1 (`c1`), which is the FPU supporting these instructions. This instruction loads a 32-bit word from `address` into the `FRdest` floating-point register. The `address` can be specified as `offset(base)` where `base` is a CPU register containing the base address. For example, the instruction

```
lwc1    $f0,0($sp)
```

loads the 32-bit word at the top of stack into the `$f0` floating-point register.

The corresponding store instruction has the following format.

```
swc1    FRdest,address
```

It stores the contents of `FRdest` in memory at `address`. For example, if we want to store the contents of `$f0` on the stack, we could do this by the following instruction.

```
swc1    $f0,0($sp)
```

Although these load and store instructions take care of the single-precision loads and stores, we have to use two of these instructions to load/store doubles. To simplify loads and stores, several pseudoinstructions are available. Let us first look at the load pseudoinstructions. The pseudoinstruction

```
l.s     FRdest,address
```

loads a single-precision floating-point number. For example, the pseudoinstruction

```
l.s     $f2,0($sp)
```

is translated as

```
lwc1 $f2,0($29)
```

Recall that `$sp` maps to `$29`. To load a double floating-point number, use `l.d` as in the following example.

```
l.d     $f2,0($sp)
```

It is translated as

```
lwc1 $f2,0($29)
lwc1 $f3,4($29)
```

We can use s.s to store a single-precision value and s.d for a double-precision value. The s.s pseudoinstruction is translated using a single swc1 instruction. The s.d instruction requires two instructions as shown in the following example.

```
s.d     $f0,0($sp)
```

is translated as

```
swc1    $f0,0($29)
swc1    $f1,4($29)
```

Two additional pseudoinstructions are available to load constants into floating-point registers. We illustrate these instructions with two examples. The li.s can be used to load single-precision values into a floating-point register. The pseudoinstruction

```
li.s    $f0,0.0
```

is translated as

```
ori     $1,$0,0
mtc1    $1,$0
```

We can load a double-precision constant using the li.d pseudoinstruction as shown below:

```
li.d    $f2,0.0
```

is translated as

```
ori     $1,$0,0
mtc1    $1,$2
ori     $1,$0,0
mtc1    $1,$3
```

Arithmetic Instructions

The FPU supports several arithmetic instructions to perform addition, subtraction, multiplication, and division on single- as well as double-precision floating-point numbers. All four instructions use the same format. We use the sub instruction to illustrate the basic format.

```
sub.s   FRdest,FRsrc1,FRsrc2   # single-precision subtract
sub.d   FRdest,FRsrc1,FRsrc2   # double-precision subtract
```

It places the result of FRsrc1−FRsrc2 in the FRdest register. For addition, use add.s or add.d as in the following example.

```
    add.s    $f0,$f0,$f2
```

This instruction adds the contents of $f0 and $f2 and places the result in the $f0 register. To divide floating-point numbers, we use div.s or div.d as shown in the example here.

```
    div.d    $f0,$f2,$f4
```

This instruction divides the double floating-point value in $f2 and $f3 by that in $f4 and $f5 and places the result in the $f0 and $f1 registers. This instruction generates exceptions to indicate conditions such as divide-by-zero, underflow, and overflow.

For multiplication, we use mul.s or mul.d depending on the precision of the numbers to be multiplied. Like the div instruction, it also generates exceptions for conditions such underflow and overflow.

In addition to these basic four arithmetic operations, the FPU also provides abs and neg instructions. The abs instruction computes the absolute value and has the following format.

```
    abs.s    FRdest,FRsrc    # for single-precision values
    abs.d    FRdest,FRsrc    # for double-precision values
```

It computes the absolute value of the number in FRsrc and places the result in the FRdest register. The negate instruction

```
    neg.s    FRdest,FRsrc    # for single-precision values
    neg.d    FRdest,FRsrc    # for double-precision values
```

reverses the sign of the number in FRsrc and places the result in the FRdest register.

Comparison Instructions

Three basic comparison instructions are available to compare floating-point numbers to establish $<$, $=$, and $\leq$ relationships. All three instructions have the same format. We use the following to illustrate their format.

```
    c.lt.s    FRsrc1,FRsrc2    # for single-precision values
    c.lt.d    FRsrc1,FRsrc2    # for double-precision values
```

It compares the two floating-point values in FRsrc1 and FRsrc2 and sets the floating-point condition flag if FRsrc1 $<$ FRsrc2.

To establish the "equal to" relationship, we use c.eq.s or c.eq.d. For the $\leq$ relationship, we use either c.le.s or c.le.d depending on the precision of the values being compared.

Once the floating-point condition flag is set to reflect the relationship, this flag value can be tested by the CPU using bc1t or bc1f instructions. The format of these instructions is the same. For example, the instruction

```
bc1t    target
```

transfers control to `target` if the floating-point condition flag is true. Here is an example that compares the values in $f0 and $f2 and transfers control to skip1 if $f0 < $f2.

```
c.lt.s  $f0,$f2  # $f0 < $f2?
bc1t    skip1    # if yes, jump to skip1
```

We don't really need instructions for the missing relationships $>$, $\neq$, or $\geq$. For example, the code

```
c.le.s  $f0,$f2  # $f0 ≤ $f2?
bc1f    skip1    # if not, jump to skip1
```

transfers control to skip1 if $f0 > $f2.

Conversion Instructions

When we have numbers of different types—integers and single-precision and double-precision floating-point values—we often need to convert numbers from one representation to the other. The final group of instructions we discuss here deals with this conversion. These instructions allow us to convert values among the integer and single and double floating-point number representations. All these instructions follow the same format. We illustrate the format using the instruction that converts from an integer to double floating-point number. The format of this instruction is shown here:

```
cvt.d.w  FRdest,FRsrc
```

This instruction converts the integer in `FRsrc` to a double floating-point number and stores it in the `FRdest` register. Typically, we move the integer to be converted from a CPU register to an FPU register using the `mtc1` instruction. The following code demonstrates the use of this conversion.

```
mtc1     $a1,$f4  # move the integer to $f4
cvt.d.w  $f4,$f4  # convert the word in $f4 to double
```

The `mtc1` instruction copies the integer in $a1 to the $f4 register. The second instruction coverts the integer in $f4 to double floating-point format. A summary of the conversion instructions is given in Table 17.2.

Our First Program

In our first floating-point program, shown in Program 17.1, we add three double-precision floating-point numbers and output their sum. We read the input values as doubles using the read_double system call (see lines 26–27, 30-31, and 34–35). This system call places the double in $f0 (i.e., in registers $f0 and $f1). We use the move instruction to copy this value into another register (see lines 28, 32, and 36).

Table 17.2 Conversion instructions

cvt.s.w	Convert integer to single-precision floating-point value.
cvt.d.w	Convert integer to double-precision floating-point value.
cvt.w.s	Convert single-precision floating-point number to integer.
cvt.d.s	Convert single-precision floating-point number to double-precision floating-point number.
cvt.w.d	Convert double-precision floating-point number to integer.
cvt.s.d	Convert double-precision floating-point number to single-precision floating-point number.

Program 17.1 A simple floating-point addition example

```
 1:  # Find the sum of three numbers              FSUM.ASM
 2:  #
 3:  # Objective: Finds the sum of three double-precision
 4:  #            floating-point numbers
 5:  #     Input: Requests three numbers.
 6:  #    Output: Outputs the floating-point sum.
 7:  #
 8:  ################## Data segment ##################
 9:          .data
10:  prompt:
11:          .asciiz     "Please enter three numbers: \n"
12:  sum_msg:
13:          .asciiz     "The sum is: "
14:  newline:
15:          .asciiz     "\n"
16:
17:  ################## Code segment ##################
18:          .text
19:          .globl main
20:  main:
21:          # data input phase
22:          la      $a0,prompt      # prompt user for input
23:          li      $v0,4
24:          syscall
25:
26:          li      $v0,7           # read 1st double into $f4
27:          syscall
```

```
28:             mov.d  $f4,$f0
29:
30:             li     $v0,7          # read 2nd double into $f6
31:             syscall
32:             mov.d  $f6,$f0
33:
34:             li     $v0,7          # read 3rd double into $f8
35:             syscall
36:             mov.d  $f8,$f0
37:
38:             # addition phase
39:             add.d  $f4,$f4,$f6
40:             add.d  $f4,$f4,$f8    # $f4 = sum
41:
42:             # result output phase
43:             la     $a0,sum_msg    # write sum message
44:             li     $v0,4
45:             syscall
46:
47:             mov.d  $f12,$f4       # output sum
48:             li     $v0,3
49:             syscall
50:
51:             la     $a0,newline    # write newline
52:             li     $v0,4
53:             syscall
54:
55:             li     $v0,10         # exit
56:             syscall
```

The three input values in $f4, $f6, and $f8 are added on lines 39 and 40 using the add.d instruction. The result of this addition is placed in $f4. This value is moved into $f12 on line 47, which is output using the print_double function (lines 48–49).

Illustrative Examples

We now give three examples to further illustrate the application of the floating-point instructions discussed in this chapter.

Example 17.1 *Find the minimum of two floating-point numbers.*

In this example, we output the minimum of the two floating-point numbers given as input to the program. The main program reads the two input numbers: the first one is read as a single-precision floating-point number using the read_float system call (lines 30–31). This number, which is in $f0, is moved to $f12 using the mov.s instruction on line 32. The second number is read as a double using the `read_double` system call (lines 34–35). This value is moved into $f14 (line 36). After this, the function `fmin` is invoked on line 38.

Program 17.2 An example to find the minimum of two floating-point numbers

```
 1:   # Find the minimum of two numbers              FMIN.ASM
 2:   #
 3:   # Objective: Finds the minimum value of two
 4:   #            floating-point numbers.
 5:   #            Uses register-based parameter passing.
 6:   #     Input: Requests two floating-point numbers.
 7:   #    Output: Outputs the minimum value.
 8:   #
 9:   #     $f12, $f14 - two numbers are passed
10:   #                 via these registers
11:   #     $f0 - minimum is returned via this register
12:   #
13:   ################## Data segment ##################
14:          .data
15:   prompt:
16:          .asciiz    "Please enter two numbers: \n"
17:   min_msg:
18:          .asciiz    "The minimum is: "
19:   newline:
20:          .asciiz    "\n"
21:
22:   ################## Code segment ##################
23:          .text
24:          .globl main
25:   main:
26:          la    $a0,prompt      # prompt user for input
27:          li    $v0,4
28:          syscall
29:
30:          li    $v0,6           # read 1st float into $f12
31:          syscall
32:          mov.s $f12,$f0
33:
34:          li    $v0,7           # read 2nd double into $f14
35:          syscall
36:          mov.d $f14,$f0
37:
38:          jal   fmin
39:
40:          la    $a0,min_msg     # write minimum message
```

```
41:          li     $v0,4
42:          syscall
43:
44:          mov.d $f12,$f0        # output the minimum value
45:          li     $v0,3
46:          syscall
47:
48:          la     $a0,newline     # write newline
49:          li     $v0,4
50:          syscall
51:
52:          li     $v0,10          # exit
53:          syscall
54:
55:  #--------------------------------------------------
56:  # FMIN receives two integers in $f12 and $f14
57:  # and returns the minimum value in $f0
58:  #--------------------------------------------------
59:  fmin:
60:          mov.s   $f0,$f12      # $f0 = holds minimum
61:          cvt.d.s $f0,$f0       # convert single to double
62:          c.le.d  $f0,$f14      # $f0 <= $f14?
63:          bc1t    done          # if yes, we're done
64:          mov.d   $f0,$f14      # else, min = 2nd number
65:  done:
66:          jr      $ra
```

The fmin function receives two floating-point numbers in $f12 (single-precision) and $f14 (double-precision). It returns the minimum of these two numbers as a double in $f0. The procedure assumes that the value in $f12 is the minimum and moves this value into $f0 (line 60). Because this is a single-precision floating-point number, it is converted to double precision on line 61. This value is compared with the second number, which is a double-precision value, using the compare instruction on line 62. If $f0 is less than or equal to $f14, we found the minimum (line 63). Otherwise, we move the value in $f14 into $f0 (line 64).

Example 17.2 *Find the average of a floating-point array.*

To illustrate the floating-point divide operation, we write a program that receives a set of floating-point values and computes the average value. The main program, shown in Program 17.3, reads the input numbers into an array. The input is terminated either by entering 40 values or by entering a zero. Space for the array is declared on lines 24 and 25, which reserves 320 bytes for 40 doubles. The array is aligned on word boundaries using the .align directive on line 23.

The read loop consists of lines 39–47. The loop count is maintained in $t1, which is initialized to 40 on line 36. The loop count is decremented on line 44 and tested for zero on line 47. The other termination condition is implemented by the following code on lines 45 and 46.

```
c.eq.d   $f0,$f2     # if number = 0,
bc1t     exit_loop   # exit loop
```

To facilitate the comparison, we initialize $f2 to zero on line 37. If the comparison is true, we exit the loop using the bc1t instruction.

The values are read using the read_double system call (lines 40 and 41). Each input double value is stored in the array on line 42. The array size is computed on lines 51 and 52. If the size is zero (tested on line 53), an error message is displayed (lines 69–72) and the program is terminated. Otherwise, the array size along with the array pointer is passed onto the array_avg procedure. After returning from the procedure, the main program outputs the average value returned by the procedure.

Program 17.3 An example to find the average of a double-precision floating-point array

```
 1:  # Find the average of an array          ARRAY_FAVG.ASM
 2:  #
 3:  # Objective: Finds the average of a double array.
 4:  #      Input: Requests doubles from the user.
 5:  #             Entering zero terminates the input.
 6:  #     Output: Outputs the average value as a double.
 7:  #
 8:  #     $a0 - array pointer
 9:  #     $a1 - array size
10:  #     $f0, $f1 - returns the average
11:  #               (64-bit double value)
12:  #
13:  ################## Data segment ##################
14:          .data
15:  prompt:
16:          .asciiz     "Please enter the numbers: \n"
17:  avg_msg:
18:          .asciiz     "The average is: "
19:  newline:
20:          .asciiz     "\n"
21:  error_msg:
22:          .asciiz     "Empty array!\n"
23:  .align 3
24:  array:
25:          .space      320         # space for 40 doubles
26:
27:  ################## Code segment ##################
```

```
28:          .text
29:          .globl main
30:  main:
31:          la       $a0,prompt        # prompt user for input
32:          li       $v0,4
33:          syscall
34:
35:          la       $t0,array         # $t0 = array pointer
36:          li       $t1,40            # $t1 = array size
37:          li.d     $f2,0.0           # $f2 = 0
38:
39:  read_loop:
40:          li       $v0,7             # read the input number
41:          syscall
42:          s.d      $f0,0($t0)
43:          addu     $t0,$t0,8         # update array pointer
44:          subu     $t1,$t1,1         # decrement loop count
45:          c.eq.d   $f0,$f2           # if number = 0,
46:          bc1t     exit_loop         # exit loop
47:          bnez     $t1,read_loop     # if loop count is not 0,
48:                                     # read more
49:  exit_loop:
50:          la       $a0,array         # $a0 = array pointer
51:          li       $a1,39
52:          subu     $a1,$a1,$t1       # $a1 = array size
53:          beqz     $a1,error         # if array size = 0, error
54:          jal      array_avg
55:
56:          la       $a0,avg_msg       # write average message
57:          li       $v0,4
58:          syscall
59:
60:          mov.d    $f12,$f0          # output average
61:          li       $v0,3
62:          syscall
63:
64:          la       $a0,newline       # write newline
65:          li       $v0,4
66:          syscall
67:          b        exit
68:
69:  error:
70:          la       $a0,error_msg     # write error message
71:          li       $v0,4
72:          syscall
73:
74:  exit:
```

```
 75:          li      $v0,10          # exit
 76:          syscall
 77:
 78:  #----------------------------------------------------
 79:  # ARRAY_AVG receives the array pointer in $a0 and
 80:  # its size $a1 and returns their sum in $f0 & $f1.
 81:  #     $t1 - array size
 82:  #     $f0,$f1 - keeps the double sum
 83:  #     $f2,$f3 - used as a temporary double
 84:  #     $f4,$f5 - array size in double
 85:  #----------------------------------------------------
 86:  array_avg:
 87:          move    $t1,$a1         # $t1 = array size
 88:          li.d    $f0,0.0         # sum = 0
 89:  add_loop:
 90:          l.d     $f2,0($a0)      # add the array element
 91:          add.d   $f0,$f0,$f2     # value to sum
 92:          addu    $a0,$a0,8       # update array pointer
 93:          subu    $t1,$t1,1       # decrement loop count
 94:          bnez    $t1,add_loop
 95:
 96:          mtc1    $a1,$f4         # move array size to $f4
 97:          cvt.d.w $f4,$f4         # convert word in $f4 to
 98:                                  # double format
 99:          div.d   $f0,$f0,$f4     # $f0 = $f0/$f4
100:          jr      $ra
```

The procedure receives the array pointer in $a0 and its size in $a1. The sum is maintained in $f0, which is initialized to zero on line 88. The add loop consists of lines 89–94. The loop count is in $t1, which is decremented on line 93 and tested for zero on line 94.

To find the average, the array size is converted to the double format using the following code on lines 96 and 97.

```
mtc1    $a1,$f4     # move array size to $f4
cvt.d.w $f4,$f4     # convert word in $f4 to double format
```

The array average is computed using the divide instruction on line 99.

Example 17.3 *Find the sum of a variable number of floating-point numbers.*

Our objective in this example is to show how floating-point numbers are passed via the stack. To meet this objective, we redo Example 11.4 given on page 208. We pass a variable number of double-precision floating-point numbers via the stack to a procedure that finds the sum of these numbers.

As in the last example, entering a zero terminates the input. The read loop consists of lines 33–41 and is similar to the read loop of the last example. The main difference is that the values are pushed onto the stack as we read them (lines 38 and 39). After exiting the read loop, we can invoke the procedure as the parameter count is in $a0 and the values are on the stack.

Program 17.4 An example to illustrate parameter passing of floating-point values via the stack

```
 1:  # Find the sum of doubles              VAR_FSUM.ASM
 2:  #
 3:  # Objective: Finds the sum of variable number of
 4:  #            doubles passed via the stack.
 5:  #            To demonstrate stack-based
 6:  #            parameter passing.
 7:  #    Input: Requests doubles from the user.
 8:  #           Entering a zero ends the input.
 9:  #   Output: Outputs the sum.
10:  #
11:  #   $a0 - number of doubles passed via the stack.
12:  #   $f0 - returns the sum as a double (in $f0,$f1).
13:  #
14:  ################## Data segment ##################
15:        .data
16:  prompt:
17:        .asciiz    "Please enter the numbers: \n"
18:  sum_msg:
19:        .asciiz    "The sum is: "
20:  newline:
21:        .asciiz    "\n"
22:
23:  ################## Code segment ##################
24:        .text
25:        .globl main
26:  main:
27:        la     $a0,prompt      # prompt user for input
28:        li     $v0,4
29:        syscall
30:
31:        li.d   $f2,0.0         # $f2 = 0
32:        li     $a0,0           # parameter count = 0
33:  read_loop:
34:        li     $v0,7           # read the input number
35:        syscall
36:        c.eq.d $f0,$f2         # if number = 0, exit loop
37:        bc1t   exit_loop
```

```
38:          subu      $sp,$sp,8        # reserve 8 bytes on stack
39:          s.d       $f0,0($sp)       # store the number on stack
40:          addu      $a0,$a0,1        # increment parameter count
41:          b         read_loop
42:
43:   exit_loop:
44:          jal       var_sum
45:
46:
47:          la        $a0,sum_msg      # write sum message
48:          li        $v0,4
49:          syscall
50:
51:          mov.d     $f12,$f0         # output sum
52:          li        $v0,3
53:          syscall
54:
55:          la        $a0,newline      # write newline
56:          li        $v0,4
57:          syscall
58:
59:          li        $v0,10           # exit
60:          syscall
61:
62:   #-----------------------------------------------------
63:   # VAR_SUM receives variable number of doubles
64:   # via the stack and the parameter count in $a0.
65:   # It returns their sum as a double in $f0.
66:   #     $a0 - parameter count
67:   #     $f0 - sum as a double (in $f0,$f1)
68:   #     $f2 - used as a temporary to hold a double
69:   #-----------------------------------------------------
70:   var_sum:
71:          li.d      $f0,0.0          # sum = 0
72:   add_loop:
73:          beqz      $a0,done
74:          l.d       $f2,0($sp)       # read the top value
75:          add.d     $f0,$f0,$f2
76:          addu      $sp,$sp,8        # update $sp
77:          subu      $a0,$a0,1
78:          b         add_loop
79:   done:
80:          jr        $ra
```

The var_sum procedure receives the parameter count in $a0. The add loop is similar to that used in the last example, except that we read the numbers off the stack. As we read the values off the stack, we update the stack pointer by adding 8 (line 76). Recall that the stack grows downward as we push values onto it. Thus, when we take values off, we have to increment the stack pointer so that, when the loop terminates, the arguments are cleared from the stack.

Summary

We presented a brief description of the floating-point unit organization. Specifically, we concentrated on the registers provided by the FPU. It provides 32 floating-point registers that can store single-precision floating-point numbers. These registers can be used in pairs to store double-precision floating-point numbers.

The floating-point instructions support the four basic arithmetic operations: add, subtract, divide, and multiply. There are also three basic comparison instructions to establish "less than", "equal to", or "less than or equal to" relationships between floating-point numbers. In addition, several conversion instructions are available. These instructions allow conversion of values among the integer and single and double floating-point number representations. Finally, we used some examples to illustrate the application of these floating-point instructions.

Appendices

A

Number Systems

This appendix introduces background material on various number systems and representations. We start the appendix with a discussion of various number systems, including the binary and hexadecimal systems. When we use multiple number systems, we need to convert numbers from one system to another. We present details on how such number conversions are done. We then give details on integer representations. We cover both unsigned and signed integer representations. We close the appendix with a discussion of the floating-point numbers.

Positional Number Systems

The number systems that we discuss here are based on positional number systems. The decimal number system that we are already familiar with is an example of a positional number system. In contrast, the Roman numeral system is not a positional number system.

Every positional number system has a *radix* or *base*, and an *alphabet*. The base is a positive number. For example, the decimal system is a base-10 system. The number of symbols in the alphabet is equal to the base of the number system. The alphabet of the decimal system is 0 through 9, a total of 10 symbols or digits.

In this appendix, we discuss four number systems that are relevant in the context of computer systems and programming. These are the *decimal* (base-10), *binary* (base-2), *octal* (base-8), and *hexadecimal* (base-16) number systems. Our intention in including the familiar decimal system is to use it to explain some fundamental concepts of positional number systems.

Computers internally use the binary system. The remaining two number systems—octal and hexadecimal—are used mainly for convenience to write a binary number even though they are number systems on their own. We would have ended up using these number systems if we had 8 or 16 fingers instead of 10.

In a positional number system, a sequence of digits is used to represent a number. Each digit in this sequence should be a symbol in the alphabet. There is a weight associated with each position. If we count position numbers from right to left starting with zero, the weight of position n in a base b number system is b^n. For example, the number 579 in the decimal system is actually interpreted as

$$5 \times (10^2) + 7 \times (10^1) + 9 \times (10^0).$$

(Of course, $10^0 = 1$.) In other words, 9 is in unit's place, 7 in 10's place, and 5 in 100's place. More generally, a number in the base b number system is written as

$$d_n d_{n-1} \ldots d_1 d_0,$$

where d_0 represents the Least Significant Digit (LSD) and d_n represents the Most Significant Digit (MSD). This sequence represents the value

$$d_n b^n + d_{n-1} b^{n-1} + \cdots + d_1 b^1 + d_0 b^0. \tag{A.1}$$

Each digit d_i in the string can be in the range $0 \leq d_i \leq (b-1)$. When we use a number system with $b \leq 10$, we use the first b decimal digits. For example, the binary system uses 0 and 1 as its alphabet. For number systems with $b > 10$, the initial letters of the English alphabet are used to represent digits greater than 9. For example, the alphabet of the hexadecimal system, whose base is 16, is 0 through 9 and A through F, a total of 16 symbols representing the digits of the hexadecimal system. We treat lowercase and uppercase letters used in a number system such as the hexadecimal system as equivalent.

The number of different values that can be represented using n digits in a base b system is b^n. Consequently, because we start counting from 0, the largest number that can be represented using n digits is $(b^n - 1)$. This number is written as

$$\underbrace{(b-1)(b-1)\ldots(b-1)(b-1)}_{\text{total of } n \text{ digits}}.$$

The minimum number of digits (i.e., the length of a number) required to represent X different values is given by $\lceil \log_b X \rceil$, where $\lceil\ \rceil$ represents the ceiling function. Note that $\lceil m \rceil$ represents the smallest integer that is greater than or equal to m.

Notation   The commonality in the alphabet of several number systems gives rise to confusion. For example, if we write 100 without specifying the number system in which it is expressed, different interpretations can lead to assigning different values, as shown below:

Number		Decimal value
100	$\xrightarrow{\text{binary}}$	4
100	$\xrightarrow{\text{decimal}}$	100
100	$\xrightarrow{\text{octal}}$	64
100	$\xrightarrow{\text{hexadecimal}}$	256

Thus, it is important to specify the number system (i.e., specify the base). One common notation is to append a single letter—uppercase or lowercase—to the number to specify the number system. For example, D is used for decimal, B for binary, Q for octal, and H for hexadecimal number systems. Using this notation, 10110111B is a binary number and 2BA9H is a hexadecimal number. Some assemblers use the prefix 0x for hexadecimal and the prefix 0 for octal.

Decimal Number System   We use the decimal number system in everyday life. This is a base-10 system presumably because we have 10 fingers and toes to count. The alphabet consists of 10 symbols, digits 0 through 9.

Binary Number System   The binary system is a base-2 number system that is used by computers for internal representation. The alphabet consists of two digits, 0 and 1. Each binary digit is called a bit (standing for *binary digit*). Thus, 1021 is not a valid binary number. In the binary system, using n bits, we can represent numbers from 0 through $(2^n - 1)$ for a total of 2^n different values.

Octal Number System   This is a base-8 number system with the alphabet consisting of digits 0 through 7. Thus, 181 is not a valid octal number. The octal numbers are often used to express binary numbers in a compact way. For example, we need 8 bits to represent 256 different values. The same range of numbers can be represented in the octal system by using only 3 digits.

   For example, the number 230Q is written in the binary system as 10011000B, which is difficult to read and error prone. In general, we can reduce the length by a factor of 3. As we show later, it is straightforward to go back to the binary equivalent, which is not the case with the decimal system.

Hexadecimal Number System   This is a base-16 number system. The alphabet consists of digits 0 through 9 and letters A through F. In this text, we use capital letters consistently, even though lowercase and uppercase letters can be used interchangeably. For example, FEED is a valid hexadecimal number, whereas GEFF is not.

   The main use of this number system is to conveniently represent long binary numbers. The length of a binary number expressed in the hexadecimal system can be reduced by a factor of 4. Consider the previous example again. The binary number 10011000B can be represented as 98H. Debuggers, for example, display information—addresses, data, and so on—in hexadecimal representation.

Conversion to Decimal

When we are dealing with several number systems, there is often a need to convert numbers from one system to another. Let us first look at how a number expressed in the base-b

system can be converted to the decimal system. To do this conversion, we merely perform the arithmetic calculations of Equation (A.1); that is, multiply each digit by its weight, and add the results. Let's look at an example next.

Example A.1 *Conversion from binary to decimal.*
Convert the binary number 10100111B into its equivalent in the decimal system.

$$
\begin{aligned}
10100111B &= 1 \cdot 2^7 + 0 \cdot 2^6 + 1 \cdot 2^5 + 0 \cdot 2^4 \\
&\quad + 0 \cdot 2^3 + 1 \cdot 2^2 + 1 \cdot 2^1 + 1 \cdot 2^0 \\
&= 167D.
\end{aligned}
$$

Conversion from Decimal

There is a simple method that allows conversions from the decimal to a target number system. The procedure is as follows.

> *Divide the decimal number by the base of the target number system and keep track of the quotient and remainder. Repeatedly divide the successive quotients while keeping track of the remainders generated until the quotient is zero. The remainders generated during the process, written in the reverse order of generation from left to right, form the equivalent number in the target system.*

Let us look at an example now.

Example A.2 *Conversion from decimal to binary.*
Convert the decimal number 167 into its equivalent binary number.

		Quotient	Remainder
167/2	=	83	1
83/2	=	41	1
41/2	=	20	1
20/2	=	10	0
10/2	=	5	0
5/2	=	2	1
2/2	=	1	0
1/2	=	0	1

The desired binary number can be obtained by writing the remainders generated in the reverse order from left to right. For this example, the binary number is 10100111B. This agrees with the result of Example A.1.   □

Binary/Octal/Hexadecimal Conversion

Conversion among binary, octal, and hexadecimal number systems is relatively easier and more straightforward. Conversion from binary to octal involves converting three bits at a time, whereas binary to hexadecimal conversion requires converting four bits at a time.

Binary/Octal Conversion   To convert a binary number into its equivalent octal number, form 3-bit groups starting from the right. Add extra 0s at the left-hand side of the binary number if the number of bits is not a multiple of 3. Then replace each group of 3 bits by its equivalent octal digit. Why three bit groups? Simply because $2^3 = 8$. Here is an example.

Example A.3 *Conversion from binary to octal.*
The following examples illustrate this conversion process.

$$1000101B = \overset{1}{\overbrace{\mathbf{001}}}\;\overset{0}{\overbrace{000}}\;\overset{5}{\overbrace{101}}\;B$$
$$= 105Q.$$
$$10100111B = \overset{2}{\overbrace{\mathbf{010}}}\;\overset{4}{\overbrace{100}}\;\overset{7}{\overbrace{111}}\;B$$
$$= 247Q.$$

Notice that we have added leftmost 0s (shown in bold) so that the number of bits is 9. Adding 0s on the left-hand side does not change the value of a number. For example, in the decimal system, 35 and 0035 represent the same value.   □

We can use the reverse process to convert numbers from octal to binary. For each octal digit, write the equivalent 3 bits. You should write exactly 3 bits for each octal digit even if there are leading 0s. For example, for octal digit 0, write the three bits 000.

Example A.4 *Conversion from octal to binary.*
The following two examples illustrate conversion from octal to binary.

$$105Q = \overset{1}{\overbrace{001}}\;\overset{0}{\overbrace{000}}\;\overset{5}{\overbrace{101}}B,$$
$$247Q = \overset{2}{\overbrace{010}}\;\overset{4}{\overbrace{100}}\;\overset{7}{\overbrace{111}}B.$$

If you want an 8-bit binary number, throw away the leading 0 in the binary number.   □

Binary/Hexadecimal Conversion The process for conversion from binary to hexadecimal is similar except that we use 4-bit groups instead of 3-bit groups because

$2^4 = 16$. For each group of 4 bits, replace it by the equivalent hexadecimal digit. If the number of bits is not a multiple of 4, pad 0s at the left. Here is an example.

Example A.5 *Binary to hexadecimal conversion.*
Convert the binary number 1101011111 into its equivalent hexadecimal number.

$$1101011111\text{B} = \overbrace{0011}^{3}\overbrace{0101}^{5}\overbrace{1111}^{F}\text{B}$$
$$= 35\text{FH}.$$

As in the octal to binary example, we have added two 0s on the left to make the total number of bits a multiple of 4 (i.e., 12).   □

The process can be reversed to convert from hexadecimal to binary. Each hex digit should be replaced by exactly four binary bits that represent its value. An example follows.

Example A.6 *Hex to binary conversion.*
Convert the hexadecimal number B01D into its equivalent binary number.

$$\text{B01DH} = \overbrace{1011}^{B}\overbrace{0000}^{0}\overbrace{0001}^{1}\overbrace{1101}^{D}\text{B}.$$ □

Unsigned Integers

Now that you are familiar with different number systems, let us turn our attention to how integers (numbers with no fractional part) are represented internally in computers. Of course, we know that the binary number system is used internally. Still, there are a number of other details that need to be sorted out before we have a workable internal number representation scheme.

We begin our discussion by considering how unsigned numbers are represented using a fixed number of bits. We then proceed to discuss the representation for signed numbers in the next section.

The most natural way to represent unsigned (i.e., nonnegative) numbers is to use the equivalent binary representation. As discussed before, a binary number with n bits can represent 2^n different values, and the range of the numbers is from 0 to $(2^n - 1)$. Padding of 0s on the left can be used to make the binary conversion of a decimal number equal exactly N bits. For example, we can represent 16D as 10000B using 5 bits. However, this can be extended to a byte (i.e., $N = 8$) as 00010000B or to 16 bits as 0000000000010000B. This process is called *zero extension* and is suitable for unsigned numbers.

A problem arises if the number of bits required to represent an integer in binary is more than the N bits we have. Clearly, such numbers are outside the range of numbers that can be represented using N bits. Recall that using N bits, we can represent any integer X such that $0 \leq X \leq 2^N - 1$.

Signed Integers

There are several ways in which signed numbers can be represented. These include

- Signed magnitude,
- Excess-M,
- 1's complement, and
- 2's complement.

Signed Magnitude Representation

In signed magnitude representation, one bit is reserved to represent the sign of a number. The most significant bit is used as the sign bit. Conventionally, a sign bit value of 0 is used to represent a positive number and 1 for a negative number. Thus, if we have N bits to represent a number, $(N - 1)$ bits are available to represent the magnitude of the number. For example, when N is 4, Table A.1 shows the range of numbers that can be represented. For comparison, the unsigned representation is also included in this table.

The range of n-bit signed magnitude representation is $-2^{n-1} + 1$ to $+2^{n-1} - 1$. Note that in this method, 0 has two representations: $+0$ and -0.

Excess-M Representation

In this method, a number is mapped to a nonnegative integer so that its binary representation can be used. This transformation is done by adding a value called *bias* to the number to be represented. For an n-bit representation, the bias should be such that the mapped number is less than 2^n.

To find out the binary representation of a number in this method, simply add the bias M to the number and find the corresponding binary representation. That is, the representation for number X is the binary representation for the number $X + M$, where M is the bias. For example, in the excess-7 system, $-3D$ is represented as

$$-3 + 7 = +4 = 0100B.$$

Numbers represented in excess-M are called *biased integers* for obvious reasons. Table A.1 gives examples of biased integers using 4-bit binary numbers. This representation, for example, is used to store the exponent values in the floating-point representation (discussed in the next section).

Table A.1 Number representation using 4-bit binary (all numbers except Binary column in decimal)

Unsigned representation	Binary pattern	Signed magnitude	Excess-7	1's Complement	2's Complement
0	0000	0	−7	0	0
1	0001	1	−6	1	1
2	0010	2	−5	2	2
3	0011	3	−4	3	3
4	0100	4	−3	4	4
5	0101	5	−2	5	5
6	0110	6	−1	6	6
7	0111	7	0	7	7
8	1000	−0	1	−7	−8
9	1001	−1	2	−6	−7
10	1010	−2	3	−5	−6
11	1011	−3	4	−4	−5
12	1100	−4	5	−3	−4
13	1101	−5	6	−2	−3
14	1110	−6	7	−1	−2
15	1111	−7	8	−0	−1

1's Complement Representation

As in the excess-M representation, negative values are biased in 1's complement and 2's complement representations. For positive numbers, the standard binary representation is used. As in the signed magnitude representation, the most significant bit indicates the sign (0 = positive and 1 = negative). In 1's complement representation, negative values are biased by $b^n - 1$, where b is the base or radix of the number system. For the binary case that we are interested in here, the bias is $2^n - 1$. For the negative value $-X$, the representation used is the binary representation for $(2^n - 1) - X$. For example, if n is 4, we can represent -5 as follows.

$$\begin{aligned} 2^4 - 1 &= & 1111\text{B} \\ -5 &= & \underline{-0101\text{B}} \\ & & 1010\text{B} \end{aligned}$$

As you can see from this example, the 1's complement of a number can be obtained by simply complementing individual bits (converting 0s to 1s and vice versa) of the number. Table A.1 shows 1's complement representation using 4 bits. In this method also, 0 has two representations. The most significant bit is used to indicate the sign. To find the magnitude of a negative number in this representation, apply the process used to obtain the 1's complement (i.e., complement individual bits) again.

Representation of signed numbers in 1's complement representation allows the use of simpler circuits for performing addition and subtraction than the other two representations we have seen so far (signed magnitude and excess-M). Some older computer systems used this representation for integers. An irritant with this representation is that 0 has two representations. Furthermore, the carry bit generated out of the sign bit will have to be added to the result. The 2's complement representation avoids these pitfalls. As a result, 2's complement representation is the choice of current computer systems.

2's Complement Representation

In 2's complement representation, positive numbers are represented the same way as in the signed magnitude and 1's complement representations. The negative numbers are biased by 2^n, where n is the number of bits used for number representation. Thus, the negative value $-A$ is represented by $(2^n - A)$ using n bits. Because the bias value is one more than that in the 1's complement representation, we have to add 1 after complementing to obtain the 2's complement representation of a negative number. We can, however, discard any carry generated out of the sign bit. For example, -5 can be represented as follows.

$$5D = 0101B \longrightarrow \text{complement} \longrightarrow 1010B$$
$$\text{add 1} \qquad \underline{1B}$$
$$1011B$$

Therefore, $1011B$ represents $-5D$ in 2's complement representation. Table A.1 shows the 2's complement representation of numbers using 4 bits. Notice that there is only one representation for 0. The range of an n-bit 2's complement integer is -2^{n-1} to $+2^{n-1} - 1$. For example, using 8 bits, the range is -128 to $+127$.

To find the magnitude of a negative number in the 2's complement representation, as in the 1's complement representation, simply reverse the sign of the number. That is, use the same conversion process: complement and add 1 and discard any carry generated out of the leftmost bit.

Sign Extension

How do we extend a signed number? For example, we have shown that -5 can be represented in the 2's complement representation as $1011B$. Suppose we want to save this as a byte. How do extend these four bits into eight bits? We have seen in Example A.5 that, for unsigned integers, we add zeros on the left to extend the number. However, we cannot use this technique for signed numbers because the most significant bit represents the sign. To extend a signed number, we have to copy the sign bit. In our example, -5 is represented using eight bits as

$$-5D = \overbrace{1111}^{\text{sign bit}} 1011.$$

We have copied the sign bit to extend the four-bit value to eight bits. Similarly, we can express -5 using 16 bits by extending it as follows.

$$-5D = \overbrace{111111111111}^{\text{sign bit}}\,1011.$$

This process is referred to as *sign extension*.

Floating-Point Representation

Using the decimal system for a moment, we can write very small and very large numbers in scientific notation as follows.

$$1.2345 \times 10^{45},$$

$$9.876543 \times 10^{-37}.$$

Expressing such numbers using the positional number notation is difficult to write and understand, error prone, and requires more space. In a similar fashion, binary numbers can be written in scientific notation. For example,

$$+1101.101 \times 2^{+11001} = 13.625 \times 2^{25}$$
$$= 4.57179 \times 10^{8}.$$

As indicated, numbers expressed in this notation have two parts: a *mantissa* (or *significand*) and an *exponent*. There can be a sign ($+$ or $-$) associated with each part.

Numbers expressed in this notation can be written in several equivalent ways, as shown below:

$$1.2345 \times 10^{45},$$
$$123.45 \times 10^{43},$$
$$0.00012345 \times 10^{49}.$$

This causes implementation problems in performing arithmetic operations, comparisons, and the like. This problem can be avoided by introducing a standard form called the *normal form*. Reverting to the binary case, a normalized binary form has the format

$$\pm 1.X_1X_2\cdots X_{M-1}X_M \times 2^{\pm Y_{N-1}Y_{N-2}\cdots Y_1Y_0},$$

where X_i and Y_j represent a bit, $1 \leq i \leq M$, and $0 \leq j < N$. The normalized form of

$$+1101.101 \times 2^{+11010}$$

is

$$+1.101101 \times 2^{+11101}.$$

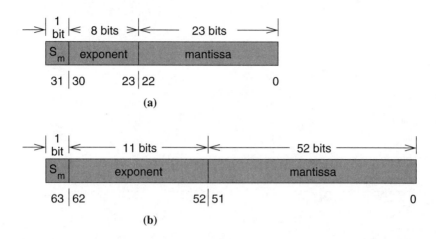

Figure A.1 Floating-point formats: (a) single-precision; (b) double-precision.

We normally write such numbers as

$$+1.101101E11101.$$

To represent such normalized numbers, we might use the format shown below:

where S_m and S_e represent the sign of the mantissa and the exponent, respectively.

Implementation of floating-point numbers varies from this generic format, usually for efficiency reasons or to conform to a standard. From here on, we discuss the format of the IEEE 754 floating-point standard. Such standards are useful, for example, to exchange data among several different computer systems and to write efficient numerical software libraries.

The single-precision and double-precision floating-point formats are shown in Figure A.1. Certain points are worth noting about these formats:

1. The mantissa stores only the fractional part of a normalized number. The 1 to the left of the binary point is not explicitly stored but implied to save a bit. This bit is always 1, therefore there is really no need to store it. However, representing 0.0 requires special attention, as we show later.

2. There is no sign bit associated with the exponent. Instead, the exponent is converted to an excess-M form and stored. For the single-precision numbers, the bias used is 127D (= 7FH), and for the double-precision numbers, 1023 (= 3FFH).

Table A.2 Representation of special values in the floating-point format

Special number	Sign	Exponent (biased)	Mantissa
$+0$	0	0	0
-0	1	0	0
$+\infty$	0	FFH	0
$-\infty$	1	FFH	0
NaN	0/1	FFH	$\neq 0$
Denormals	0/1	0	$\neq 0$

Special Values   The representations of 0 and infinity (∞) require special attention. Table A.2 shows the values of the three components used to represent these values. Zero is represented by a zero exponent and fraction. We can have a -0 or $+0$ depending on the sign bit. An exponent of all ones indicates a special floating-point value. An exponent of all ones with a zero mantissa indicates infinity. Again, the sign bit indicates the sign of the infinity. An exponent of all ones with a nonzero mantissa represents a not-a-number (NaN). The NaN values are used to represent operations such as 0/0 and $\sqrt{-1}$.

The last entry in Table A.2 shows how *denormalized values* are represented. The denormals are used to represent values smaller than the smallest value that can be represented with normalized floating-point numbers. For denormals, the implicit 1 to the left of the binary point becomes a 0. The smallest normalized number has a 1 for the exponent (note zero is not allowed) and 0 for the fraction. Thus, the smallest number is 1×2^{-126}. The largest denormalized number has a zero exponent and all 1s for the fraction. This represents approximately $0.9999999 \times 2^{-127}$. The smallest denormalized number would have zero as the exponent and a 1 in the last bit position (i.e., position 23). Thus, it represents $2^{-23} \times 2^{-127}$, which is approximately 10^{-45}. A thorough discussion of floating-point numbers can be found in [8].

Summary

We discussed how numbers are represented using the positional number system. Positional number systems are characterized by a base and an alphabet. The familiar decimal system is a base-10 system with the alphabet 0 through 9. Computer systems use the binary system for internal storage. This is a base-2 number system with 0 and 1 as the alphabet. The remaining two number systems—octal (base-8) and hexadecimal (base-16)—are mainly used for convenience in writing a binary number. For example, debuggers use the hexadecimal numbers to display address and data information.

When we use several number systems, there is often a need to convert numbers from one system to another. Conversion among binary, octal, and hexadecimal systems is simple and straightforward. We also discussed how numbers are converted from decimal to binary and vice versa.

The remainder of the chapter was devoted to internal representation of numbers. Representation of unsigned integers is straightforward and uses binary representation. There are, however, several ways of representing signed integers. We discussed four methods to represent signed integers. Of these four methods, current computer systems use the 2's complement representation.

Floating-point representation on most computers follows the IEEE 754 standard. There are three components of a floating-point number: mantissa, exponent, and the sign of the mantissa. There is no sign associated with the exponent. Instead, the exponent is stored as a biased number.

B

Character Representation

This appendix discusses character representation. We identify some desirable properties that a character-encoding scheme should satisfy in order to facilitate efficient character processing. Our focus is on the ASCII encoding; we don't discuss other character sets such as UCS and Unicode. The ASCII encoding, which is used by most computers, satisfies the requirements of an efficient character code.

Character Representation

As computers have the capability to store and understand the alphabet 0 and 1, characters should be assigned a sequence over this alphabet; that is, characters should be encoded using this alphabet. For efficient processing of characters, several guidelines have been developed. Some of these are mentioned here.

1. Assigning a contiguous sequence of numbers (if treated as unsigned binary numbers) to letters in alphabetical order is desired. Upper- and lowercase letters (A through Z and a through z) can be treated separately, but a contiguous sequence should be assigned to each case. This facilitates efficient character processing such as case conversion, identifying lowercase letters, and so on.
2. In a similar fashion, digits should be assigned a contiguous sequence in numerical order. This would be useful in numeric-to-character and character-to-numeric conversions.
3. A space character should precede all letters and digits.

These guidelines allow for efficient character processing including sorting by names or character strings. For example, to test if a given character code corresponds to a lowercase letter, all we have to do is to see if the code of the character is between that of a and

z. These guidelines also aid in applications requiring sorting, for instance, sorting a class list by last name.

Because computers are rarely used in isolation, exchange of information is an important concern. This leads to the necessity of having some standard way of representing characters. Most computers use the American Standard Code for Information Interchange (ASCII) for character representation. The standard ASCII uses 7 bits to encode a character. Thus, $2^7 = 128$ different characters can be represented. This number is sufficiently large to represent uppercase and lowercase characters, digits, special characters such as !,^, and control characters such as CR (carriage return), LF (linefeed), and the like.

We store the bits in units of a power of 2, therefore we end up storing 8 bits for each character, even though ASCII requires only 7 bits. The eighth bit is put to use for two purposes.

1. *To parity encode for error detection:* The eighth bit can be used to represent the parity bit. This bit is made 0 or 1 such that the total number of 1s in a byte is even (for even parity) or odd (for odd parity). This can be used to detect simple errors in data transmission.

2. *To represent an additional 128 characters:* By using all eight bits we can represent a total of $2^8 = 256$ different characters. This is referred to as the extended ASCII. These additional codes are used for special graphics symbols, Greek letters, and so on.

The standard ASCII character code is presented in the following two tables. You will notice from these tables that ASCII encoding satisfies the three guidelines mentioned earlier. For instance, successive bit patterns are assigned to uppercase letters, lowercase letters, and digits. This assignment leads to some good properties. For example, the difference between the uppercase and lowercase characters is constant. That is, the difference between the character codes of a and A is the same as that between n and N, which is 32. This characteristic can be exploited for efficient case conversion.

Another interesting feature of ASCII is that the character codes are assigned to the 10 digits such that the lower-order four bits represent the binary equivalent of the corresponding digit. For example, digit 5 is encoded as 0110101. If you take the rightmost four bits (0101), they represent 5 in binary. This feature, again, helps in writing an efficient code for character-to-numeric conversion. Such a conversion, for example, is required when you type a number as a sequence of digit characters.

ASCII Character Set

The following tables give the standard ASCII character set. We divide the character set into control and printable characters. The control character codes are given next and the printable ASCII characters follow.

Control Codes

Hex	Decimal	Character	Meaning
00	0	NUL	NULL
01	1	SOH	Start of heading
02	2	STX	Start of text
03	3	ETX	End of text
04	4	EOT	End of transmission
05	5	ENQ	Enquiry
06	6	ACK	Acknowledgment
07	7	BEL	Bell
08	8	BS	Backspace
09	9	HT	Horizontal tab
0A	10	LF	Line feed
0B	11	VT	Vertical tab
0C	12	FF	Form feed
0D	13	CR	Carriage return
0E	14	SO	Shift out
0F	15	SI	Shift in
10	16	DLE	Data link escape
11	17	DC1	Device control 1
12	18	DC2	Device control 2
13	19	DC3	Device control 3
14	20	DC4	Device control 4
15	21	NAK	Negative acknowledgment
16	22	SYN	Synchronous idle
17	23	ETB	End of transmission block
18	24	CAN	Cancel
19	25	EM	End of medium
1A	26	SUB	Substitute
1B	27	ESC	Escape
1C	28	FS	File separator
1D	29	GS	Group separator
1E	30	RS	Record separator
1F	31	US	Unit separator
7F	127	DEL	Delete

Printable Character Codes

Hex	Decimal	Character	Hex	Decimal	Character	Hex	Decimal	Character
20	32	Space	40	64	@	60	96	`
21	33	!	41	65	A	61	97	a
22	34	"	42	66	B	62	98	b
23	35	#	43	67	C	63	99	c
24	36	$	44	68	D	64	100	d
25	37	%	45	69	E	65	101	e
26	38	&	46	70	F	66	102	f
27	39	'	47	71	G	67	103	g
28	40	(	48	72	H	68	104	h
29	41	)	49	73	I	69	105	i
2A	42	*	4A	74	J	6A	106	j
2B	43	+	4B	75	K	6B	107	k
2C	44	,	4C	76	L	6C	108	l
2D	45	−	4D	77	M	6D	109	m
2E	46	.	4E	78	N	6E	110	n
2F	47	/	4F	79	O	6F	111	o
30	48	0	50	80	P	70	112	p
31	49	1	51	81	Q	71	113	q
32	50	2	52	82	R	72	114	r
33	51	3	53	83	S	73	115	s
34	52	4	54	84	T	74	116	t
35	53	5	55	85	U	75	117	u
36	54	6	56	86	V	76	118	v
37	55	7	57	87	W	77	119	w
38	56	8	58	88	X	78	120	x
39	57	9	59	89	Y	79	121	y
3A	58	:	5A	90	Z	7A	122	z
3B	59	;	5B	91	[	7B	123	{
3C	60	<	5C	92	\	7C	124		
3D	61	=	5D	93	]	7D	125	}
3E	62	>	5E	94	^	7E	126	~
3F	63	?	5F	95	_			

Note that 7FH (127 in decimal) is a control character listed in the Control Codes table.

C

MIPS Instruction Set Summary

This appendix lists the MIPS instructions implemented by the SPIM simulator. These instructions can be divided into two groups: instructions and pseudoinstructions. The first group consists of the instructions supported by the processor. The pseudoinstructions are supported by the assembler; these are not the processor instructions. These pseudoinstructions are translated into one or more processor instructions. For example, abs is a pseudoinstruction, which is translated into the following two-instruction sequence.

```
bgez    Rsrc,8
sub     Rdest,$0,Rsrc
```

In this appendix, as in the main text, the pseudoinstructions are indicated by a †. In the following, instructions are presented in alphabetical order.

Also note that, in all the instructions, Src2 can be either a register or a 16-bit integer. The assembler translates the general form of an instruction to its immediate form if Src2 is a constant. For reference, we also include the immediate form instructions. In these instructions, Imm represents a 16-bit integer.

---

abs[†] — Absolute value

Format: abs   Rdest,Rsrc

Description: Places the absolute value of Rsrc in Rdest.

---

add — Add with overflow

    Format: add   Rdest,Rsrc1,Src2

Description: Rdest receives the sum of Rsrc1 and Src2. The numbers are treated as signed integers. In the case of an overflow, an overflow exception is generated.

---

addi — Add immediate with overflow

    Format: addi   Rdest,Rsrc1,Imm

Description: Rdest receives the sum of Rsrc1 and Imm. The numbers are treated as signed integers. In the case of an overflow, an overflow exception is generated.

---

addiu — Add immediate with no overflow

    Format: addiu   Rdest,Rsrc1,Imm

Description: Rdest receives the sum of Rsrc1 and Src2. The numbers are treated as signed integers. No overflow exception is generated.

---

addu — Add with no overflow

    Format: addu   Rdest,Rsrc1,Src2

Description: Rdest receives the sum of Rsrc1 and Src2. The numbers are treated as signed integers. No overflow exception is generated.

---

and — Logical AND

    Format: and   Rdest,Rsrc1,Src2

Description: Bitwise AND of Rsrc1 and Src2 is stored in Rdest.

---

andi — Logical AND immediate

    Format: andi   Rdest,Rsrc1,Imm

    Description: Bitwise AND of Rsrc1 and Imm is stored in Rdest.

---

b[†] — Branch

    Format: b   label

    Description: Unconditionally transfer control to the instruction at label. Branch instruction uses a signed 16-bit offset. This allows jumps to $2^{15} - 1$ instructions (not bytes) forward, or 2^{15} instructions backward.

---

bczf — Branch if coprocessor Z is false

    Format: bczf   label

    Description: Conditionally transfer control to the instruction at label if coprocessor's Z flag is false.

---

bczt — Branch if coprocessor Z is true

    Format: bczt   label

    Description: Conditionally transfer control to the instruction at label if coprocessor's Z flag is true.

---

beq — Branch if equal

    Format: beq   Rsrc1,Src2,label

    Description: Conditionally transfer control to the instruction at label if Rsrc1 = Src2.

---

beqz[†] — Branch if equal to zero

Format: beqz   Rsrc,label

Description: Conditionally transfer control to the instruction at label if Rsrc $= 0$.

---

bge[†] — Branch if greater or equal (signed)

Format: bge   Rsrc1,Src2,label

Description: Conditionally transfer control to the instruction at label if Rsrc1 $\geq$ Src2. The contents are treated as signed numbers.

---

bgeu[†] — Branch if greater or equal (unsigned)

Format: bgeu   Rsrc1,Src2,label

Description: Conditionally transfer control to the instruction at label if Rsrc1 $\geq$ Src2. The contents are treated as unsigned numbers.

---

bgez — Branch if greater than or equal to zero

Format: bgez   Rsrc,label

Description: Conditionally transfer control to the instruction at label if Rsrc ≥ 0.

---

bgezal — Branch if greater than or equal to zero and link

Format: bgezal   Rsrc,label

Description: Conditionally transfer control to the instruction at label if Rsrc ≥ 0. Save the next instruction address in register 31.

---

bgt[†] — Branch if greater (signed)

Format: bgt   Rsrc1,Src2,label

Description: Conditionally transfer control to the instruction at label if Rsrc1 > Src2. The contents are treated as signed numbers.

---

bgtu[†] — Branch if greater (unsigned)

Format: bgtu   Rsrc1,Src2,label

Description: Conditionally transfer control to the instruction at label if Rsrc1 > Src2. The contents are treated as unsigned numbers.

---

bgtz — Branch if greater than zero (signed)

Format: bgtz   Rsrc,label

Description: Conditionally transfer control to the instruction at label if Rsrc > 0. The contents are treated as signed numbers.

---

ble[†] — Branch if less than or equal (signed)

Format: blt   Rsrc1,Src2,label

Description: Conditionally transfer control to the instruction at label if Rsrc1 ≤ Src2. The contents are treated as signed numbers.

---

bleu[†] — Branch if less than or equal (unsigned)

Format: bltu   Rsrc1,Src2,label

Description: Conditionally transfer control to the instruction at label if Rsrc1 ≤ Src2. The contents are treated as unsigned numbers.

---

blez — Branch if less than or equal to zero (signed)

Format: `bltz     Rsrc,label`

Description: Conditionally transfer control to the instruction at `label` if `Rsrc` ≤ 0. The contents are treated as signed numbers.

---

blt[†] — Branch if less than (signed)

Format: `blt     Rsrc1,Src2,label`

Description: Conditionally transfer control to the instruction at `label` if `Rsrc1` $<$ `Src2`. The contents are treated as signed numbers.

---

bltu[†] — Branch if less than (unsigned)

Format: `bltu     Rsrc1,Src2,label`

Description: Conditionally transfer control to the instruction at `label` if `Rsrc1` $<$ `Src2`. The contents are treated as unsigned numbers.

---

bltz — Branch if less than zero (signed)

Format: `bltz     Rsrc,label`

Description: Conditionally transfer control to the instruction at `label` if `Rsrc` < 0. The contents are treated as signed numbers.

---

bltzal — Branch if less than zero and link

Format: `bltzal     Rsrc,label`

Description: Conditionally transfer control to the instruction at `label` if `Rsrc` < 0. Save the next instruction address in register 31.

---

bne — Branch if not equal

    Format: bne   Rsrc1,Src2,label

Description: Conditionally transfer control to the instruction at label if Rsrc1 $\neq$ Src2.

---

bnez[†] — Branch if not equal to zero

    Format: bnez   Rsrc,label

Description: Conditionally transfer control to the instruction at label if Rsrc $\neq$ 0.

---

break — Exception

    Format: break   n

Description: Causes exception n. Exception 1 is reserved for the debugger.

---

div — Divide (signed)

    Format: div   Rsrc1,Rsrc2

Description: Performs division of two signed numbers in Rsrc1 and Rsrc2 (i.e., Rsrc1/Rsrc2). The quotient is placed in register lo and the remainder in register hi. If an operand is negative, the remainder is unspecified by the MIPS architecture. The corresponding SPIM value depends on the machine it is running.

---

divu — Divide (unsigned)

    Format: div   Rsrc1,Rsrc2

Description: Same as div above except that the numbers in Rsrc1 and Rsrc2 are treated as unsigned.

---

div[†] — Divide (signed)

Format: div   Rdest,Rsrc1,Src2

Description: Performs division of two signed numbers in Rsrc1 and Src2 (i.e., Rsrc1/Src2). The quotient is placed in register Rdest. Src2 can be a register or a 16-bit immediate value.

---

divu[†] — Divide (signed)

Format: divu   Rdest,Rsrc1,Src2

Description: Same as the last div pseudoinstruction except that the numbers in Rsrc1 and Src2 are treated as unsigned.

---

j — Jump

Format: j   label

Description: Unconditionally transfer control to the instruction at label. Jump instruction uses a signed 26-bit offset. This allows jumps to $2^{25} - 1$ instructions forward, or 2^{25} instructions backward.

---

jal — Jump and link

Format: jal   label

Description: Unconditionally transfer control to the instruction at label. Save the next instruction address in register 31.

---

jalr — Jump and link register

Format: jalr   Rsrc

Description: Unconditionally transfer control to the instruction whose address is in Rsrc. Save the next instruction address in register 31.

jr — Jump register

Format: jr   Rsrc

Description: Unconditionally transfer control to the instruction whose address is in Rsrc. This instruction is used to return from procedures.

---

la[†] — Load address

Format: la   Rdest,address

Description: Load address into register Rdest.

---

lb — Load byte (signed)

Format: lb   Rdest,address

Description: Load the byte at address into register Rdest. The byte is sign-extended.

---

lbu — Load byte (unsigned)

Format: lbu   Rdest,address

Description: Load the byte at address into register Rdest. The byte is zero-extended.

---

ld[†] — Load doubleword

Format: ld   Rdest,address

Description: Load the doubleword (64 bits) at address into registers Rdest and Rdest+1.

---

lh — Load halfword (signed)

Format: lh   Rdest,address

Description: Load the halfword (16 bits) at address into register Rdest. The halfword is sign-extended.

lhu — Load halfword (unsigned)

Format: lhu   Rdest,address

Description: Load the halfword (16 bits) at address into register Rdest. The halfword is zero-extended.

---

li[†] — Load immediate

Format: li   Rdest,Imm

Description: Load the immediate value Imm into register Rdest.

---

lui — Load upper immediate

Format: lui   Rdest,Imm

Description: Load the 16-bit immediate Imm into the upper halfword of register Rdest. The lower halfword of Rdest is set to 0.

---

lw — Load word

Format: lw   Rdest,address

Description: Load the word (32 bits) at address into register Rdest.

---

lwcz — Load word from coprocessor z

Format: lwcz   Rdest,address

Description: Load the word (32 bits) at address into register Rdest of coprocessor z.

lwl — Load word left

    Format: `lwl    Rdest,address`

    Description: Load the left bytes from the word at `address` into register `Rdest`. This instruction can be used along with `lwr` to load an unaligned word from memory. The `lwl` instruction starts loading bytes from (possibly unaligned) `address` until the lower-order byte of the word. These bytes are stored in `Rdest` from the left. The number of bytes stored depends on the address. For example, if the address is 1, it stores the three bytes at addresses 1, 2, and 3. As another example, if the address is 2, it stores the two bytes at addresses 2 and 3. See `lwr` for more details.

---

lwr — Load word right

    Format: `lwr    Rdest,address`

    Description: Load the right bytes from the word at `address` into register `Rdest`. This instruction can be used along with `lwl` to load an unaligned word from memory. The `lwr` instruction starts loading bytes from (possibly unaligned) `address` until the higher-order byte of the word. These bytes are stored in `Rdest` from the right. As in the `lwl` instruction, the number of bytes stored depends on the address. However, the direction is opposite to that used in the `lwl` instruction. For example, if the address is 4, it stores just one byte at address 4. As another example, if the address is 6, it stores the three bytes at addresses 6, 5, and 4. In contrast, the `lwl` instruction with address 6 would load the two bytes at addresses 6 and 7.

        As an example, let us look at an unaligned word stored at addresses 1, 2, 3, and 4. We could use the `lwl` with address 1 to store the bytes at addresses 1, 2, 3; the `lwr` with address 4 can be used to store the byte at address 4. At the end of this two-instruction sequence, the unaligned word is stored in `Rdest`.

---

mfcz — Move from coprocessor z

    Format: `mfcz    Rdest,CPsrc`

    Description: Move contents of coprocessor z's register `CPsrc` to CPU register `Rdest`.

mfhi — Move from hi

    Format: `mfhi`   `Rdest`

    Description: Copy contents of `hi` register to `Rdest`.

---

mflo — Move from lo

    Format: `mflo`   `Rdest`

    Description: Copy contents of `lo` register to `Rdest`.

---

move[†] — Move

    Format: `move`   `Rdest,Rsrc`

    Description: Copy contents of `Rsrc` to `Rdest`.

---

mtc$z$ — Move to coprocessor z

    Format: `mtcz`   `Rsrc,CPdest`

    Description: Move contents of CPU register `Rsrc` to coprocessor z's register `CPdest`.

---

mthi — Move to hi

    Format: `mfhi`   `Rsrc`

    Description: Copy contents of `Rdest` to `hi` register.

---

mtlo — Move to lo

    Format: `mflo`   `Rsrc`

    Description: Copy contents of `Rdest` to `lo` register.

mul[†] — Signed multiply (no overflow)

Format: mul   Rdest,Rsrc1,Src2

Description: Perform multiplication of two signed numbers in Rsrc1 and Src2. The result is placed in register Rdest. Src2 can be a register or a 16-bit immediate value. No overflow exception is generated.

---

mulo[†] — Signed multiply (with overflow)

Format: mulo   Rdest,Rsrc1,Src2

Description: Perform multiplication of two signed numbers in Rsrc1 and Src2. The result is placed in register Rdest. Src2 can be a register or a 16-bit immediate value. If there is an overflow, an overflow exception is generated.

---

mulou[†] — Signed multiply (with overflow)

Format: mulou   Rdest,Rsrc1,Src2

Description: Perform multiplication of two unsigned numbers in Rsrc1 and Src2. The result is placed in register Rdest. Src2 can be a register or a 16-bit immediate value. If there is an overflow, an overflow exception is generated.

---

mult — Multiply (signed)

Format: mult   Rsrc1,Rsrc2

Description: Perform multiplication of two signed numbers in Rsrc1 and Rsrc2. The lower-order word of result is placed in register lo and the higher-order word in register hi.

---

multu — Multiply (unsigned)

Format: multu   Rsrc1,Rsrc2

Description: Same as mult but treat the numbers as unsigned.

neg[†] — Negation (with overflow)

Format: neg   Rdest,Rsrc

Description: Place the negative value of the integer in Rsrc in Rdest. This pseudoinstruction generates overflow exception.

---

negu[†] — Negation (no overflow)

Format: neg   Rdest,Rsrc

Description: Place the negative value of the integer in Rsrc in Rdest. No overflow exception is generated.

---

nop — No operation

Format: nop

Description: Do nothing.

---

nor — Logical NOR

Format: nor   Rdest,Rsrc1,Src2

Description: Place the logical NOR of Rsrc1 and Src2 in Rdest.

---

not[†] — Logical NOT

Format: not   Rdest,Rsrc

Description: Place the logical NOT of Rsrc in Rdest.

---

or — Logical OR

Format: or   Rdest,Rsrc1,Src2

Description: Place the logical OR of Rsrc1 and Src2 in Rdest.

ori — Logical OR immediate

Format: ori   Rdest,Rsrc1,Imm

Description: Place the logical OR of Rsrc1 and Imm in Rdest.

---

rem[†] — Remainder (signed)

Format: rem   Rdest,Rsrc1,Src2

Description: Place the remainder from dividing two signed numbers in Rsrc1 and Src2 (Rsrc1/Src2) in register Rdest. Src2 can be a register or a 16-bit immediate value. If an operand is negative, the remainder is unspecified by the MIPS architecture. The corresponding SPIM value depends on the machine it is running.

---

remu[†] — Remainder (unsigned)

Format: remu   Rdest,Rsrc1,Src2

Description: Same as rem except that the numbers are treated as unsigned.

---

rol[†] — Rotate left

Format: rol   Rdest,Rsrc1,Src2

Description: Rotate the contents of register Rsrc1 left by the number of bit positions indicated by Src2 and place the result in Rdest.

---

ror[†] — Rotate left

Format: ror   Rdest,Rsrc1,Src2

Description: Rotate the contents of register Rsrc1 right by the number of bit positions indicated by Src2 and place the result in Rdest.

sb — Store byte

Format: sb   Rsrc,address

Description: Store the lowest byte from register Rdest at address.

---

sd — Store doubleword

Format: sd   Rsrc,address

Description: Store the doubleword (64 bits) from registers Rdest and Rdest+1 at address.

---

seq[†] — Set if equal

Format: seq   Rdest,Rsrc1,Src2

Description: Set register Rdest to 1 if Rsrc1 is equal to Src2; otherwise, Rdest is 0.

---

sge[†] — Set if greater than or equal (signed)

Format: sge   Rdest,Rsrc1,Src2

Description: Set register Rdest to 1 if Rsrc1 is greater than or equal to Src2; otherwise, Rdest is 0. Rsrc1 and Src2 are treated as signed numbers.

---

sgeu[†] — Set if greater than or equal (unsigned)

Format: sgeu   Rdest,Rsrc1,Src2

Description: Same as sge except that Rsrc1 and Src2 are treated as unsigned numbers.

sgt[†] — Set if greater than (signed)

Format: sgt   Rdest,Rsrc1,Src2

Description: Set register Rdest to 1 if Rsrc1 is greater than Src2; otherwise, Rdest is 0. Rsrc1 and Src2 are treated as signed numbers.

---

sgtu[†] — Set if greater than (unsigned)

Format: sgtu   Rdest,Rsrc1,Src2

Description: Same as sgt except that Rsrc1 and Src2 are treated as unsigned numbers.

---

sh — Store halfword

Format: sh   Rsrc,address

Description: Store the lower halfword (16 bits) from register Rsrc at address.

---

sle[†] — Set if less than or equal (signed)

Format: sle   Rdest,Rsrc1,Src2

Description: Set register Rdest to 1 if Rsrc1 is less than or equal to Src2; otherwise, Rdest is 0. Rsrc1 and Src2 are treated as signed numbers.

---

sleu[†] — Set if less than or equal (unsigned)

Format: sleu   Rdest,Rsrc1,Src2

Description: Same as sle except that Rsrc1 and Src2 are treated as unsigned numbers.

---

sll — Shift left logical

    Format: `sll     Rdest,Rsrc1,count`

Description: Shift the contents of register `Rsrc1` left by `count` bit positions and places the result in `Rdest`. Shifted-out bits are filled with zeros.

---

sllv — Shift left logical variable

    Format: `sllv     Rdest,Rsrc1,Rsrc2`

Description: Shift the contents of register `Rsrc1` left by the number of bit positions indicated by `Rsrc2` and places the result in `Rdest`. Shifted-out bits are filled with zeros.

---

slt — Set if less than (signed)

    Format: `slt     Rdest,Rsrc1,Src2`

Description: Set register `Rdest` to 1 if `Rsrc1` is less than `Src2`; otherwise, `Rdest` is 0. `Rsrc1` and `Src2` are treated as signed numbers.

---

slti — Set if less than immediate (signed)

    Format: `slti     Rdest,Rsrc1,Imm`

Description: Set register `Rdest` to 1 if `Rsrc1` is less than `Imm`; otherwise, `Rdest` is 0. `Rsrc1` and `Imm` are treated as signed numbers.

---

sltiu — Set if less than immediate (unsigned)

    Format: `sltiu     Rdest,Rsrc1,Imm`

Description: Same as `slti` except that `Rsrc1` and `Imm` are treated as unsigned numbers.

sltu — Set if less than (unsigned)

Format: sltu   Rdest,Rsrc1,Src2

Description: Same as slt except that Rsrc1 and Src2 are treated as unsigned numbers.

---

sne[†] — Set if not equal

Format: sne   Rdest,Rsrc1,Src2

Description: Set register Rdest to 1 if Rsrc1 is not equal to Src2; otherwise, Rdest is 0.

---

sra — Shift right arithmetic

Format: sra   Rdest,Rsrc1,count

Description: Shift the contents of register Rsrc1 right by count bit positions and place the result in Rdest. Shifted-out bits are filled with the sign bit.

---

srav — Shift right arithmetic variable

Format: srav   Rdest,Rsrc1,Rsrc2

Description: Shift the contents of register Rsrc1 right by the number of bit positions indicated by Rsrc2 and place the result in Rdest. Shifted-out bits are filled with the sign bit.

---

srl — Shift right arithmetic

Format: srl   Rdest,Rsrc1,count

Description: Shift the contents of register Rsrc1 right by count bit positions and place the result in Rdest. Shifted-out bits are filled with zeros.

---

srlv — Shift right arithmetic variable

    Format: `srlv`   `Rdest,Rsrc1,Rsrc2`

Description: Shift the contents of register `Rsrc1` right by the number of bit positions indicated by `Rsrc2` and place the result in `Rdest`. Shifted-out bits are filled with zeros.

---

sub — Subtract with overflow

    Format: `sub`   `Rdest,Rsrc1,Src2`

Description: `Rdest` receives the difference of `Rsrc1` and `Src2` (i.e., `Rsrc1−SRc2`). The numbers are treated as signed integers. In case of an overflow, an overflow exception is generated.

---

subu — Subtract with no overflow

    Format: `subu`   `Rdest,Rsrc1,Src2`

Description: Same as `sub` but no overflow exception is generated.

---

sw — Store word

    Format: `sw`   `Rsrc,address`

Description: Store the word from register `Rsrc` at `address`.

---

swc$z$ — Store word coprocessor z

    Format: `sw`   `Rsrc,address`

Description: Store the word from register `Rsrc` of coprocessor z at `address`.

---

swl — Store word left

    Format: `swl     Rsrc,address`

    Description: Copy the left bytes from register `Rsrc` to memory at `address`. This instruction can be used along with `swr` to store a word in memory at an unaligned address. The `swl` instruction starts storing the bytes from the most-significant byte of `Rsrc` to memory at `address` until the lower-order byte of the word in memory is reached. For example, if the address is 1, it stores the three most significant bytes of `Rsrc` at addresses 1, 2, and 3. As another example, if the address is 2, it stores the two most significant bytes of `Rsrc` at addresses 2 and 3.

---

swr — Store word right

    Format: `swr     Rsrc,address`

    Description: Copy the right bytes from register `Rsrc` to memory at `address`. This instruction can be used along with `swl` to store a word in memory at an unaligned address. The `swr` instruction starts storing the bytes from the least-significant byte of `Rsrc` to memory at `address` until the higher-order byte of the word in memory is reached. For example, if the address is 1, it stores the two least significant bytes of `Rsrc` at addresses 1 and 0. As another example, if the address is 2, it stores the three least significant bytes of `Rsrc` at addresses 2, 1, and 0.

---

ulh[†] — Unaligned load halfword (signed)

    Format: `ulh     Rdest,address`

    Description: Load the halfword (16 bits) from the word at `address` into register `Rdest`. The address could be unaligned. The halfword is sign-extended.

ulhu[†] — Unaligned load halfword (unsigned)

Format: ulhu   Rdest,address

Description: Load the halfword (16 bits) from the word at address into register Rdest. The address could be unaligned. The halfword is zero-extended.

---

ulw[†] — Unaligned load word

Format: ulw   Rdest,address

Description: Load the word (32 bits) at address into register Rdest. The address could be unaligned.

---

ush[†] — Unaligned store halfword

Format: ush   Rsrc,address

Description: Store the lower halfword (16 bits) from register Rsrc at address. The address could be unaligned.

---

usw[†] — Unaligned store word

Format: usw   Rsrc,address

Description: Store the word (32 bits) from register Rsrc at address. The address could be unaligned.

---

xor — Logical XOR

Format: xor   Rdest,Rsrc1,Src2

Description: Place the logical XOR of Rsrc1 and Src2 in Rdest.

---

xori — Logical XOR immediate

Format: xori   Rdest,Rsrc1,Imm

Description: Place the logical XOR of Rsrc1 and Imm in Rdest.

D

Programming Exercises

This appendix gives several programming exercises. These exercises can used to practice writing programs in the MIPS assembly language.

1. Modify the `addigits.asm` program given in Example 10.1 on page 174 such that it accepts a string from the keyboard consisting of digit and nondigit characters. The program should display the sum of the digits present in the input string. All nondigit characters should be ignored. For example, if the input string is

   ```
   ABC1?5wy76:~2
   ```

   the output of the program should be

   ```
   sum of individual digits is: 21
   ```

2. Write an assembly language program to encrypt digits as shown below:

input digit:	0 1 2 3 4 5 6 7 8 9
encrypted digit:	4 6 9 5 0 3 1 8 7 2

   Your program should accept a string consisting of digit and nondigit characters. The encrypted string should be displayed in which only the digits are affected. Then the user should be queried whether he or she wants to terminate the program. If the response is either "y" or "Y" you should terminate the program; otherwise, you should request another input string from the keyboard.

   The encryption scheme given here has the property that when you encrypt an already encrypted string, you get back the original string. Use this property to verify your program.

3. Write a program to accept a number in the hexadecimal form and display the decimal equivalent of the number. A typical interaction of your program is (user input is shown in bold):

Please input a positive number in hex (4 digits max.): **A10F**
The decimal equivalent of A10FH is 41231
Do you want to terminate the program (Y/N): **Y**

You can refer to Appendix A for an algorithm to convert from base b to decimal. You should do the required multiplication by the left-shift instruction. Once you have converted the hex number into the equivalent in binary, you can use the `print_int` system call to display the decimal equivalent.

4. Write a program that reads an input number (given in decimal) between 0 and 65,535 and displays the hexadecimal equivalent. You can read the input using the `read_int` system call.

5. Modify the above program to display the octal equivalent instead of the hexadecimal equivalent of the input number.

6. Write a procedure `locate` to locate a character in a given string. The procedure receives a pointer to a NULL-terminated character string and the character to be located. When the first occurrence of the character is located, its position is returned to `main`. If no match is found, a negative value is returned. The `main` procedure requests a character string and a character to be located and displays the position of the first occurrence of the character returned by the `locate` procedure. If there is no match, a message should be displayed to that effect.

7. Write a procedure that receives a string and removes all leading blank characters in the string. For example, if the input string is (⊔ indicates a blank character)

   ⊔ ⊔ ⊔ ⊔ ⊔Read⊔⊔my⊔lips.

it will be modified by removing all leading blanks as

   Read⊔⊔my⊔lips.

Write a main program to test your procedure.

8. Write a procedure that receives a string and removes all leading and duplicate blank characters in the string. For example, if the input string is (⊔ indicates a blank character)

   ⊔ ⊔ ⊔ ⊔ ⊔Read⊔ ⊔ ⊔my⊔ ⊔ ⊔ ⊔ ⊔lips.

it will be modified by removing all leading and duplicate blanks as

   Read⊔my⊔lips.

Write a main program to test your procedure.

9. Write a procedure to read a string, representing a person's name, in the format

   first-name⊔MI⊔last-name

and display the name in the format

   last-name,⊔first-name⊔MI

where ⊔ indicates a blank character. As indicated, you can assume that the three names—first name, middle initial, and last name—are separated by single spaces. Write a main program to test your procedure.

10. Modify the last exercise to work on an input that can contain multiple spaces between the names. Also, display the name as in the last exercise but with the last name in all capital letters.

11. Write a complete assembly language program to read two matrices **A** and **B** and display the result matrix **C**, which is the sum of **A** and **B**. Note that the elements of **C** can be obtained as

$$\mathbf{C}[i,j] = \mathbf{A}[i,j] + \mathbf{B}[i,j] \,.$$

Your program should consist of a main procedure that calls the `read_matrix` procedure twice to read data for **A** and **B**. It should then call the `matrix_add` procedure, which receives pointers to **A**, **B**, **C**, and the size of the matrices. Note that both **A** and **B** should have the same size. The `main` procedure calls another procedure to display **C**.

12. Write a procedure to perform multiplication of matrices **A** and **B**. The procedure should receive pointers to the two input matrices (**A** of size $l \times m$, **B** of size $m \times n$), the product matrix **C**, and values l, m, and n. Also, the data for the two matrices should be obtained from the user. Devise a suitable user interface to read these numbers.

13. Modify the program of the last exercise to work on matrices stored in the column-major order.

14. Write a program to read a matrix (maximum size 10×10) from the user and display the transpose of the matrix. To obtain the transpose of matrix **A**, write rows of **A** as columns. Here is an example.

If the input matrix is

$$\begin{bmatrix} 12 & 34 & 56 & 78 \\ 23 & 45 & 67 & 89 \\ 34 & 56 & 78 & 90 \\ 45 & 67 & 89 & 10 \end{bmatrix},$$

the transpose of the matrix is

$$\begin{bmatrix} 12 & 23 & 34 & 45 \\ 34 & 45 & 56 & 67 \\ 56 & 67 & 78 & 89 \\ 78 & 89 & 90 & 10 \end{bmatrix}.$$

15. Write a program to read a matrix (maximum size 10×15) from the user and display the subscripts of the maximum element in the matrix. Your program should consist of two procedures: `main` is responsible for reading the input matrix and for

displaying the position of the maximum element. Another procedure `mat_max` is responsible for finding the position of the maximum element. For example, if the input matrix is

$$\begin{bmatrix} 12 & 34 & 56 & 78 \\ 23 & 45 & 67 & 89 \\ 34 & 56 & 78 & 90 \\ 45 & 67 & 89 & 10 \end{bmatrix}$$

the output of the program should be

    The maximum element is at (2,3),

which points to the largest value (90 in our example).

16. Write a program to read a matrix of integers, perform cyclic permutation of rows, and display the result matrix. Cyclic permutation of a sequence $a_0, a_1, a_2, \ldots, a_{n-1}$ is defined as $a_1, a_2, \ldots, a_{n-1}, a_0$. Apply this process for each row of the matrix. Your program should be able to handle up to 12×15 matrices. If the input matrix is

$$\begin{bmatrix} 12 & 34 & 56 & 78 \\ 23 & 45 & 67 & 89 \\ 34 & 56 & 78 & 90 \\ 45 & 67 & 89 & 10 \end{bmatrix},$$

the permuted matrix is

$$\begin{bmatrix} 34 & 56 & 78 & 12 \\ 45 & 67 & 89 & 23 \\ 56 & 78 & 90 & 34 \\ 67 & 89 & 10 & 45 \end{bmatrix}.$$

17. Generalize the last exercise to cyclically permute by a user-specified number of elements.

18. Write a complete assembly language program to do the following.

- Read the names of students in a class into a one-dimensional array.
- Read test scores of each student into a two-dimensional marks array.
- Output a letter grade for each student in the format:

       `student name`   `letter grade`

You can use the following information in writing your program:

- Assume that the maximum class size is 20.
- Assume that the class is given four tests of equal weight (i.e., 25 points each).
- Test marks are rounded to the nearest integer so you can treat them as integers.
- Use the following table to convert percentage marks (i.e, sum of all four tests) to a letter grade.

Marks range	Grade
85–100	A
70–84	B
60–69	C
50–59	D
0–49	F

19. Modify the program for the last exercise to also generate a class summary stating the number of students receiving each letter grade in the following format:

A = number of students receiving A,
B = number of students receiving B,
C = number of students receiving C,
D = number of students receiving D,
F = number of students receiving F.

20. If we are given a square matrix (i.e., a matrix with the number of rows equal to the number of columns), we can classify it as a diagonal matrix if only its diagonal elements are nonzero; as an upper triangular matrix if all the elements below the diagonal are 0; and as a lower triangular matrix if all elements above the diagonal are 0. Some examples are:

Diagonal matrix:

$$\begin{bmatrix} 28 & 0 & 0 & 0 \\ 0 & 87 & 0 & 0 \\ 0 & 0 & 97 & 0 \\ 0 & 0 & 0 & 65 \end{bmatrix};$$

Upper triangular matrix:

$$\begin{bmatrix} 19 & 26 & 35 & 98 \\ 0 & 78 & 43 & 65 \\ 0 & 0 & 38 & 29 \\ 0 & 0 & 0 & 82 \end{bmatrix};$$

Lower triangular matrix:

$$\begin{bmatrix} 76 & 0 & 0 & 0 \\ 44 & 38 & 0 & 0 \\ 65 & 28 & 89 & 0 \\ 87 & 56 & 67 & 54 \end{bmatrix}.$$

Write an assembly language program to read a matrix and output the type of matrix.

21. In Appendix A, we discussed the format of the single-precision floating-point numbers. Write a program that reads the floating-point internal representation from the user as a string of eight hexadecimal digits and displays the three components—mantissa, exponent, and sign—in binary. For example, if the input to the program is 429DA000, the output should be:

    sign = 0
    mantissa = 1.0011101101
    exponent = 110.

22. Modify the program for the last exercise to work with the double-precision floating-point representation.

23. Ackermann's function $A(m, n)$ is defined for $m \geq 0$ and $n \geq 0$ as

$$
\begin{array}{ll}
A(0, n) = N + 1 & \text{for } n \geq 0 \\
A(m, 0) = A(m - 1, 1) & \text{for } m \geq 1 \\
A(m, n) = A(m - 1, A(m, n - 1)) & \text{for } m \geq 1, n \geq 1.
\end{array}
$$

Write a recursive procedure to compute this function. Your main program should handle the user interface to request m and n and display the final result.

24. Write a program to solve the Towers of Hanoi puzzle. The puzzle consists of three pegs and N disks. Disk 1 is smaller than disk 2, which is smaller than disk 3, and so on. Disk N is the largest. Initially, all N disks are on peg 1 such that the largest disk is at the bottom and the smallest at the top (i.e., in the order N, $N - 1$, ..., 3, 2, 1 from bottom to top). The problem is to move these N disks from peg 1 to peg 2 under two constraints: you can move only one disk at a time and you must not place a larger disk on top of a smaller one. We can express a solution to this problem by using recursion. The function

    ```
    move(N, 1, 2, 3)
    ```

moves N disks from peg 1 to peg 2 using peg 3 as the extra peg. There is a simple solution if you concentrate on moving the bottom disk on peg 1. The task move(N, 1, 2, 3) is equivalent to

    ```
    move(N-1, 1, 3, 2)
    ```
    move the remaining disk from peg 1 to 2
    ```
    move(N-1, 3, 2, 1)
    ```

Even though the task appears to be complex, we write a very elegant and simple solution to solve this puzzle. Here is a version in C.

```c
void move (int n, int x, int y, int z)
{
    if (n == 1)
        printf("Move the top disk from peg %d to %d\n",x,y};
```

```
          else
              move(n-1, x, z, y)
              printf("Move the top disk from peg %d to %d\n",x,y};
              move(n-1, z, y, x)
      }


      int main (void)
      {
          int    disks;

          scanf("%d", &disks);
          move(disks, 1, 2, 3);
      }
```

Test your program for a very small number of disks (say, less than 6). Even for 64 disks, it takes hundreds of years on whatever PC you have!

25. Write a procedure str_str that receives two pointers to strings string and substring and searches for substring in string. If a match is found, it returns the starting position of the first match. Matching should be case sensitive. A negative value is returned if no match is found. For example, if

> string = Good things come in small packages.

and

> substring = in

the procedure should return 8 indicating a match of in in things.

26. Write a procedure str_ncpy to mimic the strncpy function provided by the C library. The function str_ncpy receives two strings, string1 and string2, and a positive integer num. Of course, the procedure receives only the string pointers but not the actual strings. It should copy at most the first num characters from string2 to string1.

27. A *palindrome* is a word, verse, sentence, or number that reads the same backward or forward. Blanks, punctuation marks, and capitalization do not count in determining palindromes. Here are some examples:

> 1991
> Able was I ere I saw Elba
> Madam! I'm Adam

Write a program to determine if a given string is a palindrome. The procedure returns 1 if the string is a palindrome; otherwise, it returns 0.

28. Write an assembly language program to read a string of characters from the user and print the vowel count. For each vowel, the count includes both uppercase and lowercase letters. For example, the input string

Advanced Programming in UNIX Environment

produces the following output:

Vowel	Count
a or A	3
e or E	3
i or I	4
o or O	2
u or U	1

29. Merge sort is a technique to combine two sorted arrays. Merge sort takes two sorted input arrays X and Y—say of size m and n—and produces a sorted array Z of size $m + n$ that contains all elements of the two input arrays. The pseudocode of merge sort is as follows.

```
mergesort (X, Y, Z, m, n)
    i := 0 {index variables for arrays X, Y, and Z}
    j := 0
    k := 0
    while ((i < m) AND (j < n))
        if (X[i] ≤ Y[j]) {find largest of two}
        then
            Z[k] := X[i] {copy and update indices}
            k := k+1
            i := i+1
        else
            Z[k] := Y[j] {copy and update indices}
            k := k+1
            j := j+1
        end if
    end while
    if (i < m) {copy remainder of input array}
        while (i < m)
            Z[k] := X[i]
            k := k+1
            i := i+1
        end while
    else
        while (j < n)
            Z[k] := Y[j]
            k := k+1
            j := j+1
        end while
```

> **end if**
> end mergesort

The merge sort algorithm scans the two input arrays while copying the smallest of the two elements from X and Y into Z. It updates indices appropriately. The first while loop terminates when one of the arrays is exhausted. Then the other array is copied into Z.

Write a merge sort procedure and test it with two sorted arrays. Assume that the user enters the two input arrays in sorted (ascending) order.

Bibliography

[1] ARM, *ARM Architecture Reference Manual*, Addison-Wesley Professional, 2000.

[2] ARM, "ARM Instruction Set Quick Reference Card," 2003. This document is available from `www.arm.com`.

[3] ARM, "ARM Milestones," 2003. This document is available from `www.arm.com/aboutarm/milestones.html`

[4] ARM, "ARM Markets," 2003. This document is available from `www.arm.com/markets/`.

[5] ARM, "The Thumb Architecture Extension," 2003. This document is available from `www.arm.com/products/CPUs/archi-thumb.html`.

[6] S.P. Dandamudi, *Fundamentals of Computer Organization and Design*, Springer, New York, 2003.

[7] S.P. Dandamudi, *Introduction to Assembly Language Programming*, Second Edition, Springer, New York, 2004.

[8] D. Goldberg, "What Every Computer Scientist Should Know About Floating-Point Arithmetic," *ACM Computing Surveys*, Vol. 23, No. 1, March 1991, pp. 5–48.

[9] IBM, "PowerPC Architecture: A High-Performance Architecture with a History," 2003. This document is available from `www.ibm.com/servers/eserver/pseries/hardware/whitepapers/power/ppc_arch.html`.

[10] Intel, *Intel Itanium Architecture: Software Developer's Manual*, Volume 1: Application Architecture, 2002. This manual is available from `www.intel.com/design/Itanium/manuals/`.

[11] Intel, *Intel Itanium Architecture: Software Developer's Manual*, Volume 2: System Architecture, 2002. This manual is available from `www.intel.com/design/Itanium/manuals/`.

[12] Intel, *Intel Itanium Architecture: Software Developer's Manual*, Volume 3: Instruction Set Reference, 2002. This manual is available from `www.intel.com/design/Itanium/manuals/`.

[13] Z. Kerekes, "History of SPARC Systems," 2003. This document is available from `www.sparcproductdirectory.com/history.html`.

[14] J.R. Larus, *SPIM S20: A MIPS R2000 Simulator,* 1997. This manual is available from `www.cs.wisc.edu/~larus/SPIM_manual/spim-manual.html`.

[15] J.K. Lee and A.J. Smith, "Branch Prediction Strategies and Branch Target Buffer Design," *Computer,* Vol. 17, No. 1, 1984, pp. 6–22.

[16] MIPS, *MIPS32 Architecture for Programmers,* Volume I: Introduction to the MIPS32 Architecture, 2003. It is available from `www.mips.com/content/Documentation/MIPSDocumentation`.

[17] MIPS, *MIPS32 Architecture for Programmers,* Volume II: The MIPS32 Instruction Set, 2003. This manual is available from `www.mips.com/content/Documentation/MIPSDocumentation`.

[18] MIPS, *MIPS32 Architecture for Programmers,* Volume III: The MIPS32 Privileged Resource Architecture, 2003. It is available from `www.mips.com/content/Documentation/MIPSDocumentation`.

[19] MIPS, *MIPS64 Architecture for Programmers,* Volume I: Introduction to the MIPS64 Architecture, 2003. It is available from `www.mips.com/content/Documentation/MIPSDocumentation`.

[20] MIPS, *MIPS64 Architecture for Programmers,* Volume II: The MIPS64 Instruction Set, 2003. It is available from `www.mips.com/content/Documentation/MIPSDocumentation`.

[21] MIPS, *MIPS64 Architecture for Programmers,* Volume III: The MIPS64 Privileged Resource Architecture, 2003. It is available from `www.mips.com/content/Documentation/MIPSDocumentation`.

[22] D.A. Patterson and C.H. Sequin, "A VLSI RISC," *Computer,* Vol. 15, No. 9, 1982, pp. 8–21.

[23] PowerPC, *PowerPC Architecture Book: PowerPC User Instruction Set Architecture,* Book I, 2003. This document is available from `www.ibm.com/developerworks/eserver/articles/archguide.html`.

[24] PowerPC, *PowerPC Architecture Book: PowerPC Virtual Environment Architecture,* Book II, 2003. This document is available from `www.ibm.com/developerworks/eserver/articles/archguide.html`.

[25] PowerPC, *PowerPC Architecture Book: PowerPC Operating Environment Architecture,* Book III, 2003. This document is available from `www.ibm.com/developerworks/eserver/articles/archguide.html`.

[26] SPARC, "SPARC History," 2003. This document is available from `www.sparc.com/history.html`.

[27] SUN, "SUN History," 2003. This document is available from `www.sun.com/aboutsun/coinfo/history.html`.

[28] A.S. Tanenbaum, "Implications of Structured Programming for Machine Architecture," *Communications of the ACM,* Vol. 21, No. 3, 1978, pp. 237–246.

Index